VISIONS

OF THE WEST

VISIONS
OF THE WEST

Art and Artifacts
from the private collections of
J.P. Bryan,
Torch Energy Advisors Incorporated
and Others

edited by
Melissa Baldridge
with an introduction by
Patricia Nelson Limerick

SALT LAKE CITY

First Edition
Copyright © 1999 by The Torch Collection
of Torch Energy Advisors Incorporated

Published by
Gibbs Smith, Publisher
P.O. Box 667
Layton, Utah 84041
Visit our Web site: www.gibbs-smith.com

Design by J. Scott Knudsen, Park City, Utah
Printed and bound in China

Library of Congress Cataloging-in-Publication Data

Visions of the West : art and artifacts from the private
collections of J.P. Bryan, Torch Energy Advisors
Incorporated, and others / edited by Melissa Baldridge.
    p. cm.
    Includes bibliographical references and index.
    ISBN 0-87905-854-4
    1. Art—North America—Catalogs. 2. Torch Energy
    Advisors—Art collections—Catalogs. 3. Art—Private
    collections—Texas—Houston—Catalogs.
    I. Baldridge, Melissa.
N6503.V65   1999
700'.978'074—DC21   99-11445
                    CIP

Contents

FOREWORD VII
J. P. Bryan, Collector

PREFACE IX
Melissa Baldridge, Curator, Torch Collection

ACKNOWLEDGMENTS XIII

"ART UNBOUNDED" 1
Patricia Nelson Limerick with Hannah Nordhaus

**"PEOPLE WITHOUT BORDERS:
NATIVES OF THE NORTH AMERICAN PLAINS"** 4
Emma I. Hansen

"THE MISSIONARY-LED INDIAN COMMUNITIES 50
Gilberto M. Hinojosa

**"FIESTAS: WHERE CONTEMPORARY MEXICAN TRIBES
AND ANCIENT CUSTOMS MEET"** 94
Marta Turok

"CHRISTIAN ART AND IMAGERY IN MEXICO" 142
Gloria Fraser Giffords

"THE BLACK WEST" 170
William Loren Katz

"COWGIRLS: THE WILD, WILD WOMEN OF THE WEST" 196
Gail Gilchriest

**"HORSEMAN, RIDE WEST!:
THE EVOLUTION OF THE SPUR"** 216
Jane Pattie

**"TOOLS OF TRIUMPH AND TRAGEDY:
FIREARMS IN THE AMERICAN WEST"** 244
Richard C. Rattenbury

"THE SEARCH FOR TEXAS" 274
Becky Duval Reese

BIOGRAPHICAL NOTES 312

INDEX 315

Foreword

This book represents thirty-five years of my personal collecting effort. Combined with the efforts of others whose collections I purchased for Torch Energy Advisors and in my international business enterprises, the objects express more than two hundred years of collecting passion.

The items themselves span more than four hundred years from the time of Spanish exploration in the 1500s through the cowboy empires of the late 1900s. The collections can be separated into three different components: first, artistic expressions such as paintings, sculptures, and photographs; second, functional items such as clothing, spurs, saddles, and bridles; and third, literary or printed items—maps, books, newspapers, and documents. In total, they make up three necessary components required to gain insight into the spirit of the people who settled western North America.

What was the makeup of these actors? They were, for the most part, Anglos from Europe and the East Coast of the United States. The foundations for their western migrations had been laid, to a large extent, by the Spanish through their irregular incursions into the United States, and to a lesser extent by the French. The documentation of their dual influence is well demonstrated in the essays in this book. Willing participants and partners with the Anglos in this western drama were blacks, Hispanics, and, over time, a virtual kaleidoscope of ethnic peoples. The essays included give importance to the often historically neglected significance that blacks and women played in the settlement of the West. Also, there is ample documentation through three essays of the importance of Catholicism and the transforming effect it had on Native American or pagan religions, and how so much of western spiritual beliefs, especially at the indigenous level, remained grounded in a combination of Catholic rituals and Native beliefs.

Since this is also a collection, let's reflect on collectors. The leaven that gives a collection meaning comes from the collector and the passion he or she has for the collection itself. A collection is, without exception, a soulful expression. It is an outward and visible manifestation of some inward, invisible spirit. The complexities that compel one to collect are as numerous as life's neuroses. It can best be explained by simply saying that a collection says as much about the collector as it does about the subject collected.

For my part, I began collecting with resolve in 1966 when I learned that my father had sold his outstanding collection of Texana to the University of Texas, thereby denying me the luxury of inheritance. While I regret not being the beneficiary and steward of the numerous rarities he had obtained through inheritance or diligent search, it did send me off on my own restless pursuit of items of Texana and western Americana. That pursuit has been a lifelong avocation that frequently had more meaning and purpose than the vocations of my life. My life as a collector has not been without its regrets and guilts—regrets always about those things I didn't buy and guilt at the financial strain my collecting addiction placed upon my family and me. But now, at a resting place in my collecting life, I can look back over the years and savor the memories—the excitement that went with the pursuit of a rarity and the satisfaction at that moment of acquisition, knowing I would have the pleasure of stewardship of some meaningful new addition to the collection. I also recall with fondness the friendships with sellers and dealers, many now deceased, who have placed their own special imprimatur on these collections. But most importantly I feel friendships with the objects themselves; in some way they express my affections to those who view them.

There is history in a collection and a personal history in the collecting itself. There is also a feeling of redemption to the collector who assembles something of significance, especially something done well at great risk of resources both personal and financial. Most importantly the struggle to satisfy an inner need can now be seen and appreciated in its entirety by others. What began as a selfish pursuit can be shared and enjoyed by many. That is the crowning blessing of collecting.

For a collection to have lasting meaning, it must have soul, which requires that the subject collected be appreciated by its audience. It should be a unique and rare expression of the subject. It should somehow reflect the collector's love for the objects and invoke and answer the question—Why did he or she care to collect this?

To be successful, a collector should have a good eye and an outstanding knowledge of the subject. There will, in fact, be no great collection assembled by a collector who does not both know his subject and also have a good eye as a component in his effort. In all probability, the collector of rare books will not have read every book in his collection, but he will know the importance of each of them. The only advice I would ever impart any collector is first, know your subject; knowledge is the key to getting value. Second, acquire the rarest first; the most common will always be available. The rarest items will carry your collection to higher plateaus of appreciation at a vigorous pace. Third, never hesitate to buy the collections of others. You will never pay so much as to cover the time, genius, and affection they put into its accumulation.

The collections I have assembled are all objects, but objects that are all about people—the people who used them or produced them and, importantly, the people who lived in the western part of North America. Theirs is a history that has been idealized precisely because it *is* romantic and was made so by those who saw in the expansiveness of the West not limitations but vast opportunities—people who worked from can't to can and had no quitting sense. They turned their faces against the odds and to western North America. In doing so they accomplished things of greatness and participated in lives of both high adventure and deep deprivation.

These collections exhibit the spirit that compelled people to live in the West and all they touched in the process. A study of these collections should be a study of the soul of western North America as it was found and then transformed by centuries of immigration. In these collections, the spirits of many cultures endure as lasting, omnipresent reminders of the courage of those who came before us—people, both Native and immigrant, the likes of whom we will never see again.

J. P. BRYAN, COLLECTOR

Preface

On the day I interviewed at Torch for their curator's position, I thought I had made a big mistake. Behind the visitors' sofa in the reception room hung an enormous painting with a lively western scene—a stagecoach with mounted cowboy to its side, both hurtling across the canvas, obviously fleeing some danger behind them. The background of the painting was a sun-bleached yellow desert with dust clouds kicked up from their flight.

My heart sank. The job had sounded like a great opportunity, but I've never had a soft spot for art depicting cowboy or "western" vignettes. I wondered if I had been wrong to show up and express an interest in the job.

I waited twenty minutes for my interviewer, J. P. Bryan, then CEO at Torch, and followed him to his corner office, a large triangular room. The longest wall was floor-to-ceiling windows with all the black venetian blinds pulled and closed, and the other two walls had glass-front bookcases full of old and rare books, shelved and stacked in all sorts of configurations. In a corner stood an antique easel with a painting resting on it. Every square inch of Bryan's large Texas pine desk was covered with bibelots: silver objects, Mexican artifacts, paperweights, and knickknacks. The room was so packed with stuff that the walls felt as though they were compressing in on us.

After our visit, I toured the top floor of Torch's two-block-long office building. It was an art-laden maze. Narrow halls were painted corporate grey with dim incandescent lights. A jumble of material jammed wall spaces—works on paper, framed manuscripts and documents, equestrian gear, maps, firearms, and religious artifacts. The effect was overwhelming. Even though I was short-circuited by the visual overload, I sensed that there was much more to this eclectic jumble than I had first thought—and I accepted the job.

My first six months at Torch bore out my hunch. As I worked with the breadth of material in the collections, I was amazed by the layers and interconnected levels of fine and decorative art and historical pieces, all from western North America. I realized that my first impression—that western Americana meant "cowboy art"—was wrong.

Though the American cowboy reigned across the plains a mere twenty-five post–Civil War years, he is still with us. From country music singers to western movie stars to advertising images of handsome, rough-hewn cattlemen, our culture is steeped in his image. Symbolic like his peers the Puritan, the revolutionary patriot, and the coonskin-capped pioneer, he has come to embody virtues we hold as our own: individuality, bravery, toughness. He inflamed the public imagination and left an indelible imprint. In the same way that our counterparts from the East Coast might assume that all Texans wear Stetsons, ride horses, and own oil wells, the visual history of the West has suffered such stereotyping and misperception.

The complex interactions between groups and cultures spill over into the realm of visual history and iconography, too. Artists such as Frederic Remington, Charles Russell, and scores of their followers memorialized life in the late-nineteenth-century American West, yet we are still held captive by their imagery. They presented a simple drama where red and white square off in mortal combat, all scenes set against a backdrop of breathtaking pristine landscape. In truth, the North American West is a much more complex place than this overplayed bit of theater suggests. For us in subsequent generations to lump all imagery from the North American West together and dismiss it as "cowboy" is rash and tragic.

Groups and cultures don't exist in isolation, and this has definitely been true in the North American West. It is a vast place where many disparate people and groups have coexisted and collided for centuries. A current trend in the retelling of the region's past, New Western History, posits that the American West has been a great patchwork of peoples and cultures, with no one perspective predominate. At the epicenter of New Western History is Patricia Nelson Limerick. In her significant work, *The Legacy of Conquest,* Limerick proposed viewing the region's history from multiple viewpoints rather than interpreting it solely through the frontier model. She compared this broader view of western history to a subway system with various hubs and lines, each important to the overall system.

Just as New Western History seeks to tell the region's history from different viewpoints, this book seeks to expand its visual legacy. *Visions of the West* is about the pluralism of the North American West as reflected in the art and cultural artifacts assembled by J. P. Bryan: in the corporate art collection of Torch Energy Advisors Incorporated in Houston, a company he founded in 1981, and in the private collections lining the trail of his international business ventures. Over the thirty-five years of his collecting life, Bryan has dramatically transformed the physical and psychic spaces he has inhabited. What holds this amazing assembly of material together is geography. The things he has collected—whether Native textiles or Mexican religious artworks or early Texas furniture—all come from the North American West. The collections present regionalism in the best and broadest sense: They span an enormous time period (550 B.C. to the present), they represent a number of groups and cultures, and they cover a huge area (the plains of western Canada to Mexico). This book presents the historical layers of some of the peoples who have lived in the North American West and the visual layers they contributed to the iconography of this broad region.

In a more simplistic rendering of western history, Native Americans are cast as curios, tragic figures, or savage impediments to white man's settlement of a frontier. In her essay, "People without Borders," Emma Hansen paints a different picture of Plains Natives as complex tribes and groups with distinct cultural traditions, influenced both by tribal interactions and by contact with whites. These Native artisans, primarily women, created beautifully decorated tools and implements for everyday or ceremonial use. Though white conquest and efforts to stamp out Native cultural traditions changed their way of life forever, Hansen tells how Native traditions were miraculously borne along by indigenous art.

In his essay, "The Missionary-led Indian Communities," Gilberto Hinojosa talks about the imposition of Spain's governmental structures on an unwieldy and often unwilling Native border population, the nomadic Coahuiltecan Indians. From centralized missions along New Spain's northern border in Texas, Spain's church and state tried to mold the Coahuiltecans into good Spanish citizens with varying degrees of success. Hinojosa reexamines the missions as Indian towns led by their conquerors. Houston photographer Gary Faye's images beautifully capture these centuries-old missions and *presidios,* many of which are still in use.

In "Fiestas: Where Contemporary Mexican Tribes and Ancient Customs Meet," anthropologist Marta Turok canvasses native myths and rituals of Mexico's religions. With the coming of the Spanish, these belief systems were overlaid by Catholicism's canon of saints. Houston photographer George O. Jackson documents Mexico's native fiestas, originally pagan and now honoring Catholic saints. In his important ethnographic record, Jackson also captures the beautiful art forms of these celebrations—costumes and body painting, fresh fruit and flower ornaments, heavily festooned crosses and *santos*—that are threatened by commercially available substitutes and debased by a carnival atmosphere. This ephemeral art is important because the colors, forms, and pageantry of Mexican celebrations saturate cultural and popular life in Mexico and the southwestern United States today.

Gloria Giffords's essay, "Christian Art and Imagery in Mexico," picks up where Marta Turok leaves off—the overlay of Catholic imagery and iconography onto native Mexican polytheism. Giffords discusses the development of Mexican Catholic religious art forms by trained and folk artists alike in a variety of media, and the roles these art forms played in the lives of the Mexican people.

Largely untold until recently is the history of African Americans in the western United States. In his essay, "The Black West," William Loren Katz details the role of important African Americans from the time of the earliest European explorers forward. The artwork in this section is by African American artists or about black life in the West, and many of the African American artists represented were self-taught.

The trend in western history of broadening the focus beyond the westering experience of white males has also brought forth the stories of western women. Gail Gilchriest examines a subset of these women—cowgirls—from their pioneer beginnings through the ranching women of today in her essay, "Cowgirls: The Wild, Wild Women of the West." Gilchriest also looks at how the pre–World War II women's rodeo circuit and the entertainment industry shaped the image of the cowgirl, elevating her to the status of pop-culture icon.

Probably no two symbols are more closely linked with the cowboy than guns and spurs. Two essays document encyclopedic collections of both. In "Tools of Triumph and Tragedy: Firearms in the American West," Richard Rattenbury explores the development of the firearm and its impact on the West. Coinciding with the industrial revolution in the East, the westward migration of European Americans provided a ready market for firearm production. The repeating revolver and rifle forever changed the face of the American West—enabling the decimation of the buffalo, dramatically tipping the balance against the Native American, and providing decided advantage in the struggle for land with Mexico. Yet the study of firearm development is a micro-view of the energy, ingenuity, and innovation of America's growing industrial muscle in the nineteenth century. Rattenbury also examines the artisanry and craftsmanship in the engineering and decoration of firearms—seductive in their beauty, deadly in purpose.

In contrast to the assembly-line production of firearms on the East Coast stands the highly personal creation of beautiful, handcrafted riding tools in the West. In her essay, "Horseman, Ride West! The Evolution of the Spur," Jane Pattie traces the huge debt of the American cowboy and his ranching heritage to his Spanish and Mexican forebears. Originally blacksmiths, many of these early spur makers worked in remote towns or outposts in the western United States and Mexico without benefit of today's laborsaving machines and processes, toiling in hot, dusty shops to create these beautiful handwrought pieces. Both Pattie's and Rattenbury's essays elevate the production of these tools to a high level of aesthetic.

If one essay reflects this book's overall goal—to convey the varied, heterogeneous character of the North American West—it is Becky Duval Reese's "The Search for Texas." Critics often miss the varied character of art from Texas, seeing only images of cowboy life. As Reese says, though, "The art of Texas is as broad-based as the state itself." Texas art draws from many sources: nineteenth-century immigration that brought people to the area from all over Europe and America, currents and trends throughout American art history, its Spanish heritage and Mexican proximity, the facts and myths of the region's long and colorful history, and the land itself—vast, varied, and extreme. Reese examines how Texas artists have viewed the state and its people over the period from 1850 to 1950, using art as a looking glass.

Ultimately this book is limited by the collections it represents. There are groups we don't cover simply because they're not represented in the collections Bryan has amassed: Asians, Czechs, Slavs, Scandinavians, among others. Bryan set out with no collecting quotas in mind, no preset numbers to buy from this group or that tribe or any particular period. In fact, he would flatly deny doing so. He has been a visceral buyer, purchasing what strikes him at the moment, and in my tenure, I have encouraged him to buy from an even broader spectrum of material. Indeed, his thirty-five-year collecting career has been a visual feast, and he has piled his plate high.

Limerick and her colleagues see the West as a complex, bumptious place washed by wave after wave of immigrants, and their scholarship has freed historians from a singular viewpoint of the region's past. "The ethnic diversity of western history asks only that: pay attention to the parts, and pay attention to the whole. It is a difficult task, but to bemoan and lament the necessity to include minorities is to engage, finally, in intellectual laziness. The American West was a complicated place for its historical participants; and it is no exercise in 'white guilt' to say that it is—and should be—just as complicated for us today."*

In the same way that New Western historians encourage us to multiply our historical models, I hope that this book surprises and expands perceptions about the visual and cultural histories of the North American West. To offhandedly dismiss those as "cowboy" is to miss the depth, variety, and texture of regionalism at its best.

MELISSA BALDRIDGE
CURATOR, TORCH COLLECTION

---

*Patricia Nelson Limerick, *The Legacy of Conquest: The Unbroken Past of the American West* (New York: W. W. Norton & Company, 1987), 292.

Acknowledgments

Just as no one stands alone, no project of this magnitude happens without an enormous amount of assistance. This book has traveled an amazing two-year path: meetings scheduled or changed to just the right time, phone calls received or not, the best people brought to the project. My deepest thanks to the many who've inspired, supported, and guided me through this perilous, wonderful peregrination.

To Mrs. Lucinda Windsor, my junior-year high school English teacher. During a miserable adolescence, you gave me my love of the written word. I've been fortunate enough to write for a living in some capacity ever since. And thanks also to Bill Camfield, my twentieth-century-art-history professor at Rice. Who would've known that a twenty-five-minute discussion over two Man Ray readymades, one made ten years later than the other, would spark an interest and lifetime pursuit of art? I've not gotten rich in my vocations (so far), but I sure have been happy and fulfilled.

To the fine people of Torch Energy Advisors Incorporated, my gratitude, in particular my colleagues in the Communications Department who've been so jazzed about the Collection and have helped me spread the good news, the people of Administration who help me showcase it so beautifully, the Accounting folks who pay my bills, the legal eagles who've made sure I dotted all i's and crossed all t's, and the propeller heads in Information Technology who've provided me with the efficient tools at my fingertips so I could work with the enormous inventory of Torch's collection. Because you so conscientiously do your jobs, you've freed me to do mine.

To Amy Parsons and Sue Aizzier. You always provided access to J. P. at the perfect time. Thanks for your watchful eyes and antennae. If I'd been left to fend for myself, this book might never have left the launch pad.

To Gail Guidry. Thank you for your years of dedication and hard work on Torch's spur collection. Having that material fully catalogued made working with it much easier. Also, the pieces we lovingly cleaned still show that TLC on these pages.

To Sherry Kafka Wagner. Thanks for your suggestions at critical times in this book's development. Who knows how this project would've evolved without them? Working with you on programs for the Torch Collection has been a delight. I'm honored to have such a great mentor, role model, and friend.

To Lonn Taylor at the Smithsonian. Thank you for helping me find Patricia Nelson Limerick for the book introduction. What a perfect fit for this project!

To Anna Gardner. Thank you for helping me organize things on the other end of this project. Your timely assistance saved me lots of headaches and scrambling later. And to Judith Toliver for your diligent fact checking. I appreciate your helping me get the information about all the private collection pieces.

To Aaronetta and Joe Pierce. Your love and focus on African American history and art are inspiring. Thanks for helping me find both William Katz and some really terrific artwork by self-taught African American artists.

Many thanks to Danielle Routhier and Arlinda Abbott at the National Cowgirl Museum and Hall of Fame for research assistance. Sedate women these cowgirls were not! I appreciate your helping and refereeing.

To Catherine Anspon. Thank you for being such a great friend both to me and to the Torch Collection. I appreciate your sprightly encouragement in this project's development and your great advice along the way.

To Linda Lennon, for your ear, your constant encouragement and occasional kick in the pants. Everyone should be so lucky to have a great friend like you.

To Bobby Gerry. You are a man of great taste and decency. The art community in Texas is lucky to have a friend and advocate like you, and so am I. Thank you for your years of support and encouragement while I've curated Torch's collection.

To Madge Baird, my coordinating editor. *Man,* you are a cool number. Thanks for your even and sage advice in the mini-crises along the way in this book's production. I'm sure you've had lots of practice. Also, my gratitude to you for your unflinching trust in me. (At least *I* never saw you flinch.) What huge motivators your trust and respect have been. I have grown much under your tutelage.

Special thanks to the Managing Directors of Torch Energy Advisors. You have done nothing but support my projects. I hope this book repays your trust and confidence.

A twenty-one-gun salute to Dick Auchinleck, Art Smith, and Roland Sledge. Mr. Auchinleck, thank you for seeing your way through to the completion of this project and for honoring the contract; Roland, for your deft negotiating; and Art, for serving as a U.N. arbitrator.

My deepest thanks to J. P. Bryan. Would either of us have believed in one million years that we'd shape and develop the Collection to this point? You preach an inspiring message about motivating the people who work for you and then freeing them to do their jobs— just getting out of their way and letting them do their work. You, sir, have walked the walk. You have done nothing but give me opportunity after opportunity after opportunity. In allowing me such latitude, you've also given me room to grow and evolve as a professional in the making of this book. I hope that this fine thing—the stories about your collecting career and the West you love so much—stands as a permanent reminder of my love and esteem for you.

And lastly from the alpha of this project to the omega, thanks to God. God the Father is the God of creation, and he has so marked each of us with a tiny area of creativity; mine a love of words and images. Thanks to him for giving me and protecting this project. Its survival is a testament to determined teamwork and the power of prayer. (John 10:10; Mark 11:23, 24; John 3:16).

MELISSA BALDRIDGE

Art Unbounded

*PATRICIA NELSON LIMERICK**

Western art has led a strenuous life, challenged and tested at every turn, and seldom permitted a moment of rest and repose. Champions of art produced in the American West need never lose their sense of mission; the comfortable sense that western art has achieved a permanent position of respect is nothing to fear. Advocates for the appreciation of western artists thus have a great advantage: they are never at risk of that thought-stopping, energy-depleting affliction known as complacency.

Western art has always had to fight to prove its sophistication; at times, it has struggled hard just to hold onto the right to claim an association with the word *art*. The supposed weaknesses have been triple: first, western art comes from the provinces and carries the inescapable brand of the hinterlands and margins; second, western art has often been useful, and, to holders of a certain point of view, even a small amount of usefulness corrodes art's purity; and third, western art carries the burden of popularity—lots of people, lacking proper certification in connoisseurship, persist in embracing it, loving it publicly and enthusiastically, and thereby calling its merit into question.

What these "weaknesses" reveal is the unexamined and, often, unchallenged snobbery that shapes conventional answers to the question, "What is art?" In truth, the creative force of the human imagination has never submitted to borders of time or place. When it comes to the crafting of objects of beauty, residents of the American West, despite their distance from Europe or from the art capital of New York, have been as active as any other human population. In the same spirit, beauty itself does not refuse the company of usefulness; in shape, color, and form, a beaded Sioux moccasin pleases the eye and even stirs the spirit, even as it eases stress and friction on the foot. In fact, much of what we recognize, unquestioningly, as high or classical European art was itself produced from a very material context of patronage and commerce, conspicuous consumption and ambitions for status. It is a truly rare artist who has, in any time period or geographical setting, entirely separated himself or herself from the down-to-earth concerns of the human species. And, despite the assumed weakness attached to popularity, the enthusiasm of the "unsophisticated" does not have to come paired with the scorn of the elite. The work of an artist such as Frederic Remington or Charles Russell can engage and reward the attention of everyone from art history professors to ranchers who want to contemplate images of open space in prints and on canvases, as well as through the windows of their homes and pickup tricks.

Rather than offering us one settled way of seeing the world, western art invites us to experiment with point of view—because no group has exclusive ownership of, or rights of definition over, the art, history, or literature of the American West. The region has been occupied by a swirl of different groups: people from many different Indian societies, Spanish missionaries and colonists, and immigrants and recent arrivals from every point on the planet. In the populating of the West, the movement from east to west represented only one vector. For the Spanish who traveled from Mexico, what we call the West was the northern borderland; for the Chinese emigrants drawn to California, "Gold Mountain" lay to their east. Even the principal participants in the traditional frontier of westward expansion, occupants of that taken-for-granted category "white American," or "Anglo," carry a very wide range of identities; Irish emigrants with a long-running hostility to England, for instance, hardly saw themselves as "Anglos." Launched from so many different directions and shaped by such varying experiences, the history of the West leaves point of view perennially unsettled. Considered seriously and realistically, the West and its art invite us to a constant reexamination of the assumptions that habit has lulled us into taking for granted.

While we have adopted the custom of clearly distinguishing Anglos from Mexicans, Indians from Euro-Americans, the lines between cultures in the American West are, in practice, insubstantial and shifting. The Mexican border is a permeable boundary, even if many Americans dream of a clearly marked border separating the United States from its southern neighbor, and even if many members of Congress formulate public policy on the basis of that dream. In practice, both people and cultural practices pass back and forth across the Mexican *frontera*. A *santo* carved in Sonora and a *santo* carved in New Mexico will not necessarily reveal their differences in national origins. Either way, the *santo* contains elements of Spanish culture, of Indian culture, of the mestizo culture of Mexico, and, now, of American commercial culture. In matters of art as much as in matters of economy or the natural environment, the border is not on one side purely Mexican and on the other purely American. It is a zone of overlap and encounter and mixture.

Consider, as well, the distinction we often draw between "Indian" and "white," as if those were two clearly differentiated categories of human identity. Setting the two categories off against each other, as if they were opposites, obscures both the diversity of the groups called "whites" and the diversity of the groups called "Indians." Intermarriage between people of Indian origin and people of European origin, moreover, has been an important demographic story in North America for five centuries. Pure lines of descent are difficult to maintain under circumstances as boisterous and unregulated as those that have characterized the populating of the West. In the same way, intellectual and cultural influences have been reciprocal and mingled far more often than they have been intact and separate. In a new book called *Playing Indian,* historian Philip Deloria makes a convincing case for the many ways in which white Americans have built their own identities by reacting to, and sometimes incorporating, elements of Indian identities. Meanwhile, Indian people have shown flexibility and enterprise in incorporating various introduced elements—horses, beads, English, pickup trucks, basketball, litigation, cowboy hats, movies—into their distinctive societies.

Strict boundaries drawn in time can be as deceptive as strict boundaries drawn to separate ethnic identity. For many Americans, the "frontier" has come to function as a hardened border dividing the past from the present. For generations, high school students have been told that western history ended when the frontier line disappeared. Frederick Jackson Turner and his many followers cast the year 1890 as the end of the nation's innocence and the beginning of America's industrial future. For the writers of western dime novels, the frontier West represented an escape from the cities, telephones, automobiles, factories, wages, and clocks of the modern era, an imagined refuge from the modernization of the nation.

Thus, the works of the most popular school of western painting—individuals such as Frederic Remington, Charles Russell, and Charles Schreyvogel—are a nostalgic record of the passing of the Old West and, simultaneously, expressions of talent and vision by individuals living quite successfully in the modern times that believers in the Old West have tried to flee. To dismissive critics, the cowboy-and-Indian paintings of the late nineteenth century have offered more in the way of a good story about a mythic western past than an aesthetic experience. It is certainly true that western art became more valued after the frontier was called "closed" and the West was declared to be "won." Painters like Russell and Remington found a much larger market for their works after Americans began to believe that the true West was disappearing. A market among white Americans for the artistic works of Indians grew at the same time that the army defeated Indians and relocated them to reservations. Cowboy spurs and Colt .45 revolvers became more ornate toward the end of the nineteenth century after the range was fenced and social order became more consistently enforced. Western artifacts only began to qualify for the category of art as the Old West seemed to be fading into history.

After the frontier "closed" in 1890, one kind of time stopped in the West. Meanwhile, another kind of time—the prosaic, much-less-romantic, tiresome kind of time by which one day follows another and historical change occurs and accumulates—proceeded steadily on. In that more secular time, the West continued to exist and to serve as both the site and the outlet for human creativity and artistic impulse. The West that is still with us remains well supplied with seemingly clear and defined lines, boundaries, definitions, and categories, all of them hard-pressed to contain and keep control of a much more complicated and changeable reality. With all of these artificial lines attempting to draw and demarcate the West, it should not be surprising that the line between the "high" art tethered to Europe or Manhattan and the "folk" art of the West proves to be an equally artificial distinction. For a long time, the United States was a colonial culture with a colonial vision that distinguished between the "art" of the conquerors (and an elite segment of the conquering society at that) and the "crafts" of the conquered. A painting by a Euro-American of education and standing is "art," while an Indian tobacco bag slides down into the category of useful craft. But the eclectic gathering of western treasures presented herein makes it abundantly clear that these distinctions call for some heavy-duty rethinking and amending. The Blackfoot leggings and Plains Indian tobacco bags, the photographs of Spanish missions, the spurs, the Mexican *santos,* the single-action Colt .45 revolvers rightfully inhabit the same collections as the works of the Texas Impressionists and of Frederic Remington. Instead of eliciting the smug protest "But this isn't art!" this assembly urges us to examine and rethink our assumptions about the purity of art and the clarity of boundaries in the North American West. Most important, these collections invite our recognition of and admiration for the creativity unleashed by the striking mix of cultures that have made the North American West their home.

WITH HANNAH NORDHAUS

PEOPLE WITHOUT BORDERS
Natives of the North American Plains

EMMA I. HANSEN

I was born on the prairie where the wind blew free, and there was nothing to break the light of the sun. I was born where there were no enclosures, and where everything drew a free breath. I want to die there, and not within walls. I know every stream and wood between the Rio Grande and the Arkansas. I have hunted and lived over that country. I lived like my fathers before me, and like them, I lived happily.

TEN BEARS, 1867[1]

At the council of Medicine Lodge Creek in 1867, Ten Bears, a Penetaka Comanche leader, eloquently expressed the sentiments of many of his generation who saw their free way of life on the Great Plains slipping away. At the council, the assembled Apache, Kiowa, Comanche, Cheyenne, and Arapaho leaders reluctantly signed a treaty that would limit their lands, their movements, and ultimately bring to a close their existence as buffalo hunters and warriors of the Plains.

The struggles of the Native people of the Plains to preserve their ways of life during the last half of the nineteenth century have been interpreted through the Wild West shows, western novels and histories, and Hollywood films. Names such as Sitting Bull, Crazy Horse, Satanta, and Chief Joseph, and events known as Sand Creek, Little Big Horn, Washita, and Wounded Knee are echoes of the past that remind the North American public of these struggles. Stories of past generations of family members who actually participated in some of these events are also recounted by tribal elders to children as a means of remembering and

Lakota Woman's Dress
Northern Plains or South
Dakota, c. 1895. Buckskin
with beads; L 35⅛" (89.2 cm.)
without fringe, chest 44¼"
(112.2 cm.).

understanding this history. Inherent in this remembrance by Plains Indian people is a spiritual connection to the land and its resources that transcends generations.

The story of the White Buffalo Woman who brought the sacred buffalo calf pipe and the buffalo hunting way of life to the Lakota embodies this symbolic connection. In the story, the White Buffalo Woman first appears as a *wakan* (holy) young woman but also represents the buffalo, who gave his flesh in order that the people might live. In 1967, Lame Deer, a member of the Brule Sioux, related the end of the story of the White Buffalo Woman in the following way:

> *The White Buffalo Woman disappeared over the horizon. Sometime she might come back. As soon as she had vanished, buffalo in great herds appeared, allowing themselves to be killed so that the people might survive. And from that day on, our relations, the buffalo, furnished the people with everything they needed—meat for their food, skin for their clothes and tepees, bones for their many tools.*[2]

THE GREAT PLAINS AND ITS TRADITIONS

The vast region of the Great Plains, stretching from the foothills of the Rocky Mountains in the west to the Mississippi River in the east and from Canada south to Texas, presents a difficult and harsh environment in which to live. This region is a land of contrasts, with frequent droughts, sudden spring thunderstorms, and extreme temperature variations ranging from hot summer days to cool but dry winter months. For the Native people of the Plains, however, the land also contained rich resources in tallgrass prairies abundant with herds of buffalo and other grazing animals and fertile river valleys that supported farming traditions.

The first written descriptions of Native people of the Plains are found in the chronicles of sixteenth-century Spanish explorers.[3] In 1541, when Francisco Vázquez de Coronado and his small Spanish army crossed the Southern Plains, he met groups of Apachean buffalo hunters. These nomadic people gathered plant foods and hunted the wandering herds of buffalo and other wild game of the region. Living in tepees of smoke-darkened buffalo hides, they traveled most of the year in small family groups in search of the buffalo. Their dogs served as pack animals, dragging travois made of tepee poles or with belongings tied on their backs. For trade, they traveled to Pueblo villages of eastern New Mexico, exchanging hides, meat, tallow, and salt for farm produce, turquoise, shell ornaments, and obsidian.

The Coronado expedition also traveled to present Kansas where they encountered the Quivirans, the ancestors of the Wichita people, who were following a way of life that continued into the eighteenth century. Near their large grass villages, women tilled their gardens while the men hunted buffalo and other game. Trade was extensive and included commodities such as glazed-paint pottery, turquoise pendants, and shell beads from the Pueblo villages of New Mexico as well as bois d'arc and engraved pottery from Caddo settlements of northeastern Texas.

The Wichita are representative of an economic orientation that existed on the Plains for centuries. Over a thousand years ago, horticulturists established villages along the Missouri, Platte, Republican, Arkansas, and other rivers and streams. By the 1700s, descendants of these Plains horticulturists were known by such tribal names as the Hidatsa, Mandan, and Arikara of the Missouri River region; the Pawnee, Omaha, Ponca, and Oto of the Central Plains region of present Nebraska and northern Kansas; and the Waco, Tawakoni, Osage, and the Wichita of the Southern Plains, including present Kansas, Oklahoma, and Texas.

Living in large semipermanent villages of grass houses (in the Southern Plains) or earth lodges (in the Central and Northern Plains), Plains village women worked gardens that produced an array of foods, including several varieties of corn, beans, squash, and melons.[4] During the fall and sometimes summer, the villages were abandoned as the people traveled into the prairies to hunt buffalo. Transporting their belongings by dogs with travois and packs, men hunted buffalo while the families lived in hide tepees, like the more nomadic Plains tribes. Gathered wild foods and other game supplemented the food resources.

The buffalo, from which the basic necessities of life were produced, was of primary economic and spiritual importance to Plains Indian people, an importance that continues symbolically to the present day. Women worked long hours with implements of sharpened bone and horn to clean, soften, and tan hides that could be used as tepee covers, clothing, robes,

and bedding. Working together, women made tepee covers that required as many as a dozen hides. Pieces of rawhide were painted with pigments to be used as parfleches to transport the families' belongings when traveling. Bones and

Northern Plains Woman's Saddle
1800s. Wood, rawhide, and buckskin; seat 10" (25.3 cm.).

horn were used for hoes, digging sticks, hide-working tools, cups, and spoons. The paunch and bladder served as containers and could be suspended over cooking fires or filled with hot stones to boil meat.

BUFFALO HUNTERS ON HORSEBACK

They were all on horseback, and the women and children, composing by far the greatest part of the cavalcade, passed us without halting. Every woman appeared to have under her care a greater or lesser number of horses, which were driven before her, some dragging lodgepoles, some loaded with packs of meat, and some carrying children.[5]

In the late seventeenth century, Plains tribes acquired horses from Spanish settlements in the Southwest and guns from French and English traders. For farmers and hunters already living on the Plains, horses allowed the bands to travel greater distances to hunt and trade, and transport larger tepees and more belongings. Trade also brought European goods, including guns, metal knives, kettles, glass beads, and needles. The horse, guns, and other trade goods as well as displacement of traditional homelands in the East by Euro-American settlements attracted other tribal groups to the region. This began the movement into the Plains by the Comanche, Kiowa, Cheyenne, Arapaho, Lakota, and others during the seventeenth and eighteenth centuries and the flourishing of the nomadic buffalo hunting and warrior traditions.

The Comanche began their movement south from the Rocky Mountains in the early 1700s. By 1836, they claimed a vast region as they forced Apachean groups to the south and west. The Comanchería, as this region was known, included present western Oklahoma and a great portion of Texas, and extended into New Mexico, Colorado, and Kansas. The Kiowa moved to

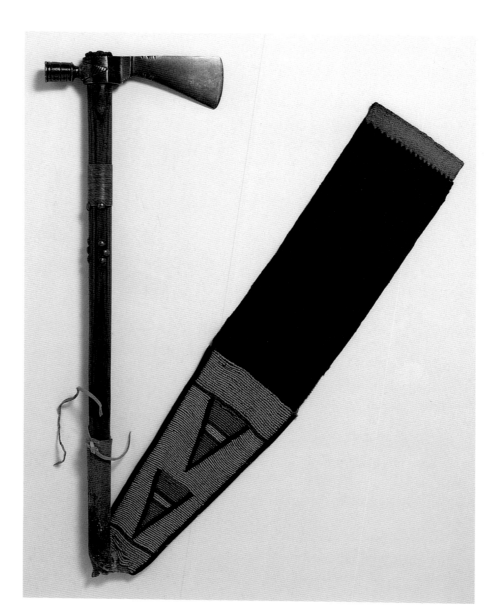

Crow Pipe Tomahawk
Northern Plains, c. 1860. Iron, brass wire and tacks, wood, rawhide, beads, and wool fabric; L 48⅛" (122.2 cm.), head W 8⅛" (20.2 cm.).

Blackfoot Buffalo Ball Rattle and Parfleche Case
Northern Plains, c. 1850. Rawhide, buckskin, and pigments; rattle L 10⅛" (25.6 cm.), case L 10½" (26.5 cm.).

Blackfoot Parfleche Northern Plains, late 1800s. Rawhide and pigment; H 15½" (39.5 cm.), W 25⅜" (63.1 cm.).

the Southern Plains from the Black Hills region of South Dakota, stopping for a period in the mountains of western Montana. With them traveled their allies, the Plains Apache, who formed a part of the Kiowa tribal council and joined their camp circle for the annual Sun Dance.

The Cheyenne came into the Plains from the Great Lakes region, where they had been horticulturists. Having gradually moved west, they began to acquire horses around 1750. By 1804, they were living in hide tepees and following the buffalo with their Arapaho allies. By 1859, the Cheyenne and Arapaho were separated into northern and southern divisions, as trading posts, Euro-American settlements, and overland routes were established between them. The northern division lived between the North and South Platte Rivers, while the southern people were located between the South Platte and the Arkansas, with hunting ranges extending into western Oklahoma and Texas.[6]

On the Northern Plains, other tribes, including the Blackfoot, Crow, and Lakota, gave up their settled farming existence to follow the herds of buffalo on the prairies. For example, the Lakota, a division of the Sioux, lived in the region of present Minnesota in the 1760s, but within thirty years, they had taken up the lives of mounted buffalo hunters, with territories in the Dakotas and south into Nebraska. The Blackfoot, a loose confederacy of three tribes, lived around the upper Missouri River basin. To the east were the Gros Ventre, and to the south were the Assiniboine. The Crow were located south of the Missouri River in the middle Yellowstone Valley of present Montana. Late in the seventeenth

century, the Plateau tribes, including the Nez Perce and the Yakima of the middle Columbia River Valley, also developed a horse culture based on hunting buffalo.[7]

The spiritual life of Plains Indian people of the nineteenth century was supreme and guided all economic and social activities. Tribal ceremonies followed a seasonal cycle based upon the yearly round of hunting and horticultural activities. For the Pawnee, ceremonies were held as corn was planted and harvested and to preserve buffalo herds and bring about successful hunts. During the winter before beginning their hunt, the Mandan and Hidatsa of the Upper Missouri held buffalo-calling ceremonies and the dramatic buffalo dance to bring the animals closer to the villages.[8]

For the nomadic buffalo hunters, such as the Lakota, Kiowa, Cheyenne, and Arapaho, the annual Sun Dance brought tribal bands together during the summer when the buffalo grazed in large herds. Called by the Cheyenne the "Sacred Lodge Dance" or "renewing the earth," the Sun Dance symbolized the rebirth of life on earth, and was held to bring good fortune to all who attended.

END OF AN ERA

Nothing lives long, except the earth and the mountains.
WHITE ANTELOPE, CHEYENNE
DEATH SONG AT SAND CREEK MASSACRE, 1864[9]

Nothing happened after that. We had lived. There were no more war parties, no capturing of horses from the Piegans and the Sioux, no buffalo to hunt. There is no more to tell.
TWO LEGGINGS, CROW, 1880[10]

The early to middle nineteenth century provided the backdrop for the dramatic rise and fall of the Plains buffalo hunters. This tradition prevailed for only 100 to 150 years in all, although the timeless image of the Plains warrior on horseback survives and often forms the popular stereotype of Indian people today.

The nineteenth-century movement of Euro-American immigrants to the West brought years of disruptive warfare and dislocation. Railroads, forts, and trails were built, and gold miners and settlers moved into tribal lands. As the Euro-American frontier moved closer to the tribes, the diseases of smallpox, cholera, and measles brought death to many.[11] Finally, the near annihilation of the once vast herds of buffalo by commercial hide hunters in the 1870s brought this dramatic period to an end.

By the 1870s, reservations had been established for Plains tribes in Canada and the United States. The massacre of Lakota adherents of the Ghost Dance at Wounded Knee in December 1890 signaled the end of the old life. The buffalo were gone, tribal populations had been reduced by as much as 90 to 95 percent, and the people faced confinement on their reservation lands.[12]

Plains people made a valiant effort to preserve and protect their traditions, ceremonies, and communities despite the poor conditions of the reservations. With the loss of the buffalo and the ability to freely hunt other game and grow traditional foods, many of the ceremonies lost their past meanings. Considering the cultural losses that occurred in this period, it is remarkable that so many traditions survive to the present.

Blackfoot Backrest
Northern Plains, 1800s. Willow reeds, beads, wool fabric, and buckskin; L 54¼" (137.8 cm.), W 31¼" (79.3 cm.).

Man's Leggings
Northern Plains, c. 1885.
Buckskin, beads, bone hair pipe,
horsehair, and yarn; L 32⅜"
(82.4 cm.), W 11⅞" (30.2 cm.).

Northern Plains Man's
War Shirt
Porcupine quill work c. 1880
applied to a later buckskin shirt;
L 26¾" (68.1 cm.), chest
43½" (110.4 cm.).

ART: THE FABRIC OF LIFE

The American Indian has tenaciously held onto his arts, not in the sense of object alone but rather as a fabric that binds and holds together many dimensions of his very existence. The arts are to him an expression of the integrated forces that tie together and unify all aspects of life.[13]

With this statement, Lakota artist and scholar Arthur Amiotte expresses the essential role of art within Native communities. As recent publications have stressed, there is no word for "art" within any North American Indian language.[14] Native American-produced objects in museum and private collections now identified as art (or artifact) have a more far-reaching significance as representations of the economic,

social, and spiritual lives of the people. Symbols of the earth and sky depicted on clothing and other materials tie the people to their homelands, beliefs, and traditions.

The distinctive material culture produced by Plains Indian people in the nineteenth century has been referred to as "an aesthetic of mobility."[15] Plains Indian clothing, household objects, and tools were transportable, functional, and practical but also were painted, quilled, and beaded to reflect tribal traditions and sense of aesthetics. Hides of buffalo, deer, elk, and other animals were the raw materials from which were made clothing, tepees, leggings and moccasins, parfleches and painted robes.

On the Southern Plains, dresses, leggings, and moccasins were painted in natural pigments of yellow, red, and blue green and trimmed in long fringes. When

Lakota Tobacco Bag
South Dakota, c. 1885. Buckskin, rawhide, beads, and porcupine quills; L 26" (66.1 cm.).

beads were introduced through trade with Euro-Americans, they were used to accent dresses, shirts, and moccasins in simple elegant designs. Porcupine quills, which had been flattened and colored with natural dyes, were wrapped or embroidered into geometric and floral designs on moccasins, pipe bags, clothing, and ornaments of Northern Plains people.

In much the same way that men were honored and recognized for their abilities in hunting and warfare, Plains Indian women were admired for their creative skills. Cheyenne, Arapaho, and Lakota women who excelled in beading or porcupine quillwork belonged to special societies or guilds. Only women of these societies had the right to make the decorations for sacred tepees or tepee liners. Before learning to work with quills, Blackfoot women were required to undergo special initiations to ensure that they would not go blind nor be harmed by the quills.[16]

Cradleboards and other baby carriers reflected the need for mobility and to provide a safe place for babies in camp when mothers worked, as well as the spiritual significance of children. Among many tribes, the making of the cradleboard was shared by both the mother's and father's relations, and represented the joining of the two families. A grandmother or another older respected woman guided the gathering of materials, design, and construction of the cradleboard.

Lakota Spoon
South Dakota, c. 1885.
Cow horn, porcupine quills, and tin cones; L 7⅞" (20.1 cm.), W 2½" (6.5 cm.).

Men recorded their accomplishments in capturing horses or in battle in pictographic hide paintings, tepee covers, and, later, drawings on paper known as ledger art. Among Plains Indian people, war deeds were accredited to assistance from more powerful beings. Retelling the stories and recording them in drawings or carvings reinforced and reminded the people of those blessings. Although such images of hunting, horse raiding, and warfare are sources of stereotypes in literature and film, for the warriors these drawings were real scenes from their own lives.[17]

During the late 1800s to early 1900s, after reservations had been established for the Plains tribes, an ironic flowering of tribal arts occurred. Just as Plains Indian people confined to the depressing conditions of the reservations seemed to have reached the low point of their existence, their creativity continued to be expressed through innovation in design and use of materials.

In reservation art, porcupine quillwork was used in combination with glass beads, fabric, tin cones, and other trade materials. During the 1890s, Lakota and Cheyenne women began to illustrate men's war deeds through pictographic beading and quillwork on tobacco bags and clothing. They also developed a new style of decoration in which entire objects were covered in beadwork. As women produced fully beaded moccasins and men's vests and even covered glass bottles with beadwork, it was said that "Sioux women beaded everything that didn't move."[18] Men's vests with pictorial designs of warriors, horses, buffalo, deer, elk, cowboys, and often the American flag were worn by Native women or sold to non-Indians.

The reasons for the flowering of Plains material culture during the early reservation period are not fully understood. Scholars have suggested that women, once they were settled on the reservations, simply had more time to produce the clothing and other materials that characterized this period. New trade materials, including silk ribbons, glass beads, cotton thread and needles, trade cloth, and brass bells, inspired innovative combinations and designs. As tribes from the northeastern woodlands were moved to Oklahoma reservations, they brought with them floral designs that influenced Kiowa and other Plains beadworkers. The Crow and the Blackfoot had earlier adopted floral designs from eastern Indians who accompanied nineteenth-century fur traders.

The reasons for this artistic embellishment, however, probably go much deeper. On the reservations, Plains Indian people struggled to maintain their tribal identities while government agencies, schools, and missionaries attempted to convince them to set aside their languages, beliefs, ceremonies, and community life. Perhaps clothing and other materials decorated with tribal designs became increasingly important as a means of establishing and maintaining identities as Plains Indian people.

Native communities in the United States and Canada today are experiencing a cultural revitalization evidenced in language-retention programs, renewed interest in the Sun Dance and other ceremonies, powwows, and the preservation of tribal dances, songs, and oral histories. While living as dynamic members of their own communities, Native people of the Plains retain an interest in their heritages that goes beyond the buffalo hunting days of the nineteenth century. The material remnants of that past found in museum and private collections speak to the people of the present not only as objects of artistic beauty but as reflections of the ancestral ideas, histories, and experiences that helped to shape their lives today.

NOTES

1. In Morris W. Foster, *Being Comanche: A Social History of an American Indian Community* (Tucson: The University of Arizona Press, 1991), 174.

2. In Richard Erdoes and Alfonso Ortiz, eds. *American Indian Myths and Legends* (New York: Pantheon Books, 1984), 52.

3. See George Parker Winship, *The Coronado Expedition, 1540–1542.* 14th Annual Report of Bureau of American Ethnology, 1892–93, pp. 329–613.

4. For a discussion of Plains village farming traditions, see *Buffalo Bird Woman's Garden: Agriculture of the Hidatsa Indians* (St. Paul: Minnesota Historical Society Press, 1987).

5. In Edwin James, "Account of an Expedition from Pittsburgh to the Rocky Mountains, Performed in the Years 1819, 1820, Under the Command of Major S.H. Long," *Early Western Travels, 1748–1846* (Cleveland: Arthur H. Clark Company, 1905).

6. For culture and history of the Cheyenne, see Donald J. Berthrong, *The Southern Cheyennes* (Norman: University of Oklahoma Press, 1963); George Bird Grinnell, *The Cheyenne Indians: Their History and Ways of Life* (New Haven: Yale University Press, 1923); and John H. Moore, *The Cheyenne Nation: A Social and Demographic History* (Lincoln: The University of Nebraska Press, 1987).

7. For Northern Plains horse traditions, see John C. Ewers, *The Horse in Blackfoot Indian Culture: With Comparative Material from Other Western Tribes* (Washington, D.C.: Smithsonian Institution Bureau of American Ethnology, Bulletin 159, 1955).

8. The artist George Catlin described and illustrated the Mandan buffalo dance. See John C. Ewers, ed., *O-Kee-Pa: A Religious Ceremony and Other Customs of the Mandan* (New Haven: Yale University Press, 1967); and Roy W. Meyer, *The Village Indians of the Upper Missouri: The Mandans, Hidatsas, and Arikaras* (Lincoln: The University of Nebraska Press, 1977).

9. In Berthrong, 1963, p. 219.

10. In Peter Nabokov, *Two Leggings: The Making of a Crow Warrior* (New York: Crowell Co., 1967) 197.

11. For a discussion of the effects of disease on North American Indian populations, see Russell Thornton, *American Indian Holocaust and Survival: A Population History Since 1492* (Norman: University of Oklahoma Press, 1987).

12. See Thornton, 1987, p. 95.

13. In Rick Hill, *Creativity is Our Tradition: Three Decades of Contemporary Indian Art at the Institute of American Indian Arts* (Santa Fe: Institute of American Indian Arts, 1992) 10.

14. See Richard West in *Creation's Journey: Native American Identity and Belief* (Washington, D.C.: Smithsonian Institution, 1994) 10; Margaret Archuleta and Rennard Strickland, *Shared Visions: Native American Painters and Sculptors in the Twentieth Century* (Phoenix: The Heard Museum, 1991). This topic has been the subject of debate among artists and art historians in recent years. In 1996, the Native Arts Network (ATLATL) entitled its sixth biennial conference "We Have No Word for Art."

15. In Ralph T. Coe, *Sacred Circles: Two Thousand Years of North American Indian Art* (Kansas City: Nelson Gallery Foundation, 1977) 159.

16. See Mary Jane Schneider, "Women's Work: An Examination of the Women's Roles in Plains Indian Arts and Crafts," *The Hidden Half* (Washington, D.C.: University Press of America, Inc., 1983) 101–22.

17. See Evan M. Maurer, Visions of the People: *A Pictorial History of Plains Indian Life* (Minneapolis: The Minneapolis Institute of Arts, 1992) 36–51.

18. In Marla N. Powers, *Oglala Women: Myth, Ritual, and Reality* (Chicago: The University of Chicago Press, 1986) 137–38.

PHOTOGRAPHY OF NATIVE AMERICAN ARTIFACTS BY BAKÓ/BECQ WORLDWIDE.

Lakota Beaded Vest
Northern Plains (South Dakota),
c. 1895. Buckskin and beads;
L 17⅜" (44.1 cm.), chest 39¼"
(99.6 cm.).

Plains Blanket Strip
c. 1890. Hide, beads, and silk
ribbon; L 60¾" (154.5 cm.).

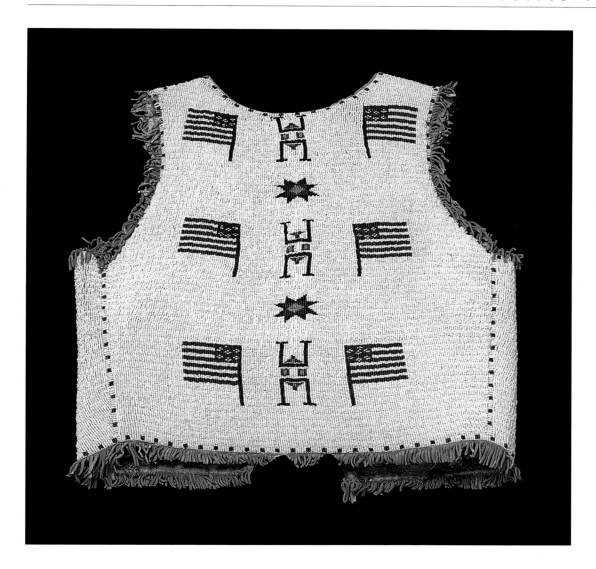

Arapaho Beaded Vest
Plains, pre-1890. Hide, beads,
and pigment; L 15½" (39.2 cm.),
chest 29" (65.2 cm.).

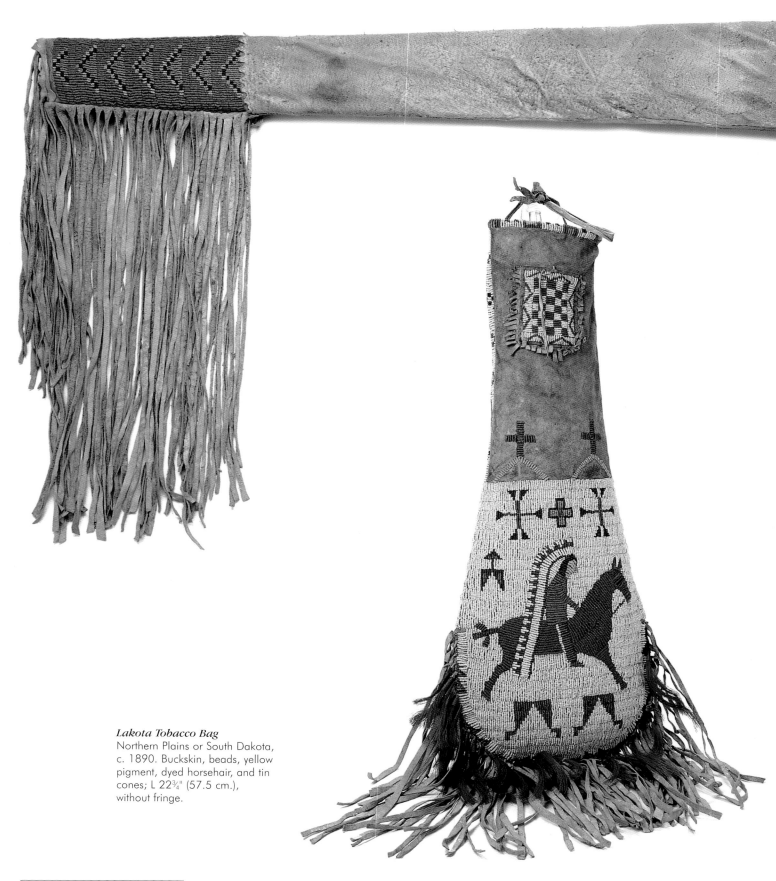

Lakota Tobacco Bag
Northern Plains or South Dakota,
c. 1890. Buckskin, beads, yellow
pigment, dyed horsehair, and tin
cones; L 22¾" (57.5 cm.),
without fringe.

Blackfoot or Flathead Gun Case
Northern Plains, 1800s. Buckskin
and beads; L 43⅜" (110.2 cm.).

Lakota Storage Bag
Northern Plains, c. 1880. Buckskin
with beads; H 14⅜" (36.3 cm.),
W 23½" (59.5 cm.).

Crow Man's Coat
Northern Plains or Montana,
c. 1890. Buckskin, beads, silk
ribbon, otter hide, yellow
pigment; L 36⅜" (92.3 cm.),
chest 40¾" (103.6 cm.).

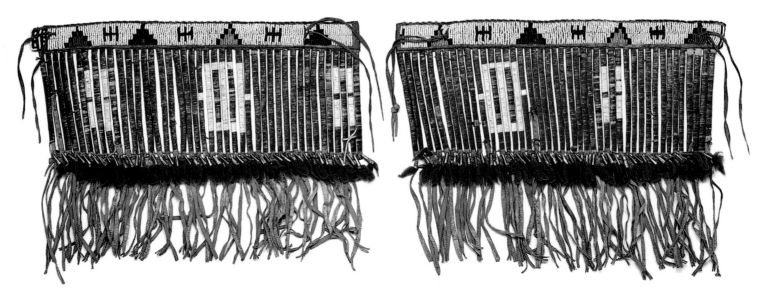

Blackfoot Man's Dance Garters
Northern Plains, late 1800s.
Buckskin, rawhide, beads, porcupine
quills, tin cones, and wool;
L 8" (20.1 cm.), W 15¼" (38.6 cm.).

Arapaho Tobacco Bag
Plains, c. 1890. Buckskin,
rawhide, beads, porcupine
quills, fiber; L 25⅞" (65.7 cm.).

Blackfoot Man's Leggings
Northern Plains, c. 1885. Buckskin
with beads; L 31⅝" (80.2 cm.).

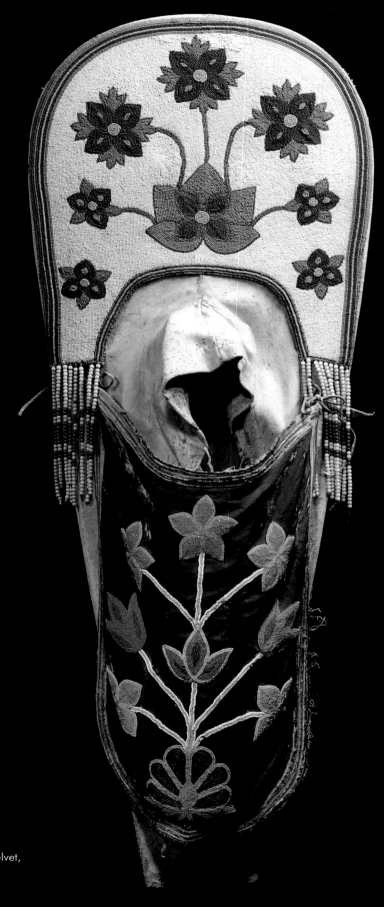

Plateau Baby Carrier
c. 1885. Buckskin, beads, velvet,
cotton cloth, and silk ribbon;
H 49¼" (125.3 cm.),
W 15¼" (38.9 cm.).

Plateau Doll Cradle
c. 1885. Buckskin and beads;
L 12¼" (30.9 cm.), W 5¾" (14.6 cm.).

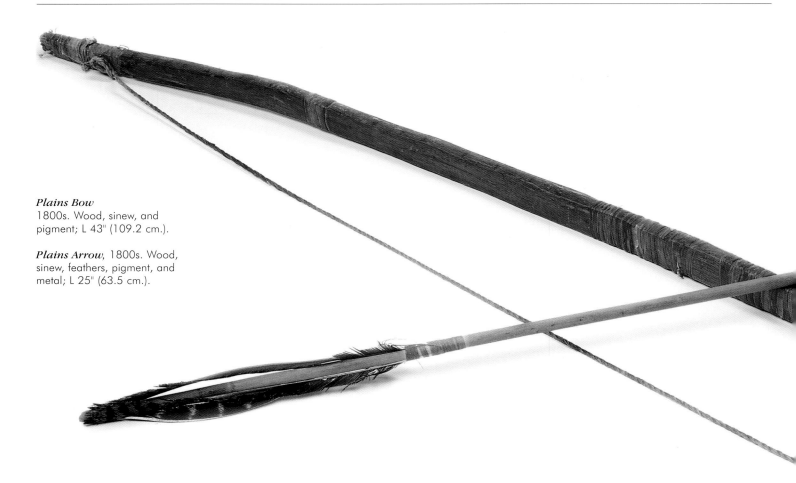

Plains Bow
1800s. Wood, sinew, and
pigment; L 43" (109.2 cm.).

Plains Arrow, 1800s. Wood,
sinew, feathers, pigment, and
metal; L 25" (63.5 cm.).

Lakota Holster
South Dakota, c. 1890.
Buckskin and beads;
L 11⅝" (29.5 cm.).

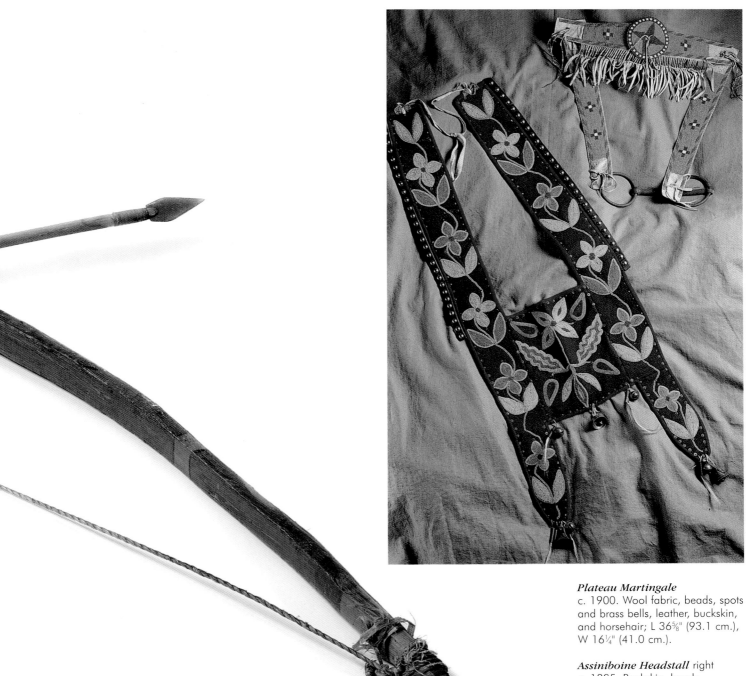

Plateau Martingale
c. 1900. Wool fabric, beads, spots
and brass bells, leather, buckskin,
and horsehair; L 36⅝" (93.1 cm.),
W 16¼" (41.0 cm.).

Assiniboine Headstall right
c. 1885. Buckskin, beads,
porcupine quills, and metal;
L 15¼" (38.6 cm.), W 16⅛"
(40.8 cm.).

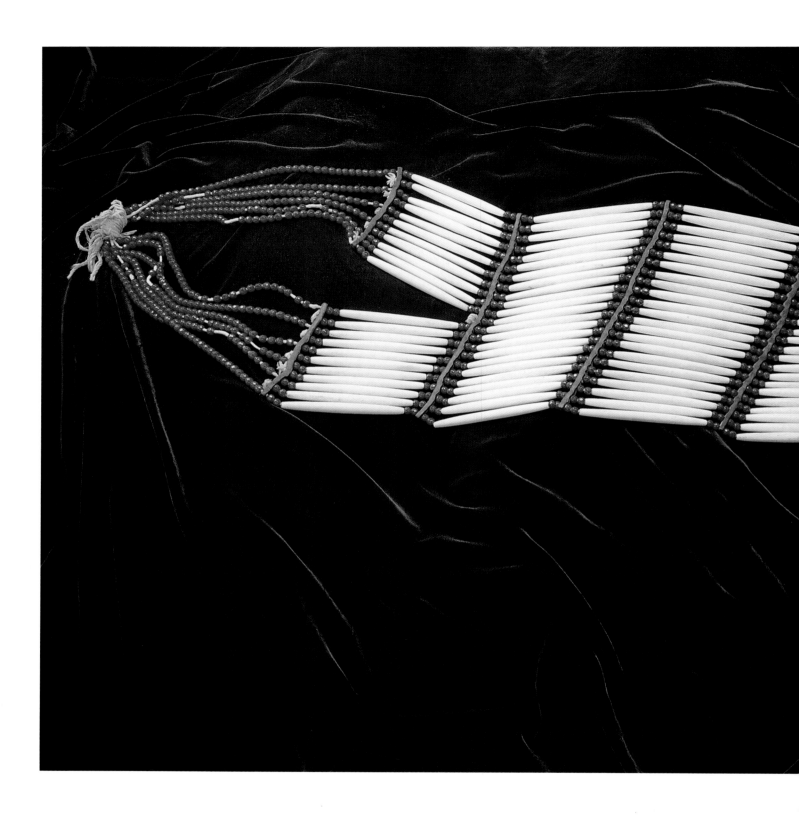

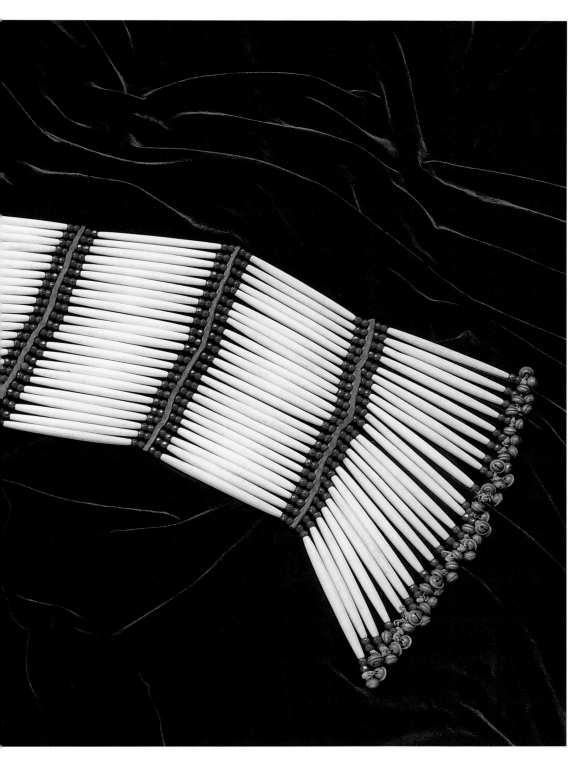

Blackfoot Woman's Breastplate,
Northern Plains, c. 1920. Bone
hair pipe, hide, beads, and brass
hawk bells; L 52¼" (132.4 cm.),
W 9⅛" (23.4 cm.).

Arapaho Pouch
Plains, c. 1885. Buckskin, beads,
tin cones, and feathers;
L 8" (20.4 cm.).

Blackfoot Porcupine Tail Hairbrush
Northern Plains, c. 1885. Wood and
beads; L 11" (28.0 cm.).

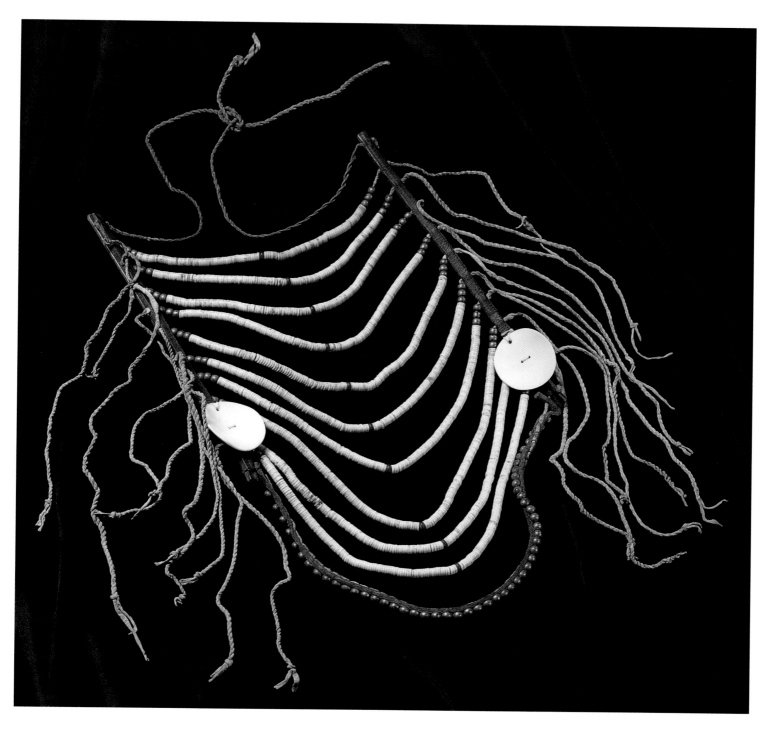

Crow Man's Necklace
Montana, c. 1880, Shells,
leather, brass spots, and beads;
L 30¼" (76.6 cm.).

Assiniboine Man's Moccasins,
Northern Plains, c. 1880. Buckskin,
cotton cloth and beads,
L 10⅛" (25.7 cm.)

Lakota Man's Moccasins,
South Dakota, c. 1890. Buckskin
and beads; L 11⅜" (28.7 cm.).

Lakota ceremonial moccasins, Southern Plains or Oklahoma, c. 1895. Buckskin, beads, tin cones, and horsehair dangles; L 10⅜" (26.3 cm.).

Hidatsa, Northern Plains 1800s. Canvas, trade cloth, porcupine quills, and rawhide, L 10¼" (26.0 cm.).

Lakota, South Dakota, c. 1885. Buckskin, beads, porcupine quills, tin cones, feathers, and fabric. L 10⅜" (26.4 cm.).

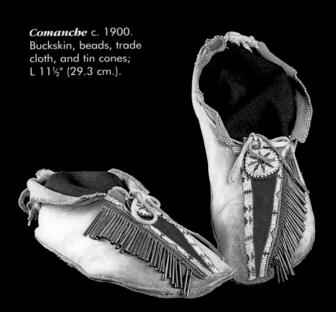

Comanche c. 1900. Buckskin, beads, trade cloth, and tin cones; L 11½" (29.3 cm.).

Lakota by Lucy White Hawk,
South Dakota, n.d. Buckskin,
beads, tin cones, and
horsehair dangles;
L 10¾" (27.4 cm.).

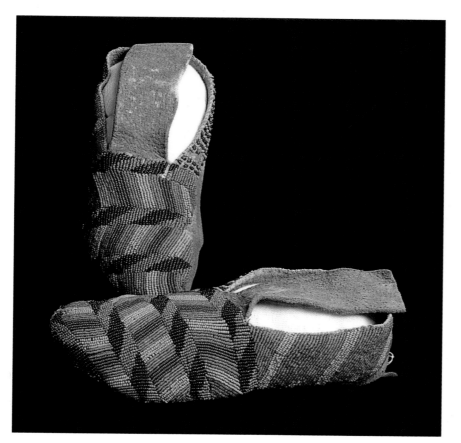

Northern Plains
c. 1875. Buckskin and
beads; L 10" (25.4 cm.).

Crow Man's Coat
Northern Plains, c. 1870.
Dyed buckskin, beads, and mink;
L 29⅜" (74.4 cm.),
chest 37¾" (96.2 cm.).

Nez Perce Woman's Dress
Plateau, c. 1890. Buckskin, beads, pigment, and abalone shell; L 43¼" (110.2 cm.), chest 37¾" (95.4 cm.).

Plateau Female Doll
c. 1910. Hide, hair, beads, tin,
and leather; H 11" (27.8 cm.),
W 5½" (13.7 cm.).

Crow Parfleche Square
Montana, c. 1900. Rawhide,
pigment, and wool strips;
H 18½" (47.2 cm.),
W 13" (32.9 cm.).

Plains Knife and Knife Case
pre-1900. Steel, wood, buckskin,
beads, porcupine quills, tin cones,
and horsehair; knife L 11½" (29.1
cm.), overall case L 20⅝" (52.2 cm.).

Cheyenne Storage or Tepee Bags, c. 1885. Buffalo hide, beads, wool cloth, tin cones, and horsehair; H 16⅜" and 15¾" (41.4 cm. and 39.9 cm.), W 23¾" and 24⅛" (60.5 cm. and 61.2 cm.).

Dakota Gauntlets
Eastern Plains, c. 1880. Buckskin
and beads; L 14¼" (35.9 cm.),
W 7⅞" (19.8 cm.).

Lakota Saddle Blanket
South Dakota, c. 1895. Buckskin,
beads, canvas, silk ribbon, and brass
hawk bells; L 82¼" (209.0 cm.),
W 30¼" (76.7 cm.).

Lakota Cradle Cover
South Dakota, c. 1890. Hide,
porcupine quills, beads, tin cones,
and horse hair; H 23⅛" (58.6 cm.),
W 12" (30.5 cm.).

***Southern Cheyenne or Kiowa
Parfleche Bonnet Case,***
Oklahoma or Southern Plains,
c. 1870. Rawhide, buckskin, and
pigment; L 27⅞" (70.7 cm.),
W 10" (25.2 cm.).

U.S. Cavalry—Blackfoot Kepi,
c. 1885. Wool, leather, and brass.

Northern Plains Saddle Pad
c. 1885. Hide, beads and yarn.

THE MISSIONARY-LED INDIAN COMMUNITIES

GILBERTO M. HINOJOSA

For many, the word *missions* evokes Spanish colonial churches, with their weathered bell towers, their earthen-colored walls, their baroque architectural trimmings. To others more familiar with the colonial period, however, the word may summon up instead the remnants of building complexes that used to house formerly nomadic Native peoples. Rarely does the term elicit what the settlers on New Spain's northern frontier actually meant in the eighteenth century when they talked about a "mission"—an Indian town founded and directed by missionaries, with its resources and its dynamic social structure. Those settlers in fact seldom used the word *mission* alone, in the abstract. Instead, they coupled the generic term *misión* with the name of a given town, or *pueblo. Mission,* then, meant an Indian community.

The term *mission* was generally used in the abstract by the missionary friars as they sought to defend the rights and prerogatives of their enterprises. It was used as well by colonial officials—governors and mayors or councilmen *(alcaldes)*—as they attacked the privileges accorded to friars and their "missions." Ecclesiastic and secular leaders on the frontier were in fact often in conflict over limited resources—that is, arable land, water rights, and Indian labor.

Their references to "mission" as an institution is the stuff from which historians have fashioned their narratives and descriptions of early Texas and what would later become the American Southwest. Naturally, then, historians have tended also to see the missions as one of the constituent units of government in New Spain or as vehicles for imperial expansion. Similarly, the role of the friar directing a particular

*Façade of Mission
Corpus Christi de la Ysleta,
El Paso, Texas.*

Priest Against Wall with Pointed Arched Windows, Mission San José y San Miguel de Aguayo, San Antonio, Texas.

town (the *padre presidente*) has usually been described by its relationship to secular authority (i.e., the governor or the viceroy).

Since by and large they have focused on the Crown's strategic objectives in New Spain, historians have tended also to characterize the settlement of the area's northern region as an attempt to hold a borderlands rather than simply to occupy a frontier. By the same token, most historians writing in the "imperial" tradition have taken for granted the role of the friar in charge of the missions, either as the leader of the mission town or as the general manager of a settlement corporation.

In fairness to such historians, it should be said that the documents that provide information for their histories seldom allude to the internal role of the Indian

towns. That may be because by the time the missions were established in Texas and the Southwest the process of structuring and organizing such towns had become prosaic or formulaic, understood by all. Alternately, the internal dynamics of mission towns may have been overlooked because historians have preferred to focus instead on the missions' conflicts with government officials. Those conflicts no doubt seemed to threaten the Crown's control of the area, and the historians who have adopted the perspective of the center (i.e., the Crown's) in their work have naturally tended to focus more on political struggles than on the social dynamics or internal administration of the Indian communities.

Recently, however, some scholars have been influenced by socioeconomic and cultural history to pose new questions of the Indian "missions" and to read the old documents in new ways. In other words, they have shifted their perspective and they have begun examining the missions on their own terms—that is, as Indian towns led by the friars. The new approach has drawn attention away from exclusively Spanish policies and from political controversies; it has sought to place the missions in the wider context of New Spain's social and economic development.

THE CONQUEST AND COLONIAL ERA SETTING

The dramatic events surrounding Hernán Cortés's seizure of Tenochtitlán, the capital of the Aztec empire (1521), have long held the attention of scholars and laymen alike. More important than Cortés's victory, though, were the long-term consequences of the conquest, which involved

the subjugation of the towns and city-states in central Mexico that the Aztecs had dominated. Those settlements, after all, had provided the labor force and the agricultural and craft products that had sustained the Aztecs' Meso-American empire. After 1521, they were to form the economic and social base for the new empire—that is, New Spain's internal economy.

Spain's policy of financing its struggles for hegemony in Europe with resources from the Americas, especially precious metals, has tended to overshadow the vicissitudes of the internal economy in the New World. This happened in large part because statesmen and politicians in Spain were concerned primarily with questions of high politics and of empire. What loomed large on the imagination of most Spanish newcomers to the Americas, on the other hand, were local resources—that is, land and Indian labor. Often the newcomers fought

Arched Breezeway Joining the Convento (missionaries' quarters) and Church, Mission San José y San Miguel de Aguayo.

53

Mission San José y San Miguel de Aguayo.

each other and the Natives for control of those resources, especially because after the conquest local products became more valuable than before.

As a consequence of such pressures, dominion over the towns and city-states in the Indian countryside (the *República de Indios*), had to be more thorough under the Spaniards than it had been with the Aztecs. The new forms of control—economic, political, religious—rested on the social structure of the self-contained, settled Indian villages.

The newcomers *(conquistadores)* depended on the indigenous towns for the procurement of labor. In return for their services in conquest expeditions, Spaniards were rewarded with land-and-labor units called *encomiendas.* The land units were not initially extensive, and they were not considered as critical as the awarding (actually, the "entrusting," as the term *encomienda* implies) of one or more Indian towns. The indigenous communities operated under *caciques,* or chiefs, who orga-

nized their townsmen's work shifts on the Spaniard owners' *(encomenderos)* lands.

The rule of the caciques, then, was critical to securing Indian labor. Without them, the Spaniards would have needed more Spanish overseers than the single manager needed (the *estanciero,* or manager of the *estancia,* the encomendero's landholding). The use of more overseers would have proven difficult because the colony did not attract Spaniards in large numbers. The alternative would have been to establish a system of slavery, but that would not have been feasible in an Indian countryside made up of autonomous Native towns.

The Crown, too, depended on the Indian towns and their managers to bolster its political control. Once the original conquistadores died out or lost their power, Spain sent into the República de Indios the same royal officials it had used to good profit in Iberia, the *corregidores,* to make sure that tribute was collected and Indian labor assigned. However, in many, if not most, towns, Indian leaders themselves

rituals and expressions of faith mixed and became inseparable.

The missionaries quickly assumed the role of protectors of the Indians. The friars resided in the Indian towns for extended periods of time and came to understand Native ways. Like the Crown and the conquistadores, they also relied on Native labor. But many of the padres were imbued with a sense of justice, and they began defending the Natives against the excesses of the encomenderos and later of the corregidores. This role came naturally in a society like that of Colonial New Spain, which was fragmented into autonomous corporations and which saw constant struggles among leaders from different sectors.

The República de Indios was not entirely Indian as its name implies; it also encompassed Spanish cities. Spaniards were lured to the countryside by pockets of silver deposits and by the need for strategic outposts; soon, regional capitals and distribution centers emerged. The Spanish towns also attracted Indian and mixed-blood laborers *(mestizos),* who sought work in the construction industries and in the service sectors. Native haulers *(cargadores)* linked the Indian and Spanish towns, making the separation between the two worlds never complete. Nevertheless, like the colony itself, the Spanish hub cities depended on the fully permanent Indian towns surrounding them.

THE FRONTIER

The flurry of explorations to the distant northern lands that followed the fall of the Aztec capital uncovered few readily available deposits of precious minerals and no kingdoms with settled Indian towns. The

managed such tasks rather than permitting the interference of outsiders. Still, the power of the Crown was very evident and quite real in the Indian communities.

Like the conquistadores and the Crown itself, missionaries also based their work on the Natives' town. For the Indians, religion was a communal bond, so that converting the caciques and other local elites was the first step to bringing all the residents into the faith. The conversion appeared simple also because the stability and discipline of the town society seemed to mirror the Christian moral order and because some Native religious practices appeared to parallel Catholic ceremonies.

But the new religion would require much more of the Indians. After their initial optimism over the many souls they were winning for the faith, the friars came to question the authenticity of the Indians' conversions, and they set about to extirpate the remaining vestiges of "pagan" practices. In time, however, a syncretism emerged in which both Catholic and Native

one such "kingdom" was the land of the Pueblos at the upper reaches of the Río Grande, and the Spaniards were not prepared to go there until 1598. That year Juan de Oñate launched the settlement of the Kingdom of New Mexico *(el Reino de Nuevo México),* so named because Oñate and his latter-day conquistadores wanted to revive and relive the glories of Spain's Meso-American empire.

Elsewhere, Spaniards found the North to be without towns *(despoblado,* also meaning "depopulated"). The area was inhabited only by Native hunter-gatherers, some belligerent but all with few resources for trade and with no immediate propensity for settlement. The discovery of mining regions in the North, however, attracted Spanish conquistadores, merchants, muleteers, and other providers. This encroachment into Native hunting and gathering territories was met with fierce resistance, so much so that in order to defend the mines and supply lines the Crown was forced to organize a costly standing military (as opposed to the ad hoc, largely self-financed, earlier conquest enterprises [*compañías*]).

To secure the area permanently, Spaniards almost reflexively set out to re-create a countryside dotted by Spanish-controlled Indian towns and dominated by strategic Spanish cities. The process started after the central highlands were occupied, and Spaniards and Hispanicized peoples spilled into the semiarid northern frontier in the mid- and late-1500s. The responsibility of gathering the Natives and re-creating the social organization of Indian communities fell on the missionaries who had worked among the natives in central

Mexico. On the frontier, the padres were expected to function as latter-day corregidores.

The Franciscans took charge of settling, acculturating, and converting the Natives in New Spain's northeastern corner and in the far north. The friars came from two Apostolic Colleges, one in Querétaro, the other in Zacatecas, which prepared them for their tasks in the wilderness. The colleges also furnished the missionaries with start-up supplies, financed by the order's benefactors in those two silver cities. Additionally, the friars received a Crown subsidy for their "civilizing" enterprises.

The Jesuits, too, accepted the challenge to evangelize the Indians of the far northern frontier. They worked among the Natives in Sonora, Arizona, and Baja California. But political developments back in Europe ended the Jesuit efforts in the Americas in 1767, and Franciscans stepped in to continue their work.

Soldiers were also sent to the frontier with the missionaries because Natives often resented Spanish intrusion and some, displaying formidable military skills, repelled the invaders. Many of the hunter-gatherers were in fact unwilling to trade their freedom for the food and security of settled existence that the padres offered, and many also failed to appreciate the social benefits of community life. The soldiers, then, were essential to protect the missionaries and to "reduce" the wanderers into missionary-led towns.

The soldiers, mostly Hispanicized mestizos accompanied by their families, were themselves also settlers who created a new kind of community on the frontier: the *presidio,* or garrison. Appealing on

Bastion at Presidio Nuestra Señora de Loreto de La Bahía, Goliad, Texas.

their service to the Crown, the soldiers requested and acquired lands that they farmed, making use of their military pay as a subsidy while they established themselves. The presidios thus functioned as soldier-settler towns that contributed significantly to stabilizing the nomadic populations.

The provincial governors, who were the commanders of the presidios, also functioned as merchants, procuring foodstuffs and other goods from the center for the settlers on the frontier. The military roads that provided security became the region's trade routes. In sum, the presidio system was an integral part of the colonization enterprise.

Spaniards and Hispanicized frontiersmen and women followed the friars and soldiers and established their own towns near the Indian and military communities. As soon as they arrived in an area, settlers in those civilian towns fought the residents of the Indian pueblos and presidios for control of rural resources. In time these newcomers won out, and their towns eventually incorporated the Indians and the soldier-settlers. Still, the presidios and, particularly, the friar-led Indian towns played important roles in the settlement of the frontier.

Graveyard and the Mission
Nuestra Señora de la Limpia
Concepción del Socorro,
El Paso, Texas.

THE MISSIONARY-LED
INDIAN TOWNS

Among the first friar-founded and -directed communities in the far northern frontier were the towns established for the Pueblos in New Mexico. These missions were aberrations of sorts, since they were established for Indians who were, for the most part, already settled. Not surprisingly, those foundations remained unstable for years. When the Pueblos revolted in 1680, Spanish settlers and the friars and their converts fell back to El Paso del Norte. There, a missionary-led community, Misión

Nuestra Señora de Guadalupe, had been established on the south bank of the Río Grande for the Natives of the area. The padres and the Pueblos who were refugees from the north replanted their mission towns of Nuestra Señora del Perpetuo Socorro and Corpus Christi de la Ysleta above the river, and there the Indian communities flourished.

When Spaniards reached the Río Grande in the northeastern frontier at the beginning of the eighteenth century, they encountered Indians who were the remnants of native groups commonly referred to as Coahuiltecans. These peoples searched for food in seasonal hunting-and-gathering migrations. Such a nomadic existence resulted in the construction of only impermanent shelters, usually small movable huts made by driving saplings into the ground and throwing animal skins or woven matting over them.

Coahuiltecans spoke a number of languages, and at times some resorted to sign language to communicate among members of different bands. Most of these Native peoples used stone and wooden tools and hunted with the bow and arrow. They crafted baskets and ceramics, so they must have developed some food-storage techniques. They held spirited celebrations *(mitotes),* enlivened by bone flutes, rattles, and other instruments and inspired by peyote beans or other hallucinogens.

At the dawning of the eighteenth century, the hunter-gatherers faced serious limits to their population growth. The semiarid region they inhabited had few natural resources, and the range of their hunting and gathering was increasingly constricted. In the late 1600s, mission towns and other settlements below the Río Grande sent flocks for grazing into the Coahuiltecans' homeland above the river. This pressure was made worse by increased Apache and Comanche raids directed at Spanish ranches but affecting the Coahuiltecans as well. Additionally, the small nomadic bands were decimated by new diseases, such as smallpox introduced by Indian intermediaries who brought trade goods north from Spanish settlements.

It was in such circumstances that the Coahuiltecans were invited to form towns under the aegis of the friars. The offers came with enticement of food and the promise that they would be taught to farm and graze, thus securing permanent resources. Such offers proved attractive to some bands, especially those who often had to go days without eating. Other bands were already prepared to settle down. They may have experimented with farming and understood that the missionary-led towns provided a ready-made social structure and the additional technical training they needed. Some of these groups actually requested the creation of mission communities.

Many Indians, particularly in the later decades, must have been coerced into the friars' towns, however. Indeed, the recruitment of Indians at times was indistinguishable from other thinly disguised Indian slave raids by Spaniards and Hispanicized settlers. Force was also used to retrieve Natives who escaped from the mission towns, and it was very likely employed at least occasionally to make sure that the work assignments were carried out.

Through a combination of such methods, the Franciscans established five missionary-led Indian towns in the plain immediately below the headwaters of the San Antonio River. The first was San Antonio de Valero, founded in 1718. It was followed by San José y San Miguel de Aguayo two years later. In 1731, three townships from east Texas (Purísima Concepción, San Juan Capistrano, and San Francisco de la Espada) were relocated to the San Antonio area. Into these towns the friars gathered the Jaranames, Pajalaches, Pampopas, Aguasalas, Tamiques, Canamas, Pitalaques and other Coahuiltecans

Mission Nuestra Señora de la Purísima Concepción de Acuña, San Antonio, Texas.

belonging to possibly as many as one hundred south Texas bands.

The friars were supported and protected by soldier-settlers in the nearby Presidio de Béxar. Additionally, the entire area was secured by another soldier town-garrison established on the Gulf Coast in 1722, the Presidio de Nuestra Señora de Loreto (commonly called Presidio de la Bahía, because of its location near the Espíritu Santo Bay). The Franciscans eventually (1747) followed the soldier-settlers to that area and founded Misión Espíritu Santo de Zúñiga for the coastal Karankawa Indians.

Upon gathering the Natives in the new towns, the friars sought out natural leaders among them. They invested those individuals with titles and symbols of authority and rewarded them with small but important privileges and with larger portions of food or finer clothing than others. The Indian governors and officials functioned as middlemen and overseers *(mayordomos)* of the work gangs that carried out the essential town-building tasks: clearing the fields; constructing the dams and irrigation canals *(acequias);* erecting the huts, storage rooms, and churches.

Each Indian town also established a ranch in the San Antonio River valley. These far-flung ranches boasted of hundreds and thousands of sheep and goats. Wild livestock *(mesteñas)* were captured, branded, and set free to graze, then rounded up and slaughtered or driven to markets to the south. The animals provided cash that was used to import foodstuffs, manufactured goods, and religious articles from central Mexico.

Spanish or mestizo building engineers

But there were others. For one thing, mission town life involved storing supplies, waiting for crops to ripen and animals to mature, and having foodstuffs and supplies doled out by the friars or their Indian subordinates. In the wilds *(el monte)* most of the Indians had perhaps already begun the process of budgeting foodstuffs, but they were still heirs to a long tradition of immediately consuming whatever was acquired.

In addition, the Natives also had to

and sculptors were brought in from the interior of the colony to direct major projects or to embellish building façades. Some area Natives took up such trades as butchering, tanning, tailoring and sewing, and smithing, and others carried out more skilled tasks. But most of the local Indians were put to work at labor-intensive assignments.

The change from nomadic to sedentary existence involved a major transformation for the Natives. The restriction of movement and the regimentation imposed by mission discipline were probably the most difficult changes for the erstwhile nomads.

adjust to new and different tools and household articles manufactured locally or imported. They had to learn new cooking techniques in preparing unfamiliar foods, although the friars allowed them to hunt wild animals such as deer, raccoons, squirrels, and wild pigs and to gather berries, nuts, prickly pears *(tunas)*, and other fruits and roots. They wove cotton and wool but continued matting with area plant fibers.

More difficult yet were the changes in sexual mores and in family structure that went along with settled existence. The formation of nuclear families and the

Mission San Juan Capistrano, San Antonio, Texas.

restriction of what had been rather free sexual activity presented formidable challenges to Natives and friars alike. The friars attempted to forbid the old and enforce the new elements of lifestyle by grilling their charges in the confessional, by using informants to gather evidence on miscreants, and possibly by making use of physical punishments as well. Such measures notwithstanding, the missionaries complained repeatedly about the difficulty of transforming the Indians' behavior in these manners.

The task of constructing the extensive town complexes and changing the life habits of the Natives at times distracted the padres from their goal of acculturating them, a process that was seen as a prerequisite for conversion. In fact, friars often gave up on the basic objective of teaching the Indians Spanish. They opted instead for a Native *lengua franca,* derived from the various Coahuiltecan dialects. The missionaries must no doubt have consoled themselves with the thought that the mere settling of the nomads would in time foster the virtues and the sexual discipline that accompanied permanent monogamous marriages.

More challenging still for both Indians and friars was the missionaries' goal to change the Natives' worldview. The hunter-gatherers saw themselves as part of the natural world, much as the other creatures surrounding them. They had no notion of a personal God, and their language lacked the concepts of the new religion. The padres considered them neophytes or children, not completely transformed barbarians *(Indios bárbaros),* who had to be permitted their ceremonies *(mitotes)* lest they run away en masse. Consequently, in

the early years they did not baptize the Natives until the hour of their death.

Acculturation and conversion efforts were more directly focused on the young. Small boys were taken from their parents and placed in boarding schools adjacent to the friar's cell, explaining the ample *convento* quarters. But even these undertakings were forsaken as town-building enterprises became more demanding of the missionaries' time.

Hence, a new strategy soon developed. The Hispanization and conversion processes, it was thought, would happen on their own through methods considered less intrusive for the Indians and less labor-intensive for the friars: the rote recitation of the catechism, the singing of hymns, the production of morality plays, the introduction of other religious and popular traditions common to central Mexico.

It is difficult to ascertain how successful such endeavors were. For one thing, acculturation usually takes place through extensive contact with the agents of cultural

Quadrangle at Presidio Nuestra Señora de Loreto de La Bahía.

change. In this context, the single friar and the single soldier-settler stationed in each mission pueblo were woefully inadequate to bring about quick change. In addition, the missionaries deemed Indian contact with neighboring Spaniards and mestizos disadvantageous, even morally detrimental, and disruptive of the smooth functioning of the Indian towns. Ironically, then, whatever their intentions, the padres' isolationist policies delayed Hispanization and ultimately full conversion.

Still, the friars appear to have succeeded in various ways. The extent of the town enterprises, with their buildings, dams, irrigation canals, productive farms, and huge ranching operations, attests to considerable acculturation. Some reports describe Indians manufacturing new products, executing new crafts, and organizing themselves along the lines of Spanish social structures. Documents also depict Natives participating fully in Christian rituals, and descendants of mission residents to this day profess the faith of the friars.

The actual construction of mission towns began with the selection, through trial and error, of the appropriate site, usually terrain elevated enough to prevent flooding but still within the gravity flow of the irrigation *(acequia)* system. The first structures erected were mud-and-stick thatched-roof huts *(jacales)* and very probably the first storage rooms. These were followed by a small stone church. Within a generation, say, by the 1740s, as the towns became productive enough to take laborers away from the fields, construction began on sizable storage rooms and on large churches. Finally, by the end of the century, the towns were enclosed with walls that gave them the appearance of fortresses. Subsequently, Indian dwellings were built along the inside of the walls.

Depending on the individual tastes of the friar in charge of a particular town and on the availability of resources, the building projects included decorative church-door and -window façades, colorfully painted exterior wall designs, and impressive towers.

The structures were all built with a local porous limestone that required continued substantial maintenance. Storage rooms and churches were apparently constructed in stages, with the earlier structures put to a different use as the community required new buildings. Some missions never completed their expansion plans.

The limits to growth were sometimes judged to be external. In the San Antonio area the friars constantly fought off encroachment by residents of the neighboring civilian and military towns of San Fernando de Béxar and the Presidio de Béxar. But the biggest obstacle, according to the padres, was the tax on livestock imposed on mission herds by the government in the 1770s. The tax allegedly wiped out any potential profit from the sale of the herds, leaving the mission Indians dependent on an agricultural production that barely sustained them. The residents then drifted away from the friars' towns, returning to the wilds or moving into San Fernando.

The actual culprit, however, was something no one could control: population limits and demographic change itself. Very few Natives resided in the missionary-led towns, even in the best of times. None of the towns ever counted more than 350 Indian residents. Surprisingly, at the very peak of the construction projects in the 1770s and 1780s, the population in all of the pueblos was already on the decline. After 1790, the numbers of residents dropped precipitously.

As in many premodern societies, population growth was hampered by a very high infant-mortality rate. At the San Antonio de Valero mission, for example, there were ten deaths for every seven births. More specifically, during a sixty-year period, of 319 individuals among the Native population whose records were found, only fifty reached the "adult" age of twelve! Of those, fourteen lived into their twenties and only eight into full maturity (their thirties and forties). Clearly, life was very precarious in the mission towns.

But the towns also lost population because many Indians, dissatisfied with the regimented life in the missions, ran away. Towards the end of the 1700s, baptisms far outnumbered burial entries, suggesting that Indians were not living out their lives in the mission towns but were abandoning them. In that period, too, the friars repeatedly recorded organizing parties to retrieve the runaways.

The same point is emphasized by the fact that the friars often undertook recruiting expeditions for new Indian settlers. By the end of the century, the expeditions reached hundreds of miles away from the San Antonio River mission towns. The

Mission Nuestra Señora del Espíritu Santo de Zúñiga, Goliad, Texas.

hunter-gatherers of central Texas, it would seem, had found alternatives to mission life. Very probably, they were joining the Norteños, or northern Indians, who were prospering by trading goods in an arc stretching from Louisiana to Texas and on to New Mexico. In any case, by the 1790s, the missionaries could no longer find recruitable Indians.

The friars in the San Antonio River Indian pueblos had no choice but to hire residents from the presidio and San Fernando communities so that the work of the mission towns could be carried out. Because of the higher costs of operation, the friars' enterprises could no longer pay for themselves, let alone make a profit. So in the 1790s the friars had to "secularize," that is, disincorporate the towns and turn the properties and lands to diocesan and government control. (The padres then shifted their operations to Sonora and especially to California where the more numerous Native populations would sustain much larger missionary-led communities.)

The secularization of the missionary enterprises along the San Antonio River and elsewhere has been judged a "failure" of sorts. In defense of the friars, some historians have argued that padres intended to secularize the missions all along. As proof, they cite an obscure reference to a goal that missions were to last for only ten years. More boldly still, such historians have also proclaimed that the Franciscans had in fact achieved their goal of converting the Natives. The problem with such explanations is that nowhere in the records is there evidence that the padres viewed their enterprises as temporary. Certainly they did not claim success when they were forced to secularize the missions; rather, they lamented their need to close down their operations.

A more plausible explanation is simply that the times and circumstances changed from an earlier age, and that in both forming the towns and closing them the friars had taken what they saw as the best options open to them. In addition to re-creating a República de Indios similar to the one in

Façade of Mission San Francisco de la Espada, San Antonio, Texas.

central Mexico, the friars saw the Indian towns as a way of preventing the immediate catastrophic decline of the hunter-gatherers and, of course, as a way of civilizing them. Additionally, the padres could not envision converting the Indians outside the mission communities.

The towns the friars created lasted for three quarters of a century—no mean feat in itself. What's more, the missionaries also succeeded, in however limited a fashion, in passing on their faith to the Natives who remained in the pueblos. When circumstances changed and the towns were not self-sustainable, the friars prepared the residents for integration into civil society. Secularization, then, should be seen as a change rather than a failure.

After the San Antonio River Indian towns were disbanded, some of the remaining former residents organized themselves into new self-directed communities and continued worshiping in the old mission-town churches. Others moved to the civilian community of San Fernando, which in the 1790s had more Natives than all the mission pueblos combined. The more recent recruits likely returned to the wilds.

The Indian towns in the Goliad and El Paso areas later experienced the same population loss that had occasioned the closing of the San Antonio missions. There, too, the padres postponed secularization until they had no other recourse. After the towns were abandoned, the walls and structures crumbled or were dismantled.

For a century the Indian pueblos lay abandoned and forgotten. As San Antonio grew in the 1800s, the Anglo-American and German population came to outnumber the Mexican American residents, and new

buildings were erected in the city's heart. Practically all the traces of the older Spanish colonial presidio and of the town of San Fernando were irrevocably lost. San Antonio de Valero, the former Indian town closest to the center of the city, became better known for its role as a fort (the Alamo) than as a pueblo.

Similar developments were unfolding along the Texas coast and in far west Texas. Anglo-Americans on the westward movement established farms on the southern coastal plains, producing cash crops that were exchanged in the thriving American economy. Small distribution centers such as Victoria and Goliad eclipsed the mission town and the presidio of La Bahía. At the other end of the state, the arrival of Anglo-Americans and the American economy gave rise to a booming El Paso. The new desert city became the center of commercial activity and population growth, quickly overshadowing the nearby Indian communities of Socorro and Ysleta.

Still, some semblance of all the friar-led pueblos remained for posterity. In the twentieth century, emigration from Mexico restored the Spanish-Mestizo character of San Antonio, Goliad, and El Paso, and sections of the former Indian towns were rebuilt—some by descendants of the mission inhabitants—as a reminder of those cities' histories, of their Native American and Hispanic origins, and of the faith that sustained the missionary founders, the Native residents, and many subsequent generations. The Indian communities had indeed perdured.

THE INVESTOR RELATIONS DEPARTMENT OF TORCH ENERGY ADVISORS DESIGNED THE 1994 ANNUAL REPORT FOR NUEVO ENERGY COMPANY FEATURING THIS COMPREHENSIVE SURVEY OF THE TEXAS MISSIONS BY PHOTOGRAPHER GARY FAYE.

Oblique View of the Mission
Corpus Christi de la Ysleta.

Mission Nuestra Señora de la Purísima Concepción de Acuña.

The Shrine at Mission San Antonio de Valero, the Alamo, San Antonio, Texas.

*Transept of the Shrine at
Mission San Antonio de Valero,
the Alamo.*

Gateway and Convento Courtyard at Mission San Antonio de Valero, the Alamo.

Rear Wall and Dome of Mission San José y San Miguel de Aguayo.

Arches in the Courtyard,
Mission San José y San Miguel
de Aguayo.

Table in the Granary at Mission San José y San Miguel de Aguayo.

*Indian Quarters at Mission San
José y San Miguel de Aguayo.*

*Arcaded Wall, Dome and
Courtyard at Mission San José y
San Miguel de Aguayo.*

*Grounds, Façade, Bell Tower,
and Dome of Mission San José y
San Miguel de Aguayo.*

*Courtyard and Cross at Mission
San José y San Miguel de
Aguayo.*

*Window in Stone Wall of
Mission San José y San Miguel
de Aguayo.*

Convento Window with View of the Dome at Mission San José y San Miguel de Aguayo.

The Rose Window at Mission San José y San Miguel de Aguayo.

Handwrought Gate Hardware,
Presidio Nuestra Señora de
Loreto de La Bahía.

San Elizario Presidio Church,
San Elizario, Texas.

*Our Lady of Loreto Chapel at
Presidio Nuestra Señora de
Loreto de La Bahía.*

Nave and Sanctuary in Our Lady of Loreto Chapel at Presidio Nuestra Señora de Loreto de La Bahía.

*Walls, Bell Towers and Dome at
Mission Nuestra Señora de la
Purísima Concepción de Acuña.*

Stone Stairway Connecting the Infirmary to the Church at Mission Nuestra Señora de la Purísima Concepción de Acuña.

Façade Detail of Mission San Francisco de la Espada with Window Above Mudéjar (Moorish) Arch.

*Bastion at Presidio Nuestra
Señora de Loreto de La Bahía.*

*Mission Nuestra Señora del
Espíritu Santo de Zúñiga.*

Mission San Juan Capistrano.

*Gate and Entrance to Mission
San Juan Capistrano.*

FIESTAS
Where Contemporary Mexican Tribes and Ancient Customs Meet

MARTA TUROK
AMACUP, A.C.

ON MYTH AND RITUAL

Myth and ritual are considered universal attributes of culture, linked to the history of ideas. They reflect the human process of symbolization of earthly, cosmic, and sacred forces and events. It is common that gods and humans exert mutual influence, mirroring their follies and virtues.

Whereas myths embody the description of the creation of the cosmos and the natural, animal, and human world, they also re-create the birth and death of heroic forefathers and mothers whose resurrection from human to sacred nurtures the pantheon of deities and gods. Together they justify an existing social system revealed through rites, customs, and moral actions. To honor the ancestors, to ask permission and forgiveness, to thank, and to invoke are all acts of humility, a reminder that we are mere mortals in a universe seeking its equilibrium by opposing forces.

Another important aspect of mythology is that it is permeable; that is, it reflects changes and incorporates new events and beliefs as people conquer or are conquered, as rulers and dynasties rise and fall, as revolts and resistance lead to social reforms. In its character of social reality, myth must be seen as a universal expression whose manifestation is specific to each social group.

Once considered to be the realm of prelogical primitive societies, as opposed to logical, scientific thought, today it is recognized that there is, in fact, a logical, historical dimension to myth as well as a spiritual depth beyond the pretensions of formulating scientific or physical theory. At the same time it is considered that

Huasteco (Huastec),
Carnaval (Carnival),
Nahua culture, Huasteca
Hidalguense. This young Indian
painted his body to mimic a
snake's skin, and in a
purification rite will shed this
painted skin to symbolize a
purging of all things old.

Turcos Quejándose al Presidente Municipal Acerca de Las Travesuras de Los Insoportables Negritos (Turks Presenting Their Case to the Village Mayor Regarding the Unbearably Annoying Conduct of the Negritos), Fiesta de San Pedro (Festival of Saint Peter), Chontal culture, San Pedro Huamelula, Oaxaca. The celebrants here participate in a ritual drama that pits *Turcos* against *Negritos* and ridicules social norms and class structure.

together with philosophy, myths and science actually apply similar logical precepts that test the axioms explaining the origin of the world, of people, animals, and plants. The development of semiotics as a science of meaning has given myth a dimension as prevalent today as its very ancient past.

Rituals are the activities rendered to the cult of these deities, spirits, and gods. They are the vehicle of communication between mortals and immortals and are performed in specific places and dates through such varied actions as prayer, chants, invocations, sacrifice, flagellation, ritual dramas and/or dances, and celebrations. Depending on the social group and the occasion, rituals may be performed exclusively or partially by a special class of person destined for performance of rites

(the priest or his equivalent), and in particular sacred places such as temples, forests, caves, springs, or mountains. Even the layman has room for individual contact with greater forces through ritual.

To recognize, to explain and interpret reality is the essence of myth. The celebrations depicted in George O. Jackson's photographs of a little-known and less-appreciated sector of Mexico are the rituals that are revealing the existence of many myths and re-creating mythical time. Celebrants are absorbed into the universe of their myths; they renew their collective consciousness and reinforce values. Above all they become immersed in the activity and enjoy the ephemeral beauty that accompany the fiestas. We will find that these concepts are fundamental in

understanding how contemporary Mexican Indians' festivities tie into their present, into their remote and recent past.

As we analyze myths and rituals, and relate them to fiestas, within a framework of pre- and post-Hispanic influence, it might be helpful to visualize the whole as a tridimensional tic-tac-toe. Each horizontal plane is a broad category such as cycles, myths, and rituals. Within each plane certain dances, ritual dramas, processions will be more representative; yet to grasp their profound meaning they must also be viewed vertically from plane to plane.

NATIVE MYTHS AND RITUALS BEFORE THE CONQUEST

The cultural and geographic regions defined as Mesoamerica and Aridamerica today encompass Mexico and part of Central America. Their joint history is of great importance, for together they were shaped by the great Olmec, Mayan, Toltec, Zapotec, Mixtec, Huastec, and Aztec civilizations, incorporating new gods as they conquered each other, or adding new attributes to existing gods. It is also important to note that an estimated one hundred and fifty ethnic groups existed in this territory, each with its own language and history, in a broad territory with one of the greatest biodiverse environments in the world. This brought about trade and interdependence of products, techniques, and ideas.

For most of the groups in this region the universe was divided into three planes: the cosmos, the earth, and the underworld—the places where the respective gods dwelt. As with many other agricultural societies around the world, they worshiped the Sun and the Moon as male and female mythical

heroes who were sacrificed during the creation, as well as the stars, who were offspring of the Moon. The concept of history, men, and gods was perceived as cyclical and in terms of duality and conflict: male powers fighting female powers, evil nocturnal forces versus benevolent diurnal ones, the sky lords and the lords of the underworld. The four corners of the universe and world were held up by giant trees, were color-coded, and were presided over by gods— Red to the East, White to the North, Black to the West, Yellow to the South—and the center was green, where the giant sacred tree's branches reached the sky and its roots were entrenched in the underworld, a place found in an intermediate plane crossing a river of an underground cave.

The central and southern groups were

Maringuilla, Fiesta de San Bartolo (Festival of Saint Bartholomew), Zapotec culture, San Bartolo Zoogocho, Sierra Ixtlan de Juárez, Oaxaca. A *maringuilla* is the female character of a dance, usually played by a man dressed as a woman.

Niños Pintados de Negro y Amarillo Contra Una Puerta Verde (Children Painted Yellow and Black Against a Green Door), Carnaval (Carnival), Huastecan Nahua culture, Huasteca Hidalguense.

Danzando Con El Oso (Dancing with the Oso), Jueves de Carnaval (Carnival Thursday), Huastec culture, Benito Juárez, Huasteca Veracruzana. The figure dressed in dried banana and corn leaves is known as the Oso, the indigenous spirit at the festival who sheds his crust, burns it, and emerges purified and renewed to begin the planting.

La Danza de los Tlacololeros (The Dance of the Tlacololeros), Fiesta del Cruz del Ocho (Festival of the Cross of the Eighth of May), Nahua Guerrerense culture, Cerro de Coaxtlahuacan, Guerrero.

the first to master the domestication and cultivation of maize, beans, and squash, whose adoption by most of the groups of the entire region was accompanied by the myths and gods that symbolized the long agricultural process: controlling the forces of nature through rituals and sacrifices to the Gods of Fire (Xiuhtecuhtli), Wind (Ehecatl), Rain (Tlaloc and Chaac); ensuring fertility of the land with rituals to the Earth Goddess Coatlicue and helpers such as Snakes, Frogs and Toads, Birds. Predators such as the Jaguar, the Raccoon, and the Squirrel were also incorporated into their rituals. Maize in itself had various

gods in accordance with the planting cycle: Centeotl (the central God of Maize) associated with Chicomecoatl (Goddess of Sustenance), Xilonen (Goddess of the Tender Ears of Corn), and Ilamatecuhtli (Old Woman Goddess of Dried Corn Ears).

The northern groups were mostly hunters and gatherers, nomadic peoples who took hundreds of years to dominate the central Highland Plateau, a broad semi-desert region rich in edible and useful flora that they also were able to cultivate, such as the cactus and agave plants, a gift of the Goddess Mayahuel. Their rituals centered around hunting themes, divination, and fertility. Their gods included Huitzilopochitl, the mythical hero who led them in the great pilgrimage from Aztlán to Tenochtitlán (present-day Mexico City), and seems to have been the first to "demand" humans be sacrificed in his honor. Perhaps a deeply entrenched concept of human responsibility contributed to the extended practice of sacrifice, and self-sacrifice through flagellation, penitence, and self-inflicted wounds.

Two types of myths form the backbone of Mesoamerican thought and ritual: the first is related to the Creation of the Universe and of Humankind, the second to the discovery of Maize.

CREATION MYTHS

There are many similarities regarding the creation of the universe and of Humankind among the peoples of Mesoamerica. For the Nahuatl peoples of central Mexico there have been four creations, or Suns, and we are presently in the fifth.

In the First Creation, 4 Ocelotl (Jaguar/Tiger), giants dominated the world until the jaguars devoured them. Tezcatlipoca (Smoking Mirror) was the Sun.

In the Second Creation, 4 Ehecatl (Wind), the winds dominated, and ended up destroying the world; the few surviving people were turned into monkeys. Quetzalcóatl was the reigning Sun.

In the Third Creation, 4 Quiautl (Rain), volcanic eruptions destroyed the world, and the surviving people who were all children turned into birds. Tlaloc was the Sun.

In the Fourth Creation, 4 Atl (Water), floods destroyed it, mountains disappeared, and people became fish. One couple survived because they were instructed by Tezcatlipoca to make a hole in the trunk of a giant ahuehuete tree. Chalchihuitlicue was the Sun.

The Fifth Creation, 4 Ollin (Movement), men were made with bones taken from the Underworld by Quetzalcóatl and given life with blood he took from his body. The gods created four people, Tezcatlipoca and Quetzalcóatl were transformed into giant trees, and together they raised the sky and stars and marked a path (the Milky Way). In the sixth year after the flood, Centéotl (God of Maize) was born, and the gods created people after that. This Fifth Sun will end with earthquakes.

Tonatiuh, the sun god, is its Sun.

Among the Maya in the First Creation, the gods molded people from clay, but they had no movement, no strength, and melted in the water.

For the Second Creation men were made from the pito tree and women from reed grass. Though they reproduced, spoke, and saw as people, they had no soul or mind, they were expressionless, and their flesh was yellow. They were annihilated as they did not recognize their lord and creator. A dense fog covered the earth, and black rain fell day and night. Objects and animals began to complain; they accused and avenged the existing wooden people for all the things they had been made to suffer. They too were destroyed, and survivors turned into monkeys.

In the Third Creation white and yellow corn were used to create the ancestors of present people, four men first and four women afterwards. They thanked their creators for having been given life and for all the wonders of life. However, there was a danger that they think they were as wise as the gods, so steam was blown into their eyes to diminish their knowledge. The Morning Star (Venus) appeared to all the gathered people, the priests burned incense, and then the wondrous Sun came out. Four Bacab Gods held the sky up at intercardinal points, and four sacred trees held Earth up at the color-coded cardinal points, including the green tree of abundance in the center.

THE DISCOVERY OF MAIZE MYTHS

Once again we find similar versions among the Aztecs and the Mayas of an important myth. Quetzalcóatl asked the red ant where he had found the corn he was carrying. At first the ant didn't want to tell him but finally indicated it came from the Tonacatepetl Mountain (Maize Mountain). Quetzalcóatl became a black ant and penetrated the rock formation, finding the deposit. He took some kernels and brought them back to the other gods, to Tamoanchan where they dwelt. Although he returned and tried carrying the whole mountain with him, it became clear through divination with corn kernels that only one god could pulverize the mountain. Nanahuatl succeeded in his endeavor to open the mountain with a thunderbolt but fainted from the effort, making it easy for the Tlalocs (the blue, the white, the yellow, and the red) to steal the food. Given the force of the thunderbolt the otherwise white corn was scorched, turning some of the ears of corn red; others were smoked, turning them yellow; and still some others were carbonized and became black.

In the Mayan variations it is the fox, the coyote, a small parrot, or the mountain cat who asks the ant for some kernels, then more animals discover what he is eating and also ask for kernels. Since there wasn't enough for all, the ants refused to give them any more, and that is when the animals told humans about the secrets of that wonderful foodstuff. The humans proceeded to trick the ants and steal some kernels to plant. When planted, the stolen kernels did not germinate (hence, a moral lesson), but humans learned that the secret of successful planting was to soak them in lime water. The indispensable role humans played in the domestication of maize from its primitive wild state as *teozintli,* and the discovery of the role of lime to make it edible by softening the inedible part of the kernels is embedded in the Mesoamerican indigenous peoples' collective consciousness. Maize and men are made from the same flesh: same-equal-same.

SYNCRETISM: THE GRAFTING OF ANCIENT AND SPANISH RITUALS

The Spanish conquistadors were, in their own way, a multicultural group of adventurers. In 1517 they were just coming out of an 800-year domination by the Moors. Centuries before, the Romans, the Celts, and the Visigoths had criss-crossed the territory. Spain had its own brand of popular Catholicism that had an analogous tradition to that of Mesoamerica, which included the flexibility to incorporate local deities. However, the fearsome Spanish Inquisition was created to supervise the unification of faith and religion in a Castilian-dominated Spain, and was transplanted to America soon after the Conquest.

The early friars were totally devoted to the evangelization of the "heathen." By sword or by faith, group after group accepted baptism, attended Mass, and nominally accepted Christianity. It has often been pointed out that at first idols were put behind altars, and many recidivists were burned at the stake or subjected to excruciating torture. In a few generations' time, the attributes of the ancient gods were transferred to the new saints and virgins: Tonantzin for the famed Virgin of Guadalupe; the Holy Cross and Saint Isidore the Husbandman for Tlaloc, the God of Rain; Jesus and Mary, the Sun and Moon Gods of Creation; Huitzilopochitl, the God of Warfare, into Saint James; Saint Michael, the God of Thunder, and so on.

Señor Santiago, Montado en Su Caballo (Saint James, Astride His Horse), Fiesta de Santiago Apóstol (Festival of Saint James), Totonac culture, Santiago Yancuictlalpan, Sierra Norte de Puebla.

Despite intensive and extensive indoctrination by numerous Catholic orders over a 300-year period and watchful supervision of fiestas and dances in the atrium of churches, the extent of cultural resistance became ever more obvious after the war of independence in 1821. During the nineteenth century, fiestas and rituals openly took over the streets, the tops of sacred mountains, and the depths of sacred caves and underground springs.

On the other hand it is clear that certain medieval concepts and beliefs became deeply entrenched into Mesoamerican religion such as the religious brotherhoods known as Cofradías or Mayordomías that sponsor the fiestas; ritual kinship through the *compadre* (godfather) and *comadre* (godmother) that took on much greater social and religious relevance in Mexico; and the *vara,* or staff of power, used by Spanish local officials that was practically deified among the indigenous groups as a symbol of religious and political authority.

The horse, a useful animal for the Spaniards, was also deified, the Maya making effigies and naming him Tzimin Chaac (lightning tapir), not only because it was the animal it most resembled but because horse and gunfire had been associated as one. Thus, when the horsemen and their horses race down in groups of four during the fiesta, with their pounding hoofs they are assuming the characteristics of Chaacs, Gods of Rain and Thunder. On another plane, in the dance-drama of the Conquest, introduced by the clergy as the Dance of Moors and Christians, it seems logical that the Moors are defeated in ritual combat, as it was meant by the Spaniards to become a permanent reminder as to which side had won. It should be of no surprise to find that in some communities the person who portrays Saint James girdles a wooden frame around his waist with a horse's head in front, a horse's tail in back so that man and horse are one as he dances and clashes (see above). And on a third plane we have also mentioned that Saint James was the new personality Huitzilopochitl, the Aztec God of War assumed. Who then defeated whom?

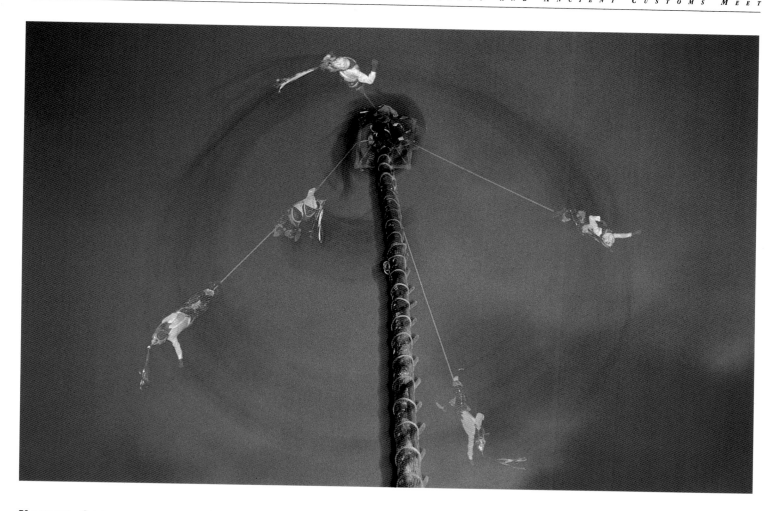

NATIVE CALENDARS AND FIESTAS

Mesoamerican calendars were quite sophisticated as Olmecs, then Mayas and Aztecs refined their astronomical observations. The calendric solar year, known as the Cempoallapoualli, added up to 365 days, divided into eighteen months of twenty days each, with five "lost days" (Nemontemi among the Aztecs and Chay K'in among the Maya). This year began and ended approximately in February. A second ritual calendar of 260 days, the Tonalpoualli (in Nahuatl) or Tzolk'in (in Maya), was divided into thirteen months of twenty days and moved like the gears of a clock with the calendric year. A third calendar, the Year Count, or Xiuhpoualli, a fifty-two-year cycle akin to a "century," was calculated by multiplying four times thirteen years, with each

group of four represented graphically as a "bundle." The symbolic importance of bundles appears in different settings: the "Year Bearer" (a fiesta steward) was designated on an annual basis to care for a ritual bundle of sacred objects that were passed on to the following official, a ritual still being enacted among Chiapas Indians. A large bundle of reeds is carried by a *penitente* as self-sacrifice in Taxco, Guerrero, during Holy Week (p. 129), whereas bundles of arrows are carried in various communities where facial and bodily mud-daubing is practiced. The Yaxk'in and Tzolk'in agricultural calendars tend to be viewed by bundles of time: a 100-day sun cult and purification cycle, four twenty-day cycles for preparing the cornfields (before the rains), and eight thirteen-day cycles for planting and growth of the corn crop (during the rains).

Voladores (Flyers), Fiesta de Santiago Apóstol (Festival of Saint James), Totonac culture, Santiago Yancuictlalpan, Sierra Norte de Puebla.

An example of continuity in the beliefs that cosmic forces can still be controlled through invocation to the four directions as well as to the rain and the sun is the significance behind the spectacular pre-Hispanic Voladores Dance (p. 103). Five Voladores (Flyers) defy gravity and dance on a small rotating platform atop a 15- to 20-meter tree, cut and embedded for the occasion. Four have wrapped rope around their bodies, and as the fifth stands atop the platform with flute and drum, they soar into space, each making thirteen turns before reaching the bottom. Four men times thirteen turns, a fifty-two-year-count cycle.

Communities tend to celebrate more than one particular date. Patron saints are associated with the founding of a town or village, and are related to the Catholic order that was present during evangelization. Other saints and virgins have been incorporated over time, each with certain attributes and their own *mayordomo,* or patron. He or she must garner great support from family and compadres in order to pay for the flowers, incense, fireworks, musicians, and food involved in the year-long sponsorship. It is within this realm of multiple saints' veneration where the association with agricultural and cosmic forces becomes most apparent. The great economic and social burden the mayordomo carries is another form of individual sacrifice for the collective good.

Processional sanctuaries, whose origins also result from a combination of pre-Hispanic and Catholic practices, have a wide distribution and are intimately related to miraculous apparitions, health, ancient trade routes, and mining. (*See* p. 135, *Procession of the Blind Child*).

FIESTA CYCLES

Mesoamerica and Aridamerica are not bound by four clear-cut seasons as other regions closer to the poles. What prevails is a dry season and a rainy season with slight variations existing in the Gulf region and the Pacific Coast. Thus the vast majority of farmers plant and harvest one corn crop per year, and are totally dependent on rain for germination. As mentioned earlier, maize is the basis of the culture. It follows that the indigenous fiesta cycles be closely related to the agricultural calendar. On the one hand we find the 100-day cycle of the Sun Cult (Yaxk'in)—characterized by the harvest, purification and penance—leading to agricultural propitiation, and on the other the Tzolk'in cycle of petition for rain and crops and abundance. If we apply the precepts to specific festivities, we find that the first cycle covers the Day of the Dead, Christmas, Candlemas, Shrovetide (or Carnival), Lent, and Easter Week. The second cycle slightly overlaps; it begins with Holy Cross day on May 3 and continues until Saint Francis on October 4, with special attention given Saint Isidore (May 15), Corpus Christi (a movable feast during June), Saint John the Baptist (June 24), Saint Peter and Saint Paul (June 29), Saint James the Apostle (July 25), the Assumption (August 15), and St. Michael Archangel (September 29).

YAXK'IN OR THE SUN CULT: PURIFICATION AND PENANCE

It begins with the Day of the Dead, a combination of ancestor worship and harvest festival. Christmas among some indigenous groups is also a time of agricultural thanks, as the shrove in the home nativity scene where Jesus was born is adorned with a sample of all the best seeds from the present crop hanging from its roof. I have witnessed a couple of chili peppers hanging from St. Joseph's hand and cotton wool from Mary among the Mixtec and Zoque. Candlemas is also transformed into a festivity of purification, not only of Mary and the presentation of the Christ Child in the temple, but also as the blessing of the seeds of corn, beans, squash, and other crops to be planted during the ensuing season.

The spectacularity of Shrovetide among the indigenous groups is a chapter in itself. Bishop Landa, a sixteenth-century chronicler of life among the Maya of Yucatán (who, unfortunately, had all the sacred books burned in a giant bonfire), reports that during the month of Mac the elders held ceremonies to the Chacs (rain gods) and Itzam Na (creation god). In the ritual, fresh mud from a *cenote* (limestone sinkwell) was daubed onto the first step of a pyramid, while blue pigment was daubed onto the rest of the steps, in a ritual where equal-produce-equal. This is a clue as to the importance and wide distribution of facial and body mud-daubing and painting during Carnival fiestas throughout Mexico. The symbolism behind the ritual washing after the dry earth has been caked on has various origins. One deals with a mythical time of a "second creation" related to the advent of Christianity (the Conquest), where they recall their life when they were "savages"; the other is related to the veneration to Xipe-Totec, the Flayed God of Young Corn for whom human skins of sacrificial victims were worn.

Easter is the festivity that closes this Yaxk'in cycle and is the epitome of suffering, penance, and sacrifice. The force of the spiritual Conquest in Mexico is reenacted in the ritual drama of the trial and crucifixion of Christ—part human, part god. His individual sacrifice was for the collective good, a concept shared by Indian cultures of yesterday and today. Death at the cross and resuscitation also mirror the rituals of sacrifice to ensure fertility and plant renovation. The meaning of renewal and hope becomes most apparent in the Indian transformation of Christ's disciples, the Apostles (p. 114), into children and their role of washing feet as in and the transition into the next rain cycle.

TZOLK'IN, OR THE DAY COUNT: AN AGRICULTURAL ALMANAC

In stark contrast to the clay and earthen colors of the Yaxk'in cycle, the Tzolk'in cycle conjures images of the color green, of bright costumes with red trimmings, multicolor ribbons and embroidery, and fresh flowers. Based on the ritual calendar used for divination and rain propitiation, ritual dramas such as the Tiger-Tecuan complex (jaguars) are reminiscent of pre-Hispanic priests who dressed as jaguars and eagles and lashed out at each other, drawing blood (pp. 123–124). Performed during the celebrations of the Sacred Cross (the symbol of fertility), the connections between flagellation and plant renewal are very consistent.

During the following eight "bundles" of thirteen days we find that there are vital agricultural activities that parallel the series of saints and fiestas mentioned before. As was pointed out in the Third Mayan Creation Myth (see p. 100), it is crucial to human survival to thank the deities for interceding favorably. The beauty behind

Una Ofrenda de Agradecimiento a Todos Los Ángeles en el Cielo (An Offering of Gratitude to All of the Angels in the Sky), Fiesta de San Mateo (Festival of Saint Matthew), Nahua Guerrerense culture, Zacualpan, Guerrero.

the photograph *An Offering of Gratitude to All the Angels in the Sky* (above), taken during the Festival of Saint Matthew in September among the Nahua of Zacualpan, is that it eloquently shows us how these precepts are applied. A single layman has set fifty places, each with an offering to accommodate the angels who dwell among the clouds high in heaven. Since Christian times, it was believed that children who die become angels, and in true syncretic format, children's tears were considered an important tribute to Tlaloc, the Rain God, spurring the sacrifice of children in ancient Teotihuacán. Thus it is through their tears that rain has fallen and propitiated the "first fruits" of the crop.

FESTIVAL SECULARIZATION

We have but scratched the surface of the meanings lurking behind the masks, the dancers, the tricksters, the offerings, the flower arches, the men dressed as women, and the fireworks. And we must end by considering the radical changes pointing towards the secularization of fiestas in many (but fortunately not all) regions.

When beer drinking to blaring record music during the day and popular music groups at night seems to dominate the scenery, the fiesta is turning into a fair. When there is a loss of cargo-holders *(mayordomos),* dances and costumes, it heralds the end, for then the religious core of the fiesta has eroded. The Huautla, or Hidalgo Shrovetide, in 1994 pointed to various tendencies: the first was that indigenous bilingual teachers sent word out to the outlying communities to come to the head town, and the fiesta was turned into a parade and contest within the school's basketball court. I couldn't help but find a likeness to the watchful clergy from 300 years ago, who contained the fiesta within the church's atrium. At the same time wonderful pastel-colored headdresses (p. 110) ushered innovation into an otherwise stark yellow, black, and red tradition. Change as survival and change as an end has remained constant over a millennium: always duality and conflict.

PHOTOGRAPHER'S STATEMENT

GEORGE O. JACKSON, JR.

***Viejita Trique (Little Old Trique Woman)**,* Fiesta de San Juan Bautista (Festival of Saint John the Baptist), Trique culture, San Juan Copala, Oaxaca.

In the tradition of Norwegian explorer Carl Lumholz, who documented the indigenous cultures of northern Mexico 100 years ago, and his contemporary Edward S. Curtis, called the "Shadowcatcher" by the western American Indians he photographed, I have set forth to document the important festivals of each of Mexico's indigenous folk cultures (which number more than sixty) as they exist in the final decade of the millennium. Being of Mexican heritage, I have been able to hone skills that enable me to enter the humble little communities I photograph and emerge with pure cultural treasure. My goal was to create an important historical collection of cultural photography of

El Milagroso (The Miraculous One), Semana Santa (Easter Week), Mestizo culture, Colatlan del Río, Morelos.

the richness and texture of the traditional festivals celebrated in their honor. Studying them has opened up a whole world of myth and ritual, from the far reaches of the legendary past to the current practices of the contemporary. I admire the magnificence of the spectacle, its strange and cryptic ways and extravagance of color, form, texture, and fragrance, which provide an attitude of escape for the celebrants and at the same time give them the opportunity to reaffirm their identity. In remote places where the culture is still reasonably intact, people still dress in their traditional best, speak their traditional language, eat traditional foods, and dance to traditional music. They are steeped in the cultural activity that defines them. In a sense the culture actually blooms, releasing its essence—*The Essence of Mexico.*

I was already somewhat aware that festivals were a way indigenous people celebrated their relationship with the earth, but only later did I realize that true traditional festivals are genuine manifestations of ancient cultural activity, originally created by the people to entreat and therefore interact with the influences that held sway over their lives. Most intriguing to me is that in many places, the same people are still dealing with the same deities for the same reasons as they were at the beginning of agriculture.

These rituals were even more important in former times. Centuries ago, a poor harvest brought about death from famine and the pestilence that usually accompanied it. Some current adaptations of pre-conquest rituals are a grim reminder of just how seriously the people took appeasing the gods: What are now animal sacrifices were

the subject, which will grant a sort of permanence to this enchanting ephemeral art form, preserving its beauty and cultural clues. The project, *The Essence of Mexico,* began in early 1990 and so far includes a photographic record of more than 200 festivals in forty-five cultures.

I have long been fascinated by the devotion the Mexican people bestow on their saints and icons, particularly through once human; the ritual combat was once genuine mortal combat: the blood offerings were once from human victims. They believed then as now that one cannot expect favors without giving something dear in return.

Pre-Hispanic cultures had a profound knowledge of astronomy, enabling them to plan their rituals very accurately, as you have read in Marta Turok's essay on the agricultural cycle and sun cult. Their festival cycle followed the periods involved with the production of corn, from pre-planting to post-harvest, each period with its own deity. The contemporary festival cycle mimics the ancient calendar, with Catholic saints overlaying the ancient deities, many of which are still reverenced. It comes in the form of food, floral and incense offerings, traditional dances, ritual, and sometimes dramatic propitiation (as ritual combat) in their honor. The festivals are celebrated in order to gain favor with the deities being honored so that they might use their influence with nature to help make the coming year a good one.

The beautiful, ingenious festival art that seems to spring directly from the souls of the people also fueled my fascination. It is usually made from the simplest and most readily available materials at hand. Because of the ephemeral nature of its components, festival art is meant to be enjoyed for the moment that it is created to embellish.

Festival art is crucial in providing the proper setting for the enactment of the important ritual that it accompanies and supports. It also serves to provide a festive mood. It can be said that the success of the art is directly related to the success of the festival. Because it is so temporary, it has

never been considered art in the highest sense and, therefore, never well documented. My project has given me the opportunity to build a nice collection of these photogenic, otherwise unpreservable, moments of artistic ingenuity:

• Sensitive offerings of exquisite fresh flowers and fruit sometimes in elegant simplicity, other times fashioned into elaborate sculpture.

• Groups of mud-covered *carnavaleros*, further embellished with black, white, and yellow natural-pigment-painted designs in the form of bandoliers, evoking their independent spirit—the wearing of charming, homemade *penachos* (headdresses) with pinwheels and streamers of brilliantly colored paper dancing in the bright morning sunlight.

• Hordes of white barite-painted *fariseos* with artistic designs painted on with purple dye, wearing white cloth hoods with traditional designs (such as crosses, scorpions, and fish) bewitchingly embroidered with purple thread, carrying colorful staffs with elaborate designs or colorful bundles of fifty-two arrows also with meticulous designs, tipped with metallic paper.

• Covering literally every street of a small town, some 4.5 kilometers, luxurious carpets made from colored sawdust, carefully stenciled with classic designs and copiously trimmed with flowers by cooperating neighbors, to receive the post-midnight mass procession of the Virgin of Charity, syncretized with Xochipilli, the Aztec Flower Prince. The procession is met at every street corner with lavish displays of imaginative pyrotechnics until it ends at daylight. By 9 A.M. the streets are spic-and-span.

Carnaval Huasteco (Huastecan Carnival), Huastecan Nahua culture, Huasteca Hidalguense.

• Wonderfully creative, cottage-made fireworks, including a war between groups of full-sized soldiers who shoot it out across a battlefield; boxers boxing; washerwomen washing; streaking, blazing, exploding *toritos* running and dancing amongst the celebrants, sometimes under firefalls from a 100-foot-high *castillo* heavily festooned with rockets, shrieking footchasers, multi-colored sparklers, pinwheels, and burning figures that appear sporadically during the course of an up-to-two-hour burn.

There are many other cultural expressions representing and elaborating the themes and subject matter on which the festivals are based. The magic of photography has given me the capability to explore and document some of Mexico's best examples.

The Mexican Indians are not easy to photograph due to the basic mistrust fomented by existing sharp socioeconomic

Comanches, Carnaval Huasteco
(Huastec Carnival), Huasteco-
mestizo culture, Ixcatepec,
Huasteca Veracruzana.

contrasts. In addition, five centuries of cruel exploitation since Spanish conquest, compounded by constant aggressive pressure on them to join the modern world, has long threatened their cultures, religion, family structure, economic systems, even their cherished relationship with the earth, and has resulted in deep resentment. If one is accepted into the community, as I have been over 200 times to date, the people are usually warm, hospitable, even generous despite, in many cases, pitiable poverty. Once they become aware of the extent of my mission, which in a sense is a form of their immortality, the people usually become enthusiastic collaborators.

Many traditional festivals are at the point of extinction due to the aggravated encroachment of a modern consumerist society. Young people of the communities, who would ordinarily be receiving and learning the traditional ways to carry on, have left their communities, lured away by the promise of a better life constantly extolled by two decades of television. Another complication comes from imported values brought back by some who have lived in the modern world and returned to traditional ways.

Indeed, modernism has already cost them some of the important luxuries they once had in their lives. Sadly, fond memories of classically dressed peasantry, dignified in comfortable radiant-white Indian cotton or wool costumes colorfully embroidered in a style that reflected their identity, have degenerated into the contemporary reality of cheap, imported modern-style polyester garments now being worn by men, women, and children alike. Shapeless, "day-glow" polyester sweat suits touted as

Amarrando Una Flor de Yuca (Tying a Yucca Flower), Fiesta de la Santa Cruz (Festival of the Holy Cross), Nahua culture, Zitlala, Guerrero.

"in-style unisex sportswear" also proliferate to further pollute the scene. Comfortable handmade leather *huaraches* are being replaced by cheaper-to-make shoes molded from inner-tube rubber. Beautiful sculptural clay pottery, developed over the millennia to keep water fresh, is losing out to flimsy plastic buckets that form slime in a few hours. Even the beautiful ephemeral offerings used in the important propitiation of their deities—traditionally fashioned from ingeniously arranged fresh flowers and luxuriously colored paper—are giving way to gaudy, more durable plastic.

"Cur rides? Nomine mutato de tu fabula," wrote the Roman poet Horace. "Why do you laugh? With the name changed, the story is about you." The cosmology of these Mexican cultures has much to offer

us since it is very near to a place that we have long departed.

How many of us realize that our own liturgical season, beginning with Christmas and ending with Easter, is a reflection of the religion of Europe's ancient Druids? The coincidence of Christmas with the winter solstice and its symbolism of the evergreen tree is not only biblical. Also, Easter, with its eggs and rabbits, once had a powerful link with fertility rituals.

The Mexican folk cultures that I photograph are particularly fascinating because in many cases the linkage of their past to their present is still intact. To our own culture, lured away from the earth and its wisdom by the siren's song of technology, these cultures should be a source of forgotten wisdom.

Cerro de Cruzco (Place of the Crosses), Fiesta de la Santa Cruz (Festival of the Holy Cross), Nahua culture, Zitlala, Guerrero.

Apóstoles (Apostles), Semana Santa (Easter Week), Coastal Mixtec culture, Pinotepa de Don Luis, Oaxaca.

Procesión de Huaves (Huave Procession), Semana Santa (Easter Week), Huave culture, San Mateo del Mar, Ismo de Tehuantepec, Oaxaca.

El Calvario (Mount Calvary), Semana Santa (Easter Week), Coastal Mixtec culture, Pinotepa de Don Luis, Oaxaca.

Fariseos (Pharisees), Semana Santa (Easter Week), Coastal Mixtec culture, Pinotepa de Don Luis, Oaxaca.

Cruces Huaves (Huave Crosses),
(detail), Semana Santa (Easter
Week), Huave culture, San Mateo
del Mar, Ismo de Tehuantepec,
Oaxaca.

Turco (Turk), Fiesta de San Pedro
(Festival of Saint Peter), Chontal
culture, San Pedro Huamelula,
Oaxaca.

*La Danza de Los Ormegas,
(The Dance of the Ormegas),* La Fiesta del Inicio de la Siembra, (Festival of the Beginning of the Planting Season), Nahua culture, San Juan Ahuacatlán, Puebla.

*Negritos Bailando Los Listones
(Negritos Dancing the Ribbon
Pole),* La Fiesta del Inicio de la Siembra (Festival of the Beginning of the Planting Season), Nahua culture, San Juan Ahuacatlán, Puebla.

*Pasando el Pañuelo—Passing
the Scarf,* La Fiesta del Inicio de la Siembra (Festival of the Beginning of the Planting Season), Nahua culture, San Juan Ahuacatlán, Puebla.

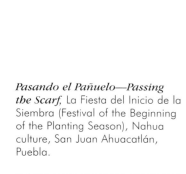

San Juan Ahuacatlán, La Fiesta del Inicio de la Siembra (Festival of the Beginning of the Planting Season), Nahua culture, San Juan Ahuacatlán, Sierra Norte de Puebla.

*La Ofrenda
(The Offering)*,
Fiesta de la
Santa Cruz
(Festival of the
Holy Cross),
Nahua culture,
Zitlala, Guerrero.

Tecoani (One Who Draws Blood), Fiesta de la Santa Cruz (Festival of the Holy Cross), Nahua Guerrerense culture, Zitlala, Guerrero.

Tecoani Acateco (Tecoani from Acatlán), Fiesta de la Santa Cruz (Festival of the Holy Cross), Acatlán, Guerrero.

123

Tecoaliztli (The Act of Drawing Blood), Fiesta de la Santa Cruz (Festival of the Holy Cross), Nahua Guerrerense culture, Zitlala, Guerrero. In the Festival of the Holy Cross, the ritual combatants here believe that one cannot ask for favors and get them without giving something dear in return. Since the villagers have nothing else to give, these fighters offer their pain as a propitiation to ensure the proper rain for a successful crop.

Diablos Recibiendo Una Bendición (Devils Receiving a Blessing), Carnival, Tepehua culture, Tepehua region, Huasteca Veracruzana.

Hombre con Penacho de Estrella, Pintado de Negro y Ruedas Amarillas (Man Wearing a Headdress with a Star, Painted Black with Yellow Circles), Carnaval Huasteco (Huastecan Carnival), Huastecan Nahua culture, Huasteca Hidalguense.

Diablo Carnavalero (Carnival Devil), Jueves de Carnaval (Carnival Thursday), Mestizo culture, Huasteca Veracruzana.

Papalotero, Domingo de Carnaval (Carnival Sunday), Mestizo-Tlaxcalteco culture, Santa Ana Chiauhtempan, Tlaxcala.

Penitentes (Penitents), Semana Santa (Easter Week), Mestizo-penitent culture, Taxco, Guerrero.

Un Castillo Chispando (Castillo Shooting Sparks), Fiesta de la Virgen de la Candelaria (Festival of the Virgin of Candlemas), Tepehua-mestizo culture, Huehuetla, Hidalgo.

Penitente Encruzado (Crucified Penitent), **Semana Santa (Easter Week)**, Mestizo-penitent culture, Taxco, Guerrero. One of the most extraordinary Easter celebrations takes place in Taxco when penitent brotherhoods come together to practice ritual penance and share Christ's crucifixion suffering. The penitent here carries an 88-pound bundle of raspberry thorns with prickly horsehair rope, and the center of the rope is in his mouth. The rest of the rope lashes him to the bundle, and burning candles drip hot wax on each of his hands.

José Lachineer, Capitán de Los Negritos (José Lachineer, Captain of the Negritos), Fiesta de San Pedro (Festival of Saint Peter), Chontal culture, San Pedro Huamelula, Oaxaca.

San Manuelito (Saint Manuelito),
Fiesta de San Manuelito (Festival of
Saint Manuelito), Nahua culture,
Zihuatetla, Sierra Norte de Puebla.

***El Señor del Perdón (Our Lord
of Forgiveness)***, Tercer Viernes de
Cuaresma (Third Friday in Lent),
Igualapa, Guerrero.

*El Paso de un Torito Chispando
(The Pass of a Torito Shooting
Sparks)*, Fiesta de San Juan
Bautista (Festival of Saint John the
Baptist), Tzotzil Maya culture, San
Juan Chamula, Chiapas.

Conchero, Fiesta de San Juan Bautista (Festival of Saint John the Baptist), Tlahuica-Ocuilteco cultures, San Juan Atzingo, Estado de Mexico.

La Piedad (Piety), Fiesta de Santiago Apóstol (Festival of Saint James),
Tlapanec culture, Zapotitlan Tablas, Sierra Tlapaneca, Guerrero.

Quetzales Haciendo la Reverencia (Quetzales Practicing Reverence),
Fiesta de Santiago Apóstol (Festival of Saint James), Totonac culture,
Santiago Yancuictlalpan, Sierra Norte de Puebla.

La Procesión del Niño Cieguecito (The Procession of the Blind Child),
Fiesta del Niño Cieguecito (Festival of the Little Blind Child), Mestizo
culture, Convento de las Capuchinas, Puebla, Puebla.

La Iglesia de Santa María Magdalena (The Church of Mary Magdalen),
Fiesta de Santa María Magdalena (Festival of Saint Mary Magdalene),
Cuicatec culture, Tlalixtac, Sierra Cuicateca, Oaxaca.

Un Torito Desintegrando (A Torito Exploding), Fiesta de la Virgen de la
Asunción (Festival of the Virgin of the Assumption), Afromestizo culture,
Santa María Huazolotitlán, Costa Chica, Oaxaca.

Un Tecuane (A Tecuane), Fiesta de San Francisco Asis (Festival of Saint Francis of Assisi), Mestizo culture, Chietla, western Puebla.

La Danza de los Bixanos (The Dance of the Bixanos), Fiesta de la Virgen del Rosario (Festival of the Virgin of the Rosary), Zapotec-Yalaltec culture, Villa Hidalgo Yalalag, Oaxaca.

La Danza de Los Malinches (The Dance of the Malinches), Fiesta de la Virgen de Guadalupe (Festival of the Virgin of Guadalupe), Pame culture, Pame region, San Luis Potosí.

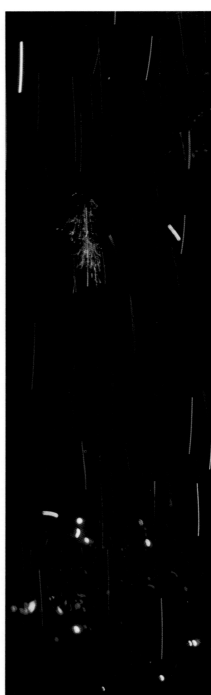

Danzantes en el Atrio de Una Iglesia (Dancers in a Churchyard), Fiesta de la Virgen del Rosario (Festival of the Virgin of the Rosary), Zapotec-Yalaltec culture, Villa Hidalgo Yalalag, Sierra Ixtlan de Juárez, Oaxaca.

Danzando en el Fuego (Dancing in the Fire), Fiesta de San Bartolo (Festival of Saint Bartholomew), Zapotec-mestizo culture, San Bartolo Zoogocho, Sierra Ixtlan de Juárez, Oaxaca.

CHRISTIAN ART AND IMAGERY IN MEXICO

GLORIA FRASER GIFFORDS

GENESIS

Christian art and imagery in Mexico played significant roles in the conversion of native peoples to Spanish domination. To the observant eye, however, Catholic saints and Christian emblems are not just merely tokens of a faith or a shorthand of the extremely intricate iconographic system developed over the past two millennia. In colonial Latin America, these icons and their symbols encompass powerful reminders of the superimposition and amalgamation of cultures and beliefs that resulted from a violent and brutal meeting of two widely diverse civilizations.

In the discovery and conquest of Mexico, the Spaniards encountered cultures rich in artistic and intellectual achievements. The pre-Columbian American in relative isolation had developed a remarkably civilized world. Without the use of the wheel and iron tools, he had erected massive temples skillfully decorated with sculpture. His ceramics, textiles, and metallurgy compared favorably with those of his European counterpart. In some places he exceeded the European with a more accurate calendar, imaginative literature, a well-developed sense of natural history, and highly sophisticated city planning and management. He had also evolved a complicated theocracy, effective laws, and educational systems.

The invading and conquering Spaniards took advantage, whenever possible, of the highly trained and skilled artisans. These people in urban centers throughout central and southern Mexico lived in a structured and well-determined hierarchical society that valued achievement and understood prolonged construction campaigns. The task of the new regime, therefore, was to destroy previous political and

Nuestra Señora, Refugio de Pecadores (Our Lady, Refuge of Sinners)
c. 1850, oil on canvas, 29½" x 24⅜" (75.0 x 61.9 cm.).

religious allegiances and set the newly generated vassals to tasks that would benefit the Spanish Catholic Church and state and, of course, their representatives.

Indigenous peoples were encouraged to believe that their leaders' downfall and the catastrophic destruction of their temples and social systems were the result of the impotency of their gods and the supremacy of the Christian belief and Spaniards. Even though evangelizing priests and secular conquerors zealously pursued a policy of *tabula rasa*—a clean slate—by which they sought to wipe from sight and sound former religious practices, the trauma of the conquest, the catastrophic dissemination of the population from European-introduced diseases, and the subsequent destruction of cultural and political systems reinforced a reliance upon previous patterns in some ways. Forced into accepting the new faith, native peoples quickly related to certain elements not dissimilar to their former beliefs. The newly conquered and marginally Christianized people of Mexico, then, were not confronted with issues of non-tolerance of images as aids to their religious development. Instead, an imposition occurred of images representing the new hierarchy of figures that expounded a belief system of their conquerors with their own idols. In several instances, the very saints who preempted native gods were merged into popular belief, sharing iconography and patronage with the preexisting panoply of deities. The Virgin of Guadalupe is commonly believed to be such a development: the vision of a woman appearing on a sacred hill of the native population to a recently converted Indian. This site was significant to the Aztec earth and fertility goddess Tonantzin (Mother of the Gods), and the dark-complexioned vision, shining like the sun and representing the mother of Christ, requested a sanctuary be constructed for her (the Virgin Mary) at that place (p. 145).

Aware of this persistence of collective memory and hoping to redirect religious energies toward the Catholic faith, tabula rasa notwithstanding, missionaries carefully sought similarities between the new and old faiths. A few aspects of native religions, especially in the more structured and politically developed cultures in Mexico, contained elements familiar to the Spaniards, such as priests' roles as interpreters of deities' wishes, performers of rites for the appeasement of divinities, supplicants for specific causes, and models of penance and sacrifice. The missionary clergy, then, appropriated certain elements of native faiths to construct bridges for belief and acquiescence. Post-conquest feast days and public celebrations that involved indigenous people consciously incorporated local elements judged to be harmless and even considered them beneficial from the standpoint of substituting the Catholic dogma for pagan practices. Indeed, many Christian holidays had equivalent calendar times as pre-Columbian religious observances, and what better way to encourage the adaptation of a new faith than to provide a continuation of attendance to some particularly significant site that now had the church and cross superimposed. The native people's love of ceremony and an enlivening of their daily, often brutal, routine was met in most part by the Christian rites and holidays, and in some instances the similarities between the two beliefs' rites and feast days were close enough that early friars suggested that there appeared to have been some previous contact by proselytizing disciples of Jesus!

Traditionally since almost the beginning of Christianity, imagery and symbolism have served as visual lessons of the faith. Paintings and sculpture, altars placed in specific locations, decorative elements, garments worn by clergy, even the shape and direction of the church all had significant meaning. The walls of churches were considered the bible of the masses. Here the paintings and sculptures of holy personages could be pointed out to the illiterate congregation. The need to possess some of the magic implied by attention and reverence to these figures with which to ameliorate some of life's uncertainties has stimulated worshippers for aeons to obtain replicas of images for their personal use. Although conscious of the danger that these paintings, sculptures, or prints themselves might be regarded as imbued with some personal power, nevertheless, the Mexican clergy encouraged the converts to have and honor them as reinforcements of Catholic beliefs as well as replacements for their former pagan talismans.

And so they did. Every home had (and many still have) some place reserved for the display and worship of the household's saints. In the most humble of circumstances, this may not have been much more than a shelf attached to the wall or a dresser top, where figures, paintings, or prints rest upon the ledge. Flowers and candles frequently accompany the images and the area becomes a devotional focus

for the family or individual—a sacred spot where one asks for help, health, and good fortune, and gives thanks for blessings received.

THE CREATORS AND THEIR INFLUENCES

For the next almost five centuries, the creation and proliferation of religious imagery in, and destined for, Mexico was enormous. Concurrently, for more than two and a half centuries, depictions of religious

Nuestra Señora de Guadalupe (Our Lady of Guadalupe) mid-to-late 19th century, oil on tinplate, 13½" x 9⅝" (34.8 x 24.4 cm.).

imagery were carefully scrutinized by authorities in order to prevent not only deliberate heretical ingredients from inclusion by artists and craftspeople but also the innocently incorrect representations of the Catholic panoply of holy figures. Whereas organizations were soon established in metropolitan centers such as Mexico City, Guadalajara, and Puebla to create guidelines, bureaucratic channels, and guild mechanisms within which artists officially functioned for commissions on churches, convents, or private chapels, the demand for religious images by lower socioeconomic classes in rural or provincial areas, as well as an innate artistic energy of the Mexican people, developed a vigorous strata of artisans creating popular religious art that was generally outside the official pale. These two streams—the officially sanctioned and stylistically up-to-the-moment "high" art produced by individuals academically trained and produced in the apprentice/journeyman/master tradition and the art of the masses, or popular art, most often associated with rudimentarily trained or self-taught craftspersons in the provinces—flow throughout much of Mexican expression even today.

Whereas the high art, with its restrictions and proscriptions, remained true to its Spanish and European origins, popular art—although drawing from the former's stylistic and iconographic roots but with little if any formal basis or supervision—almost immediately begins to achieve a look of its own. As the mixtures of the bloods of Spaniards and indigenous peoples created the Mestizo, or Mexican, race, so did the blending of the cultures nurture a distinct essence detectable in artistic expressions,

also referred to as *Mestizo.* Elements such as localized flora and fauna, ages-old forms and shapes, materials and techniques particular to specific regions appeared in the designs, decorations, and in the essential matrix of articles produced in New Spain. In the case of the production of religious imagery, although striving to fulfill clients' wishes for familiarly represented images, the popular artists' expressions are far less static and predictable than their "official" models. Examples vibrate with color, exuberance and vigor; naïve solutions to the arrangement of figures in hierarchical scale, perspective, and anatomy increase their appeal. Many of these characteristics are present in the *retablos* in the collections of J. P. Bryan. *Retablo* is a popular name given to a unique type of religious imagery—paintings on small pieces of tinplate—that flourished during the nineteenth century in the upper- and mid-central rural areas and mining towns of Mexico.[1]

Sheets of tinplate were abundantly imported from England after Mexico's independence from Spain. They were primarily intended as an inexpensive material from which to create items such as pails, lamps, stove and drain pipes, cups, plates and hundreds of other types of cheap household items. The exact reason for the selection of this unorthodox type of support by the provincial artists for painting religious images is not known. It may have been by sheer accident or the ingenuity of the Mexican artist to see the possibility of other uses for this attractive, flat, and durable medium. Wherever and whenever the first one appeared, the use of tinplate for retablos was fairly ubiquitous and it continues to be used today by painters of ex-votos.

Popular, or folk, retablos fall into two categories: images of religious personages intended for use in domestic shrines or walls of homes (hereafter referred to as *retablos*), and ex-votos—thanks given a specific religious personage and placed in a church near that image. From approximately 1820 until the first decades of this century, hundreds of thousands of retablos of Christ, the Virgin Mary, saints, and certain religious iconographic themes were created, as were literally millions of ex-votos.[2] With the increasing popularity of their chromolithographic counterparts, the retablo ceased being made during the early decades of this century. The ex-voto, even though competing with photographs, X-rays, crutches, and *milagros* (small metal or wax representations of body parts or other objects relevant to the blessing),[3] continues to be produced, and there are a number of shrines in Mexico festooned with these examples of thanksgiving.

Frequently disturbing is the amount of blood and anguish portrayed with images of Christ or martyrs. Religious art of Spain, in response to the Counter-Reformational dictates, sought to impart to the viewer the greatest emotional impact possible. This was achieved through startlingly realistic and horrific scenes of torture and death. It can be convincingly argued that if these artistic influences had fallen on a more prosaic group of people other than the constantly warring nations of Mexico, and if colonization methods had been gentle and undemanding, there may have been less acceptance or an amelioration of the subject matter. As it was, there appears to have occurred an immediate association by indigenous people of their

misery with the almost lifelike representations of other individuals in painful and humiliating circumstances, especially Christ. This embracing of the exaggeration of the torture and agony seen in the Counter-Reformational and baroque art of Spain struck responsive chords within indigenous aesthetic sensibilities, the vernacular of death as seen on pre-Columbian monuments and sculpture having preceded the enforcement of Christianity and the imposition of *its* icons. Because of the

Manus Incorruptae San Matrís (The Incorruptible Hand of San Matrís), 19th century, oil on tinplate, 13¾" x 10" (34.9 x 25.4 cm.).

control Spain exerted, prohibiting any out-side influences within her provinces, the mystical and dramatic elements of Spanish Catholicism (reinforced by the politics and economy of Mexico of the last half of the millennium) have remained throughout.

Beginning in the first half of the six-teenth century with a number of elements of the late Renaissance, European influ-ences upon Mexican art soon introduced the baroque, which, mutating through a number of stages, lasted almost 200 years. Coinciding with various philosophical movements, the baroque gave way to neo-classicism in metropolitan centers toward the end of the eighteenth century but hung on in the provinces. The attraction for the rich, saturated colors; the opulent, gold-leafed retablos, altars, and statues; and the drama of sudden light and shadow con-trasts, as well as the emotions portrayed of the baroque era, were deeply rooted within the Mestizo consciousness. Resonating from the magnificence of former cultures, experi-encing the holocaust of the conquest, and being conscious of the beauty and vastness of their natural environment, the baroque was not only a response but also a mirror. The cool and reserved neoclassicism could never match the enthusiasm for, or accep-tance of, the baroque by the Mexican artist.

Spanish or European motifs, styles, and designs and native and imported materials and techniques, however, were not the only sources of inspiration or aesthetic determi-nates. Almost immediately, with the con-quest momentum still cresting, trade and religious missions were attempted through-out the Orient. These points of contact in the Philippines, China, and Japan unlocked sources and developed channels for won-

drously exotic goods and materials that impacted New Spain's acquisitive consumer class. Silk, ivory, dense and lustrous woods, precious stones, and shells were either imported in finished goods or simply as materials. Other items, such as lacquered wood, brass, and porcelain, were imported in manufactured products. The amount of goods imported was highly significant, and all of this provided stimulus to the artist, artisan, decorator, collector, and con-sumer—both church and secular. With access to this array of sensuous stimuli, nascent baroque style acquired additional nuances.

THE COLLECTION

Items in the Torch Collection reflect the dichotomy between academically trained and self-taught artisans coexisting in time and place—the metropolitan/guild-governed craftsperson and his provincial equivalent from the eighteenth through the nineteenth centuries. The sculpture, paint-ings, and silverwork encompass a sweep of influences from every continent except Australia and Antarctica and represent items intended for churches and both upper and lower classes' private holy spaces. Nowhere is this more evident than in the comparison between the silver pro-cessional cross and the tin retablos (p. 149). In the processional cross, one sees the grandeur and dignity of the church as expressed by workmanship of high quality and from guilds who were among the most powerful and influential, while the retablos have the informal and humble quality of most folk art. San Jerónimo (Saint Jerome, translator of the Vulgate Bible and one of the doctors of the

Church), his environment and his attributes have been reduced to decorative essentials. The first was unquestionably created for an important church by metropolitan craftsmen; the second by provincial artists to sell during religious fairs.

Sculpture

We do not know the name or gender of the creators of any of these works. In fact, the vast majority of religious art, sculpture, and painting throughout Mexico is anonymous. Reasons for this perhaps lie within the mentality of a society that regarded these items more as mechanisms for worship or manifestations of faith rather than opportunities to celebrate individual personalities. Furthermore, until the late nineteenth century, religious sculpture and painting were regarded as adjunct to altarpieces rather than individual expressions of skills in manipulating materials. Most times in large workshops, works were the result of the combined efforts of a number of craftspeople, each doing a specialized task. The image of *San Cayetano* (Saint Cajetan), founder of the Theatines Regular Clerks (p. 167), serves as an excellent

San Jerónimo, Defensor de la Fé y Abogado para la Buena Muerte (Saint Jerome, Defender of the Faith and Intercessor for a Holy or Peaceful Death) late 19th century, oil on tinplate, 14" x 10" (35.6 x 24.5 cm.).

Spanish 18th-century Silver Processional Cross early 18th century with 19th-century additions, silver and alloy, overall height 33½" (84.8 cm.).

example. Judging from the high quality of the *estofado* (the punch work and gold-leaf treatment of the garments), it may be safely surmised that this piece was done in a guild-regulated workshop. Because the carving, preparation of the wood, gold leafing, painting of fabrics, and *encarnación* (painting of the flesh) were skills that fell under separate guild domains, it is likely that this figure is the result of a group effort of from four to five different individuals working under the supervision of a *maestro de taller de escultura* (owner or head sculptor in a workshop or studio) or a *maestro de obras* (artistic overseer or project foreman). Consequently, if there *ever* had been a maker's name associated with this piece, it most likely would have been the foreman or workshop owner—someone who was the responsible party for contractual purposes. The figure of *La Inmaculada* (The Immaculate Conception) (p. 164), although much smaller than the sculpture of *San Cayetano,* was probably crafted in the same manner.

The artistic guild system, however, gradually disintegrated toward the end of the eighteenth century and was officially disbanded in the first decade of the nineteenth. Now, makers of polychromed statuary, if they wished, could construct and decorate a piece in its entirety. The nineteenth- or early-twentieth-century crucifixes (pp. 151 and 165) would not, therefore, have been under those constraints. However, the *poblano-* (popular)-style crucifix (p. 165), because it was most likely made in a village or environs away from metropolitan centers (dates notwithstanding), would probably never have fallen under official scrutiny anyway. These sculptured figures graphically demonstrate the variances likely to be found throughout Mexico—sophisticated and academic as opposed to naïve and popular. Comparisons between the two crucifixes elegantly demonstrate the wide range of expressions. It should be noted that the larger "folkish" piece loses nothing from its lack of correct anatomy; instead, its stiffness and stylization imbue it with vigor and pathos.

Among the ivory pieces there are also differing degrees of technical refinement. It is obvious that the maker of the allegorical cross (p. 162) is not in the same technical category as the makers of the figure of *Santa Rosa de Lima* (Saint Rose of Lima, Perú) (p. 152), the head of *El Niño Jesús* (the Christ Child), or *La Inmaculada* (both p. 166). Yet, what he lacked in technical skill he made up in a good sense of arrangement of elements and angles, his rather personal interpretation of the symbols of the Passion, and, as a bonus, the inclusion of figures on the base—possibly representing *animas solas* (lone souls), persons in purgatory. The sculptor of the figure of *Santa Rosa de Lima* was well aware of the qualities of the material with which he was working and respected the natural curve of the tusk to create a female body with a slight sway. Of particular interest is the fact that the head of *El Niño Jesús* exhibits oriental characteristics reflecting its Asian origin. While the figure of *La Inmaculada* has no overt Asian physical qualities, the lotus-like pedestal and manner in which the robe is tied in the front tips it toward its oriental heritage.

Just as the sculpted wooden figures were *always* intended to be covered with

Corpus, bone or wood,
6½" x 6¾" (16.7 x 17.2 cm.).

paint and gilding, the sensibilities of the Spanish/Mexican client demanded that the ivory figures also include color; therefore, pupils, hair, and sometimes clothing were painted and, in the case of hair or clothing, gold leaf was occasionally applied.

Paintings

Religious paintings were done on any number of different types of supports, and the Torch Collection has examples on canvas, wood, and tinplate. While all of them served much the same purpose, their sizes, themes, and inscriptions indicate an intention for different audiences. Large paintings of a singular saint, such as *San Juan Nepomuceno* (Saint John Nepomuk, patron of lawyers, Bohemia, and bridges) (p. 159), were customarily included as part of a series in altar screens. Each altarpiece has a specific dedication or theme; therefore, religious orders would have representations of "their" saints in their churches. Because the devotion of *San Juan Nepomuceno* was promulgated by the Jesuits, it is entirely possible that this painting had been intended for a Jesuit church or private chapel of individuals supportive of the Jesuit order. Similarly, the smaller painting of *San Anastacio* (Saint Anastasius) (p. 169) may well have belonged to a convent of Carmelites. Out of context, the significance of subjects is frequently lost. While the painting of *San Miguel* (Saint Michael, chief of the archangels) (facing page) or of *La Mater Dolorosa* (The Sorrowful Mother) (p. 155) could easily have been a singular object in a small shrine in a domestic setting, either also may originally have been part of a much larger scheme—as part of an altarpiece: San Miguel with the other six

Santa Rosa de Lima (Saint Rose of Lima, Perú), late 18th to early 19th century, ivory, 9½" (24.1 cm.).

archangels or Mary and scenes from her life or the seven joys and seven sorrows.

Mary's enormous popularity is testified to by the large number of her images, outnumbering all other figures, including Jesus. *Nuestra Señora, Refugio de Pecadores* (Our Lady, Refuge of Sinners) (p. 143), whose cult status received the greatest impetus after the image was placed in the Cathedral of Zacatecas and nearby at the Convent of Guadalupe in the early decades of the eighteenth century, enjoyed enormous popularity during the nineteenth century. The figure on page 143 charmingly displays the distinctive ciphers of Jesus, Mary, and Joseph on this particular Virgin's robe as well as the delicate handling of the gilding of lace, crowns, and halos.

Didactic script, not uncommon in religious paintings in Mexico, helps identify not only the image's identity, but also elucidates the painting's function. *El Divino Rostro* (The Divine Face or Veil of Veronica) (p. 161) announces 12,000 years of pardon granted pontifically for devotion to this image and the recitation of The Lord's Prayer and Hail Marys; the shield at the foot of San Anastacio (p. 169) proclaims his unshod Carmelite affiliation, that he was a martyr, and that not only did demons flee from his presence but he healed all illnesses. Smaller and more intimate is the mnemonic device of examining one's conscience (p. 147) taken from a devotion based upon the relic of the undecaying hand of *San Matrís*. Similarly, the painting of the head of *Santa Teresa de Jesús* (Saint Theresa) (p. 161) that is venerated in a Carmelite convent includes text explaining the image as well as providing a decorative frame for the object. The painting of

San Joaquín y la Niña María (Saint Joachim and the Virgin as a Child) (p. 168) contains biblical references in Latin as well as the Spanish text giving Joachim's title and patronage nicely incorporated within a painting loaded with attributes of the Virgin Mary as found in the litanies to the Virgin. The smallness of the script, the details within these last three paintings, as well as the delicacy of elements, strongly support

San Miguel (Saint Michael, Archangel), late 18th century, oil on canvas, 12½" x 8½" (31.7 x 21.5 cm.).

El Divino Rostro
(The Divine Face of Christ)
19th century; wood, gesso, paint,
and glass; panel 13 x 19½"
(32.6 x 24.0 cm.).

the proposition that these were intended
for personal devotion within a home or
private chapel or a more intimate environment than the nave of a church.

The subject matter of the retablo can
be divided into two main categories, and
the Torch Collection holds both: images of
the Holy Family (Mary, Joseph, Jesus and
God the Father) and the saints. The various

images are painted in a straightforward
manner with the proper colors and gar-
ment types proscribed by canonical law or
tradition, and generally the figures hold or
are depicted in association with some
attribute that is particular to them. Usually
there is only one image or theme per
panel, but instances do occur where
another image, unrelated except that it is

Mater Dolorosa con Instrumentos de la Pasión (Our Lady of Sorrows with Symbols of the Passion), 18th century,
oil on wood panel, 12¾" x 12"
(32.3 x 30.6 cm.).

also regarded as a holy personage, shares the format. The artistic quality ranges from academically inspired or trained artists to naïfs, and in baroque, neoclassic, and even Italo-Byzantine styles, depending upon the sources of inspiration used.[4] Certain saints or images of the Virgin and Christ were immensely popular and make up a large percentage of the overall production. The figure on page 145 of *N.S. de Guadalupe* (Our Lady of Guadalupe, patron of Mexico) illustrates a typical use of clear, bright colors; fluid handling of paints; and the delightful inclusion of decorative elements found in many of the paintings on tinplate. The figure on page 157 of *San Antonio de Padua* (Saint Anthony of Padua, patron for infertile women and girls seeking husbands and finder of lost objects) contains some of the above elements but also clearly demonstrates the naïf artist's misuse, or lack of, perspective and shadowing—characteristics that somehow endear the image and make these small, popular paintings on tin more appealing and approachable than the larger and academic works done on canvas.

The Torch Collection contains an unusual set of other paintings on tin—*Vías Cruces* (the Stations of the Cross) (p. 158). A devotion alluding to the fourteen different incidents of the Passion of Christ was initiated in the latter half of the fifteenth century. Later, in the seventeenth century, this became regarded as a substitute for perilous pilgrimages to the Holy Land. Since about the eighteenth century, fourteen small paintings and/or crosses have been required in every Catholic church. This particular set has much of the "folk" quality of the retablos.

The format of the ex-voto is almost undeviating. A scene appears in the center of the painting that shows the devotees either in prayer or at the moment during some horrific incident when they appeal to a particularly efficacious religious personage for deliverance. In an area of the painting, usually isolated from the human, the image from which help is sought is placed. At the bottom appears a text giving grateful testimony for the miracle, explaining the incident, and giving the place and date. Frequently, as evidenced by the ex-voto depicted on page 160, the artist goes beyond merely including the above requisites. The angles of the landscape and building have been manipulated to give the viewer the best view possible, and loving attention has been given to details of the supplicant's, as well as *N.S., Refugio de Pecadores'* clothing and to the vegetation and fences. It is in this genre of Mexican religious painting that the greatest amount of ingenuity and creativity are demonstrated.

CONCLUSION

Within the scope of J. P. Bryan's Mexican religious art are numerous objects reflecting varying materials, technical solutions, and aesthetic approaches. Each of these objects, moreover, projects different levels of emotional and philosophical expressions. While some are just simply images of a particular religious personage, others are abstract and require the viewer to process symbols in order to understand their significance. While they all express the Catholic dogma of the times, interpretation varies—sometimes in direct correlation to the level of sophistication of the piece. As a group, they give the viewer a good idea of the range and scope of the influences upon, skills acquired, and mediums used by Mexican artists from the seventeenth through nineteenth centuries. Individually, there are a number of pieces that transcend their religious messages and, through their appealing designs, colors, and humanity, speak to the heart.

BIBLIOGRAPHY

Carrillo y Gariel, Abelardo. *Téchnica de la pintura de Nueva España.* México: Universidad Nacional Autónoma de México, 1946.

Egan, Martha J. *Milagros: Votive Offerings from the Americas.* Santa Fe: Museum of New Mexico, 1991.

Giffords, Gloria Fraser. *Mexican Folk Retablos.* Rev. ed. Albuquerque: Museum of New Mexico, 1992.

Lange, Yvonne. "Lithography: An Agent of Technological Change in Religious Folk Art: A Thesis." *Western Folklore* 33, no. 1 (January 1974): 51–64.

NOTES

1. The word *retablo* (from Latin *retro-tabulum*, "behind the altar") originally referred to altar screens of Spanish and Spanish Colonial churches.
2. Although they have been collected in Guatemala and a similar tradition exists in Bolivia, Mexico was by far the greatest producer of retablos on tinplate. There were, however, some ex-votos painted on tinplate in mid-nineteenth-century southern Italy.
3. See Egan, Milagros.
4. In a time-honored tradition, retablo artists used black-and-white prints as sources of inspiration. (See Lange, "Lithography.") Lange puts forth the theory that a significant amount of nineteenth-century New Mexican and Mexican painting and sculpture was influenced by prints produced throughout Europe and exported to Mexico, and feels that certain distinctly Byzantine devices of rendering drapery and anatomy found on any number of retablos can logically be explained in this manner. (See also Carillo y Gariel, *Téchnica . . .* , pp. 126–31.)

PHOTOGRAPHY OF MEXICAN RELIGIOUS ART BY BAKÓ/BECQ WORLDWIDE AND FRANK WHITE.

San Antonio de Padua (Saint Anthony of Padua), mid-to-late 19th century, oil on tinplate, 13⅞" x 10⅛" (35.3 x 25.5 cm.).

Vía Cruces No. 1 (First Station of the Cross), Jesus is Condemned to Death, 19th century, oil on tinplate, 8½–9" x 13½" (22.4-23.0 x 34.5 cm.).

Vía Cruces No. 12 (Twelfth Station of the Cross), Jesus Dies on the Cross, 19th century, oil on tinplate, 9" x 13½" (23.1 x 34.4 cm.).

San Juan Nepomuceno
(Saint John Nepomuk),
c. 1860, oil on canvas,
33¼" x 24½" (84.5 x 62.2 cm.).

Ex-voto, 1883, oil on canvas mounted on paper 16⅝" x 22¼" (42.2 x 56.4 cm.). This ex-voto depicts María Simón Serrato, ill with pneumonia. Dying, she received the Last Sacrament but was then miraculously healed of her illness. She commissioned this ex-voto to honor Our Lady, Refuge of Sinners, to whom she credited her amazing recovery.

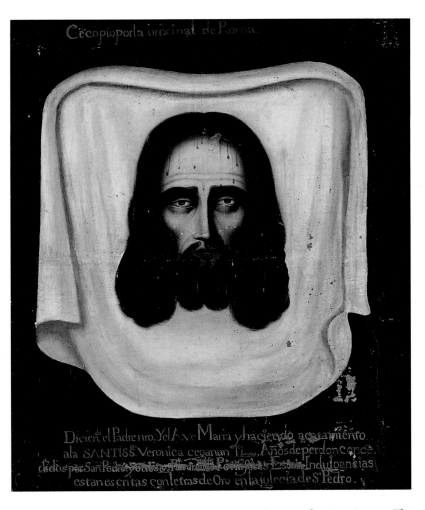

Santa Teresa de Ávila (Saint Teresa of Avila), early 19th century, oil on canvas, 6¾" x 4⅞" (17.2 x 12.2 cm.).

Verónica o El Divino Rostro (The Veil of Veronica or the Divine Face), 18th century, oil on canvas, 29¾" x 23" (75.5 x 58.5 cm.).

Carved Cross, late 18th to early 19th century, ivory, 18½" x 8⅝" (47.0 x 22.0 cm.).

La Cruz de Ánimas (The Cross of Souls), 19th century, painted wood, 50" x 27¼" (127.6 x 69.1 cm.).

***La Inmaculada (The Most
Immaculate Virgin Mary),***
18th century; wood, gesso, paint,
gilding, silver, and glass;
18¼" (45.9 cm.).

Corpus on Cross, 19th century; wood, plaster, paint, glass, rope, and nails; 60" x 43¼" (151.8 x 111.1 cm.).

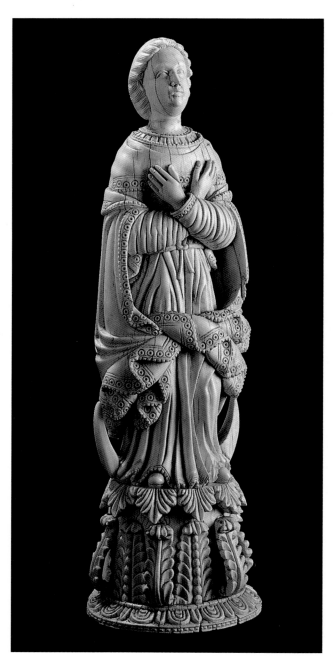

La Inmaculada (The Most Immaculate Virgin Mary)
late 18th to early 19th century,
ivory, 11¾" (30.0 cm.).

El Niño Jesús (The Christ Child)
18th century; ivory, silver, paint,
2⅝" (6.5 cm.).

San Cayetano (Saint Cajetan)
17th century; wood with gesso,
paint, and gilding; 15¼" x 12½" x
5¼" (38.8 x 31.8 x 13.3 cm.).

San Anastacio (Saint Anastasius),
late 18th century, oil on canvas,
19½" x 14¼" (49.3 x 36.2 cm.).

Jesús, San Joaquín y María
(Jesus, Saint Joachim and Mary),
18th century, oil on canvas,
41⅜" x 33⅛" (105.1 x 84.1 cm.).
In this work, San Joaquín holds the
infant María, and Christ is present
as the radiant "IHS" above them.

S. Anastasio Monje
Carmelita Descalzo, y Mar
tir de cuya presencia huyen
los demonios, y sana de todas
enfermedades como lo contex
tan el Concilio Niceno, y
Calendario Romano y
special Avogado de las
que es tan de
esto

Ike Edward Morgan, *John Wayne*, c. 1985, pastel and ballpoint pen, 18" x 12½" (46.1 x 32.0 cm.).

THE BLACK WEST

WILLIAM LOREN KATZ

In the nineteenth century, scholars transformed our frontier saga from a grim duel with nature that unleashed the worst and best in people into a national mythology to honor Europeans for building a nation in the wilderness. This revised tale was not subject to Indian claims and omitted people of African descent, even denying them a place in dime novels, school texts, or other tales of pioneer life. When Hollywood's central casting selected actors to race across silver screens, African Americans were not considered.

This has finally begun to change. Like the dark, mysterious figures in "horse operas" who suddenly ride into town only to be recognized as missing earlier settlers, African American men and women of the West have come home. Scholarly diligence has cleared a path for these long-neglected pioneers to begin to enter the public consciousness.

From the misty dawn of the earliest foreign landings Africans were a crucial force in the New World. Their presence has been affirmed in explorers' diaries, viceroys' letters, church records, government reports, fur company ledgers, recollections of Indians and whites, newspaper accounts, and census reports. Their faces have been captured occasionally in sketches by artists Charles Russell and Frederic Remington, and by early professional and amateur cameramen, military and civilian. Some sat for portraits in pencil or oil and others kept diaries, notes or wrote letters. Black families forded rivers, scaled mountains, and slogged through marshes to enrich the culture and economy of each American frontier. The black frontier role that has been buried, strayed, or lost from view, is now clear.

Pietro Alonzo il Negro, traveling with Columbus in 1492, was pilot of the *Niña*. In 1513 African laborers marched with Vasco Balboa when he stumbled on a village of black people near Panama whose existence has never been fully explained. Other Africans marched into the wilderness behind, alongside, or a little ahead of Father Serra, Chief Pontiac, Ponce de León, and Davy Crockett. Slaves, fugitive slaves, or free, they entered the continent as explorers, fur trappers, adventurers, schoolmarms, homesteaders, sheriffs, cowboys, soldiers, outlaws, miners, journalists, and entrepreneurs.

Europeans first had built their American labor system on Native American enslavement, and added Africans after 1502 to the inflammable mixture. The two peoples of color became husbands, wives, sisters, and brothers, and with Native Americans showing the way, together they fled their chains. In 1503, when Governor Ovando of Hispañola reported his African slaves fled to the rain forest, his complaint that they "never could be captured" probably meant, at this early date, they had found a red hand of friendship. Africans were welcomed by an Indian adoption system that drew no color lines, and arrived with some unique agricultural skills and a familiarity with European weapons and diplomacy.

In a history filled with ironies, the subjugation of the New World was led by Spain, a nation of mixed bloods since 711 and the Moorish invasion of the Iberian peninsula. The opening of Africa by European merchants in 1442 and Spain's expulsion of the Moors in 1492 enabled the invaders to turn the New World into a massive experiment in colonization and enslavement.

Africans, slave and free, traveled as soldiers or laborers with foreign expedition to the Americas. They landed in Florida with Ponce de Leon, and, in 1519, Africans dragged the cannons that Hernán Cortés used to vanquish the Aztec empire. Others marched under the Pizarro brothers in their conquest of Perú and still others aided Francisco de Montejo in subduing Honduras. In 1539 Estevanico, a daring African Moor with a command of Indian languages, served as the scout for a southwestern exploration led by Father Marco de Nizza. Estevanico, accompanied by 300 Indians, became the first foreigner to enter Arizona and New Mexico.

Though colonial officials warned about bringing Africans where they might associate with Native Americans, Africans served in the European armies of occupation. Many took the opportunity to flee to Indian villages beyond the European bastions that dotted the coastlines. A European report from Mexico in 1537 noted: "The Indians and the Negroes daily wait, hoping to put into practice their freedom from the domination and servitude in which Spaniards keep them." That year black miners in Amatepeque, Mexico, revolted, elected a ruler, and, assisted by Native Mexicans, militarily challenged Spanish hegemony.

In 1579 four Africans accompanied Sir Francis Drake when he landed in San Francisco. In 1588 Africans helped Juan de Oñate colonize New Mexico and remained to take part in its civil wars two generations later. They joined the Pueblo Indian uprising of 1680 that overthrew Spanish rule, and a dozen years later fought against the Africans who helped Spain's armies crush the revolt. Beginning in 1769 Africans helped Father Junípero Serra's Jesuits build a string of missions in California. Some remained and appear in church birth, marriage, and death records, while others melted into Native villages.

From North Carolina's Great Dismal Swamp to Brazilian rain forests, two peoples of color fled together and formed outlaw "maroon societies." Though most maroon communities were committed to trade and/or agriculture rather than banditry, Europeans termed them "the gangrene of colonial society" and conducted a clockwork of legal and military assaults on their right to survive as alternative societies. By the American Revolution hundreds of armed Africans and Seminoles had settled along Florida's Appalachicola River. The Africans arrived first and taught the Seminoles—a breakaway segment of the Creek nation—methods of rice cultivation they had learned in Senegambia and Sierra Leone. On this basis the red and black people formed an agricultural and military alliance that held the United States Army, Navy, and Marines at bay for half a century.

The New World's first written racial protest was an affidavit signed in 1600 by Isabel de Olvera before she accompanied Juan Guerra de Resa's expedition to New Mexico. Born of an African father and Indian mother, Olvera said she had "some reason to fear I may be annoyed [because of race]." In words that still resonate, she wrote, "I demand justice."

In 1781 Los Angeles was founded by forty-six people (eleven different families), twenty-six of African descent. One, Manuel Camero, served on the city council from 1781 to 1816. Another, Francisco Reyes, owned the San Fernando Valley and sold it

to become the city's first mayor. María Rita Valdez, daughter of a black founder, owned Beverly Hills, and still others owned huge tracts of land and large herds of cattle. In 1790 a Spanish census of California uncovered a significant African presence: San Francisco, 18 percent; San Jose, 24 percent; Santa Barbara, 20 percent; Monterey, 18 percent.

Texas also had a richly diverse population. San Antonio was founded in 1718 by 72 people, many of African descent, and in 1777, 151 Africans were listed among its 2,060 residents. In 1789, of Laredo's 708 residents, 119 were of African parentage. However, after 1795, when Spain's King Charles III declared African blood inferior to Spanish blood and the Crown sold certificates allowing residents to claim greater Spanish blood, the census reported a drop in the number of black people.

In the 1820s people of African descent, slaves, free people of color, and runaways, some responding to Stephen Austin's invitation, entered east Texas from the United States. Fugitive slaves and others sought the liberty promised by some antislavery Mexican officials. In 1829 Vicente Guerrero, a revolutionary hero born of African and Indian parents, became president of Mexico, wrote its new constitution, and liberated its slaves.

By the 1830s free African Americans in Texas began to make their mark. In the southeast the four Ashworth brothers owned almost two thousand acres of land and 2,500 head of cattle, and were able to avoid military service by hiring substitutes. Greenbury Logan traveled to Texas with Stephen Austin where he volunteered for and was severely wounded in the war that

John Willard Banks; *Blacks Fought at the Alamo Too!* 1986; graphite pencil, wax crayon, felt tip and ballpoint pens, and liquid concealer; 28" x 44⅛" (71.2 x 112.2 cm.). Joe, the slave of William Barret Travis, reportedly attested that there were several black women and children in the Alamo at the time of the battle. The only woman killed in the battle was black, and she died in the open space in front of the church, an area now known as Alamo Plaza. John Banks memorialized these unknown defenders in this artwork, which was commissioned for the Texas sesquicentennial.

freed Texas from Mexico. He found, however, that the slaveholders who ruled the Lone Star Republic had no respect for the rights of a wounded black veteran. During the Mexican War, untold numbers of Texas slaves fled plantations to the Colorado, the Nueces, and the Red Rivers, or to Santa Anna's armies or the Comanches. Pio Pico, born to a prominent family of mixed African descent, was the last Mexican governor of California, serving from 1845 to 1846 when he was deposed by the victorious U.S. armies.

In San Francisco, William Leidesdorff of Danish-African descent, a wealthy and fervent U.S. Partisan, in 1845 was appointed a U.S. vice-consul by President Polk. He secretly plotted to overthrow Mexican rule and not only welcomed U.S. Captain John Montgomery and his army but spent a night translating the proclamation on the transfer of power that Montgomery read to the assembled citizens at the plaza the next day.

For adventurous souls in the east, the end of the American Revolution led to settlement of the Ohio and Mississippi Valleys. Some black people arrived as missionaries, others as trappers, schoolteachers, adventurers, and runaways. In 1779 Jean Baptiste Point Du Sable built a trading post near a lake in the Illinois territory, married a Potawatomie woman, made friends with Chief Pontiac and Daniel Boone, and watched as his settlement grew into the city of Chicago. Colonel James Stevenson, who lived for thirty years among Native Americans, in 1888 wrote: "The old fur trappers always got a Negro if possible to negotiate for them with the Indians, because of their 'pacifying effect.' They could manage them better than white men, with less friction."

James P. Beckwourth, a handy man with a Bowie knife, gun, or hatchet, cut a jagged path from St. Louis to California and back across the continent to Florida as a fur trader, army scout, and warrior-for-hire. In April 1850 he discovered a pass in the Sierra Nevadas important to the forty-niners, and the pass, the nearby town, and a peak still bear his name. In the age of Daniel Boone, Jim Bowie, and Davy Crockett, a western writer believed Beckwourth was "the most famous Indian fighter of this generation."

Thousands of slave runaways lived among the Six Nations of the northeast or the Five Civilized Nations of the southeast. Frontier artist George Catlin described their offspring as "the finest looking people I have ever seen." When the U.S. government forced 14,000 Cherokees into a "Trail of Tears" midwinter march from Georgia to Oklahoma, the Cherokees had 1,600 African members.

During the gold rush two thousand African Americans flocked to California and one thousand called themselves miners. Some were free, but others who were enslaved were sent or taken by their gold-seeking masters; a few black men gathered enough gold nuggets to purchase their freedom. In cities some African Americans became noted chefs, entrepreneurs, and land investors, and California soon boasted the wealthiest black community in the country.

California's black intellectuals built a two-story "Athenaeum" as an educational center, complete with 800 books and a black museum, and developed a civil rights agenda. In 1855 the new capital at Sacramento hosted the first of three annual black state conventions to demand the right to testify in court, to vote, and to have their children educated in public schools. The next year's black convention created a newspaper, *Mirror of the Times,* to carry news of their campaigns to the state's thirty counties.

California became an early battleground over human rights. In 1846 Mary, a Missouri slave, sued for liberty in a Mexican court in San Jose and won. During gold rush days other enslaved people, often assisted by white attorneys, took their masters to court or tried to flee to Canada. Slave Biddy Mason reached California the hard way: she walked all the way from Mississippi in charge of her owner's livestock. Aided by a white Los Angeles sheriff, she served her master with a writ of *habeas corpus* and, after two days in court, was granted liberty for herself and her three daughters. After becoming a successful midwife, she invested wisely in Los Angeles real estate and became a noted philanthropist.

Of all the western territories, only Utah made slavery legal. In 1848 the 1,700 Mormons who settled in the Salt Lake Valley clung to a belief that the Scriptures condemned blacks to servitude. But Mormons and their four dozen enslaved black people began by sharing scarce food, crowded shelters, and the punishments of nature. Two years later, black Mormons were able to hold assemblies for social and political purposes in their own Salt Lake City building. Though the Mormons promulgated a "slave code" in 1852, it focused on masters and required them to provide the enslaved decent clothing, food, and opportunities, and permitted sales only with their consent. In the spring of 1862

Congress ended slavery in Utah and other western territories.

By then, more than a few slaves had freed themselves and headed west. Clara Brown arrived by covered wagon in Denver in 1859 when it was still called Cherry Creek, began a laundry, started the first Sunday school, and used her home to organize the Saint James Methodist Church. After the Civil War, Brown used money she had saved to search for her relatives lost during slavery. She found only one daughter but brought dozens of other former slaves to Colorado where she helped them gain an education and find jobs. In 1885 her funeral was attended by the governor of Colorado and the mayor of Denver and was conducted by the Colorado Pioneers Association.

Long before they had become free, African Americans in the Southwest were roping and branding cattle. After the Civil War they were among 35,000 cowboys who drove Texas cattle up the Chisholm Trail to rail depots in Kansas. In 1925 George Saunders, president of the Old Time Drivers Association, recalled "about one third of the trail crews were Negroes and Mexicans."

Most cowpunchers were ordinary men, such as Nat Love, a former Tennessee slave later known as Deadwood Dick, who journeyed west to hone his skill on the long drives and work for $30 a month and grub. Few were as lucky as former slave D. W. Wallace of Texas, who made the transition from a penniless teenage cowhand to wealthy ranch owner.

Very few had the exceptional skills of Bill Pickett. Called "the greatest sweat and dirt cowhand that ever lived" by Zack

John Willard Banks; *The Cattle Drive*; c. 1980; wax crayon, felt tip and ballpoint pens; 13¾" x 22" (34.8 x 55.9 cm.).

Deacon Eddie Moore, *Bill Pickett, First Bull, Dogger, 1906*, c. 1992, wood and paint, 11⅜" x 14¼" x 13" D (28.9 x 36.2 x 33.0 cm. D).

Miller, boss of the sprawling 101st Ranch in Oklahoma, Pickett created the rodeo sport of "bull-dogging," or steer wrestling, one of the seven traditional rodeo contests. Billed as "The Dusky Demon," Pickett was the 101st Rodeo's star attraction when it performed in Oklahoma, England, Mexico, and at New York's Madison Square Garden. His daring finale had Pickett biting into the steer's lip to show his only grip on the beast was with his teeth.

Most cowhands tried to follow the law but some rode in to break it. In 1877 the Texas wanted list with five thousand names included every race. The first man shot in Dodge City was a black cowhand named Tex, an innocent bystander to a gun duel between two whites. The first man thrown into Abilene's new stone prison was not innocent and he was black, but his black and white trail crew shot up the town and rescued him. Black desperadoes such as Cherokee Bill and the Rufus Buck gang who roamed the Oklahoma Territory were cut in the mold of Billy the Kid and the Dalton gang: they killed without regard to race, color, or creed, and paid with their lives.

Some black men pinned on a lawman's badge. Dozens of black deputies served under "Hanging Judge" Isaac Parker. One, Bass Reeves, became a legend in his time. In thirty-two years he shot fourteen men but largely relied on his disguises, detective skills, and a knowledge of Indian languages and customs to outwit and arrest dozens of criminals. In 1874 Willie Kennard convinced a skeptical mayor of Yankee Hill, Colorado, to hire him as marshal before facing down Casewit, a deranged killer and rapist. Shooting the two guns from Casewit's hands, Kennard marched him to jail.

Law and order first rode into the western territories with the U.S. Cavalry. The black Ninth and Tenth Regiments—a fifth of the U.S. Cavalry soldiers in the West—and the 24th and 25th U.S. Infantry Regiments were called "Buffalo Soldiers" by Native Americans, who named them after the animal they relied on for food, clothing, and shelter. The Buffalo Soldiers patrolled from the Rio Grande to the Canadian border, from the Mississippi to the Rockies, and won the respect of every military friend and foe they encountered. For acts beyond the call of duty more than a dozen black troopers earned the Congressional Medal of Honor, though many in Texas faced harassment and assault from the townspeople they defended.

Rarely did African American women head west alone, but in 1868 Elvira Conley arrived in Sheridan, Kansas, a raucous railroad town ruled by vigilantes. She began a laundry and wisely made friends with two of her best customers, Wild Bill Hickok and Buffalo Bill. In Sheridan she also met the wealthy Sellar-Bullard merchant family and spent more than half a century serving as a governess to generations of their children.

The first major black migration from the southern states began in 1879 when an estimated eight thousand African American men, women, and children, who agreed "It is better to starve to death in Kansas than be shot and killed in the South," headed West. Mobilized largely by women, often widows of men slain by white marauders in the Deep South, they saw Kansas as a promised land of safety, education, farms, and decent work. Founded in 1877, Nicodemus, Kansas, served as a beacon, especially after Mrs.

Walter Frank Cotton, *Freedman's Aid School*, c. 1938, oil on cardboard, 32¾" x 66¼" (83.2 x 168.5 cm.). In *Freedman's Aid School,* Walter Cotton depicts his grandmother as a little girl coming through the door of this freedman's school in Limestone County, Texas.

Francis Fletcher began a one-room school for fifteen black boys and girls with donated books and a curriculum of literature, hygiene, moral values, and mathematics.

Like the European emigrants who poured into the United States at this time, black pioneers largely rejected rural life—which they associated with slavery—for town jobs. Black women pioneers were mostly in their twenties to forties, older and more likely to be married than white women, and had a lower childbearing rate than either white women or black women in the East. They were five times as likely

to have jobs (usually as domestic servants) as white women and twice as likely to be employed as Indian women—initially a minority within a minority on the frontier.

In 1889 another great land rush in Oklahoma attracted thousands of people of color. Most came from the Deep South and fled mounting violence for a chance to see their women and children protected, gain an education, and look for economic opportunities. Leaving home in kinship and friendship caravans of a hundred or more people, their travel arrangement provided the many women a protective, comforting blanket. Since the large bands included

many skilled artisans, the early days of settlement went much smoother in black towns than in white towns. Residents did not have to solicit or wait for missing artisans as did white communities. The simultaneous arrival of so many family and friends also ensured cooperation, minimized conflict, and spurred town growth and spirit.

In the dramatic political career of Edwin P. McCabe, one can chart the ebbs and flows of power brought by the black migration to Kansas. Republicans twice nominated and elected McCabe state auditor, only to deny him a third term. In 1890

he arrived in Oklahoma, helped found Langston City the next year, and championed Oklahoma as a black refuge from the South's racist violence. He evidently planned to settle a black majority in each congressional district and had set his eyes on Oklahoma's territorial governorship. Within eight years Langston City boasted a public school, later a college, and within a decade had virtually eliminated illiteracy among its fifteen- to forty-five-year-old men (5 percent) and women (6 percent).

Boley, Oklahoma, formed in 1904 on land owned by Abigail Barnett, a black Indian, in two years had a school with two

Frederic Sackrider Remington, *A Pool in the Desert*, c. 1888, oil on canvas mounted on board, 17¾" x 27⅝" (45.1 x 70.2 cm.). Frederic Remington painted *A Pool in the Desert* about the 10th U.S. Cavalry, also known as the Buffalo Soldiers, on a pack trip to San Carlos from Fort Grant in the Arizona Territory desert. Remington accompanied the 10th Cavalry for an illustrated article that he wrote for *The Century Magazine* in April 1889.

teachers, and later a high school that sent half of its graduates to college. In 1908 Booker T. Washington called Boley "striking evidence" of "land-seekers and home-builders . . . prepared to build up the country." By World War I a thousand black people lived in Boley, and several thousand ran nearby farms.

Between 1890 and 1910 thirty-two all-black towns sprouted in Oklahoma. Men ran the governments but women organized community events; built schools, churches, and self-help societies; and enshrined middle-class values. Then, in 1907, Oklahoma entered the Union as another white supremacy state, the first to segregate telephone booths. Black towns still elected local officials but not national or state officers, and quickly fell under the bigoted hand of the new state's justice system. Segregation laws and declining agricultural prices spelled ruin, turning most black towns into ghost towns. McCabe's political goal sputtered to earth, and he left for Chicago where in 1920 he died in poverty. But his dream lived on in black migrants' flight from racism and in their resounding victories over illiteracy.

Women remained a major reservoir of black community strength. They put up the walls and nailed down the floors of frontier schools, churches, and self-help societies. In 1864 women in Virginia City, Nevada, began the First Baptist Church with a new bound Bible and a dozen hymn books. These pioneers went on to demand public education for their children, to begin literary societies for both men and women, and in 1874 to hold a Calico Ball for the 374 blacks living largely in western Nevada.

In Montana, in 1888, black women started St. James Church and the next year the Methodist Episcopal Church. By 1924 thirty-one delegates assembled in Bozeman as representatives of Montana's Federation of Black Women's Clubs. In Denver, Colorado, in 1906 the Colored Women's Republican Club proudly reported that a larger percentage of black women voted in the city election than white women. By 1910, and largely due to the efforts of women, illiteracy among African Americans in California, Oregon, and the Mountain States had been reduced to less than 10 percent. Even in western prisons, 87 percent of black women inmates knew how to read and write.

In many locales, black women were so rare that black bachelors would meet incoming stagecoaches and trains, seeking a marriage partner. Western women were far more likely to marry than their sisters in the East. In Arizona mining towns it was married black women who, distressed by the single men who disturbed the peace at night and on weekends, formed the "Busy Bee Club." Their strategy was to make arrangements with black churches and newspapers in the East for the importation of mail-order brides-to-be for unmarried miners. Young women, promising to wed the men who paid their fare, boarded trains for Arizona. Among those waiting were men whose wives had died under primitive conditions, often leaving many children. Young brides survived tense wedding days to meet the challenges of family life on the frontier. By 1900 black women outnumbered black men in Denver and Los Angeles.

As Boley and Langston City struggled to survive, other black towns sprouted in the

West. California gave birth to Albia, Allensworth, Bowles, and Victorville; Texas produced Andy, Booker, Board House, Cologne, Independence Heights, Kendleton, Oldham, Mill City, Roberts, Shankleville, and Union City. The last high-plains black settlement was Dearfield, Colorado, founded in 1910 by Oliver and Minerva Jackson and settled by seven hundred poor, older women and men with little capital and scant farming experience. During World War I Dearfield prospered only to be struck by a water shortage and searing winds, finally to be toppled by the postwar agricultural depression.

Black farming communities had marched into battle without the necessary weapons. Black pioneers, having less capital than whites, were unable to purchase the large acreage required for survival. Denied easy credit, they became less able to weather economic and natural disasters. And, like rural whites, in the age of the automobile and movies, the jobs and bright lights of cities constantly lured their young.

The West produced unusual and distinguished women and men of color. In 1866 Cathy Williams dressed as a man and, as "William Cathy," served for two years in the Buffalo Soldiers. Barney Ford built a palatial Inter-Ocean Hotel in Denver and then another in Cheyenne, Wyoming. An African American cowpuncher named Williams taught a New York City tenderfoot named Theodore Roosevelt how to break in a horse, and another black cowboy named Clay taught movie star Will Rogers his first rope tricks. Mifflin Gibbs rose from a California bootblack to start the state's first black newspaper, graduate from college, and become a judge in Little Rock, Arkansas.

In Texas, Sutton Griggs, at twenty-six, became a Baptist minister and a published novelist, and went on to write seven books of fiction and essays. Born a slave in Texas, Lucy Gonzales Parsons became the first

prominent socialist revolutionary of color, advocate for the wretched of the earth, and voice of the working class in the United States. As editors of the popular *Seattle Republican,* Susan and Horace Cayton became wealthy leading citizens of the new state of Washington. Six-foot, 200-pound Mary Fields ran a restaurant and laundry in Cascade, Montana, and in her sixties, as "Stagecoach Mary," delivered the U.S. Mail and drove a stagecoach. In 1898 widow May Mason of Seattle rushed off to the Yukon, Alaska, gold rush and returned with $5,000 in gold and a $6,000 land claim. Oscar Micheaux wrote seven novels, including two fictionalized autobiographies of his life in South Dakota, and as a pioneer moviemaker in the 1920s and 1930s wrote and produced forty-five films that cast his people as cowboys, detectives, and doctors.

African American pioneers were a hearty breed; they had to be, for they faced more than their white counterparts. To live

at peace on the frontier, they had to survive the raging storms of nature and man, and overcome a bony hand of bigotry that could rise at any time from white strangers or neighbors. Like other pioneers, African Americans strode across the broad plains and mountains seeking their dream, and some found it by dint of hard work and luck. But their sojourn often was a frontier experience with a difference. Their families needed a place where skill would count more than skin color; where women and children would find safety, education, and a chance in the race for life; and where men would find decent jobs. Most black pioneers sought to avoid the genocidal bigotry and murderous land-hunger that stained European trails into the wilderness, and tried to be good neighbors on all sides.

With undaunted spirit, raw courage, and an unfailing persistence, black pioneers added a new dimension to western life and had their chance to ride off into the sunset.

Isaac Smith, *Diamond Back Rat'ler,* c. 1992, wood and paint, 49" L (124.5 cm.).

John Coleman, *Camping Time*,
1986, oil on board, 29⅞" x 40"
(76.1 x 101.5 cm.).

Rev. Johnnie Swearingen,
The Red Bull, c. 1973, oil on board,
15⅞" x 20" (40.3 x 50.8 cm.).

John Willard Banks; *Lone Oak;*
1984; wax crayon, felt tip and
ballpoint pens; 14⅛" x 22"
(35.8 x 56.0 cm.).

John Willard Banks, *Stagecoach Robbery*; 1986; graphite pencil, felt tip and ballpoint pens; 16" x 20" (41.0 x 50.9 cm.).

John Willard Banks; *1859 Overland Stagecoach at Fort Kearney, Nebraska*; n.d.; wax crayon, felt tip and ballpoint pens; 11" x 14⅛" (28.2 x 36.1 cm.).

John Willard Banks; *Bustin' A Bronco*; 1987, colored pencil, felt tip and ballpoint pens, and graphite pencil; 22" x 28⅛" (56.3 x 71.3 cm.).

Fronzell L. "Doc" Spellmon,
The Rescue of Lt. Bullis, c. 1981,
oil on canvas, 24 x 30" (60.9 x 76.1
cm.). In *The Rescue of Lt. Bullis*, "Doc"
Spellmon depicts the Seminole Negro
Indian Scouts battling Comanche
Indians near the Pecos River with
Lt. John Bullis, their white commander,
rescued by one of his troops.

Ike Edward Morgan; *Western Scene*; c. 1995; pastel, felt tip pen and graphite on paper; 23¾" x 18" (60.9 x 45.7 cm.). Ike Morgan's inspiration for *Western Scene* came from a *TV Guide* image from the movie *Giant*.

Ezekiel Gibbs; *Hog Butchering*; c. 1978; gouache, crayon, and graphite on black construction paper; 26⅛" x 20" (66.3 x 50.9 cm.).

Ike Edward Morgan, *Solemn Horse*, c. 1985, pastel and ballpoint pen, 18" x 12½" (45.9 x 31.7 cm.).

Ike Edward Morgan, *Rifleman*, c. 1985, pastel and graphite, 24"x 18" (60.8 x 45.7 cm.).

Carl Dixon, *Horse Race*, 1997, wood and paint, 18" x 24" (45.6 x 61.1 cm.).

Ronald Cooper; *Hell Skull,*
c. 1990; horse's skull, enamel paint,
and clothespins; 6½" x 9⅜" x 20¼"
L (16.3 x 23.4 x 51.8 cm. L).

The Only Way, 1903, chromolithograph on paper. The Chicago & Alton Railway Company from a promotional calendar in 1904.

COWGIRLS
The Wild, Wild Women of the West

GAIL GILCHRIEST

Not long ago, a second grader in Connecticut grappled with the troubling question of what costume to choose for Halloween. She'd already been a princess, a witch, a ballerina, and now—at the ripe old age of seven—she felt sure that all the truly great trick-or-treat roles were behind her.

Her mother offered a suggestion: "Why don't you be a cowgirl?"

"A what?" demanded the child. A Yankee through and through, and a young one at that, she had not yet ventured south of the Mason-Dixon or west of the Appalachians. And so, the appellation "cowgirl" reached her little ears for the very first time.

"A cowgirl rides horses, shoots guns, sleeps under the stars, and isn't afraid of anything," the mother explained. "She wears a pretty neat outfit too."

The little girl's eyes widened. "Why hasn't anyone told me about this before? *Of course, I want to be a cowgirl! Who doesn't?!*"

Exactly! In some way, we all want to be cowgirls, to blaze new trails, to conquer our own personal Wild Wests. And yet today, just a handful of women cowgirl (and yeah, that's a verb) in the traditional, most literal sense. The approaching millennium finds only a small number of people—male or female—actually wrangling cattle for a living. Sure, some gals still ride the rodeo, and a lucky few croon western songs in Nashville, but the ranching-roping cowgirl of folklore has ridden into the sunset. Her myth, however, endures. No longer an occupation, cowgirl thrives today as a maverick state of mind.

Admission Certificate of Jane Hughs, July 29, 1831. A widow, Jane Hughs came to Texas to settle in Stephen F. Austin's third colony. It was unusual for a woman to be named a land grantee, and Hughs brought fifty-nine family members with her to Texas.

according to her own lights, she trampled over anyone who attempted to trim her wings or squeeze her into a corset.

At the dawn of cowgirl time came the pioneer woman, the Prairie Madonna, a sunbonneted Ma Ingalls type. This prairie homemaker went west reluctantly. She braved hunger, disease, wicked weather, harsh environment, and the loneliness of frontier life in a dutiful, stand-by-your-man sort of way. And while she didn't always embrace life on the frontier, she did often rise to meet its challenges. Sometimes circumstance arose when she had to mount a horse and help with "man's" work. And sometimes she found that she liked it. Not too surprisingly, quite a few pioneer women discovered that sitting tall in the saddle under the big western sky beat the hell out of housework.

You might even say that the Women's Movement started when a ranch woman first climbed atop a good cutting horse. The view from the saddle changed her whole outlook, gave her a fresh perspective on the world. As a farm wife back East, she'd lived at ground level behind a plow, gazing at a mule's rump for hours on end; but out West, on horseback, ah! from there she could see the horizon—and imagine far beyond. The new vista inspired confidence and competence and courage.

Even though some women in Mexico and the American Southwest were known to have worked cattle almost from the moment those regions were settled, *cowgirl* remained more or less an unlabeled feminization of a male occupation until 1899 when humorist Will Rogers witnessed the cowboyish antics of little Lucille Mulhall,

Non-ranching women imbued with the cowgirl spirit dot the contemporary cultural landscape like wildflowers on the prairie. Artist Donna Howell-Sickles, writer Pam Houston, former Texas governor Ann Richards, and many other gutsy women from all walks of life, follow—with varying degrees of conscious intent—in the boot-steps of the premiere female American role model: the cowgirl of yesteryear.

The fact of the cowgirl evolved out of the western experience, and the fiction of the cowgirl flowered from that fact.

An amalgam of many different western types, from the long-suffering prairie housewife to the quick-tempered lady gun-slinger, the cowgirl represents the ultimate female individualist, the embodiment of womanly valor. Blazing her own trail, living

daughter of an affluent Oklahoma rancher. Legend has it that Rogers, upon meeting Lucille, was the first to merge the words *cow* and *girl,* thereby creating an all-new noun to describe the daring women of the West.

Cowgirl, the obvious feminine of *cowboy,* hardly sparkled as inspired verbal coinage—not Will Rogers at his pearly best with the language, to be sure. More than likely, he was not the very first human to speak the word. Lucille Mulhall certainly wasn't the first woman to do the work. Nevertheless, she created quite a stir.

Lucille qualified as a sure-enough western prodigy, riding at age two and sticking like a postage stamp to the back of any horse she mounted by the time she turned eight. Before she reached her twelfth birthday, she could lasso a running jackrabbit, rope a full-grown steer, and use her reata to pick up the hind legs of a calf on the run. When her father once jokingly promised Lucille she could keep any cattle she could rope and brand all by herself, the little girl quickly amassed a nice-sized herd of her very own. Theodore Roosevelt, a dinner guest at the Mulhall's ranch one evening, bet young Lucille an invitation to his upcoming presidential inaugural celebration that she couldn't rope a wolf. He lost the bet.

Roosevelt, Will Rogers, and other visitors to the Mulhall spread went away so impressed by the cowboying Lucille, that Colonel Mulhall organized a touring Wild West act around her and his four other children. In addition to performing at local cowboy contests, the family played the St. Louis World's Fair in 1904. Will Rogers was part of the Mulhall troupe, as was future movie star Tom Mix. But Lucille always topped the marquee. In 1905, throngs of adoring fans trailed her and her pretty sisters wherever they went in New York City. The first time she roped in public there, the skeptical audience mobbed her and tore at her clothing in an attempt to discern whether she was actually a man.

Rogers's term *cowgirl* seemed a fairly straightforward description when compared with some of the other silly handles newspapermen penned in an effort to characterize the Lucille phenomenon. They called her "Queen of the Range," the "Female Conqueror of Beef and Horn," a

Dismounted Woman Stroking Her Horse, c. 1920.

Robert Wade, *Sheridan Cowgirls*, 1996, acrylic on photo linen. From left to right: Reva Gray, Grace Runyon, Fox Hastings, Betty Meyers, Tad Lucas, Ruth Roach, and Ruth Benson.

"Lassoer in Lingerie," or the "Cowboy Cowgirl." While journalists scrambled for ever-more-apt descriptions, Lucille and other fearless women of the Wild West shows put the finishing touches on the cowgirl image.

Lucille Mulhall may have been the first woman publicly described as "cowgirl," but the womanly western ideal had blasted onto the stages, stadiums, and front pages of the world a few years earlier in the person of Phoebe Ann Moses—better known as Annie Oakley.

Annie, the original cowgirl media darling, wasn't a cowgirl at all. She was a petite city slicker who had never set foot west of Cincinnati. She knew nothing of ranching, riding, or roping, yet her finesse with a firearm, coupled with her feminine charms, made Annie Oakley the first cowgirl star. Former Indian fighter William F. "Buffalo Bill" Cody recognized the boffo box-office

potential in the paradox that Annie embodied. He built an immensely popular Wild West revue around the then revolutionary contrast between her womanly appearance and manly marksmanship.

Dead-eye Annie's crowd-pleasing gunplay involved feats such as shooting a coin from her husband's hand, and puncturing a playing card with a bullet from ninety feet away. Once, she even blasted a cigarette from the mouth of German Crown Prince Wilhelm without disturbing so much as a whisker in the royal mustache. The famous Sioux chief Sitting Bull dubbed her "Little Sure Shot"—"little" because she stood only five feet tall, and "sure shot" . . . well, with a weapon in hand, tiny Annie towered above any man.

Though Buffalo Bill ran the largest and most widely known Wild West show of his time, his wasn't the only game in town. Audiences hungered for anything western, and as Wild West shows began touring the

Andy Warhol, *Cowboy and Indian Series: Annie Oakley,* 1986, serigraph.

Vivian White's Professional Rodeo Cowboy Association gold card. Champion cowgirls like Vivian White received recognition for their accomplishments decades after male peers in the sport. White received her life membership in the PRCA in 1984.

caught on in the United States, the contests typically featured bronc riding, steer bull-dogging, and wild horse racing. And on both sides of the Rio Grande, these amazing feats were sometimes undertaken by women.

At first, many of the stars featured in Wild West shows and rodeos were actual ranchers, real-life cowboys and cowgirls taking time out from their chores to dazzle crowds and pocket some coin. But increasingly the performers were just that—performers—full-time entertainers who found show business more profitable than beef business.

Barbara "Tad" Lucas—a rodeo cowgirl from Fort Worth, Texas—exemplified the trend. Like most of the early Wild Westers and rodeo hands, Tad hailed from a ranching background. The youngest of two dozen children she cut her cowgirl teeth on her parents' spread in Nebraska. At age thirteen, she rode wild cows at a gathering of local ranchers. Soon afterwards she found work as a jockey, eventually earning the then royal sum of $25 for staying atop a wicked steer at a community fair. It didn't take a sharp gal like Tad too long to discover that good horse sense mixed with a touch of showmanship could combine for a very exciting and somewhat lucrative lifestyle. She wowed audiences at New York's Madison Square Garden and London's Wembley Stadium with her trick-riding exhibitions, and she conquered several All Around Cowgirl Championships in places as far away as Sydney, Australia.

The fame of women such as Lucille Mulhall, Annie Oakley, and Tad Lucas spread internationally. By the dawn of the Jazz Age, the cowgirl was recognized

country around 1883 they managed more than entertainment. They also etched into the national psyche a highly romanticized version of the western myth. Part rodeo, part county fair, part vaudeville, the shows were sort of specialty circuses with a western theme. The program typically included impressive demonstrations of roping and riding and shooting along with a simulated pony express ride, a staged buffalo hunt, plus assorted depictions of Native American customs. "Step right up," ringmasters like Buffalo Bill implored, "and see the curious creatures of the West: the Indian, the buffalo, and the women in trousers riding wild horses and shooting guns."

Parallel to the thundering popularity of the Wild West shows galloped rodeo. From the Spanish word *rodear,* "to go around," rodeo originated south of the border where Mexican *caballeros* often engaged in good-natured contests of cowboying skill as after-hours recreation. By the time rodeo around the world as a genuine American original. The iconoclast became an icon.

The show-business cowgirl of the Wild West show and early rodeo glossed her machismo with a veneer of glamour and daintiness. This seemingly contradictory combination of masculine bravery and feminine sex appeal thrilled audiences. And once the cowgirl started sewing sequins on her chaps, it was just a short trot from the rodeo arena to the silver screen.

In 1898, the Edison Company produced the first western movie, *Cripple Creek Barroom.* The silent film was little more than a skit performed in costume as cameras rolled, but it portended bigger and better things to follow. By the 1930s, moguls churned out low-budget assembly-line western movies at quite a clip, often finishing an entire picture in only a few days. The scripts of these so-called "B" Westerns relied on tried-and-true formula plots. The stories rarely varied, and the cowboy's horse was always his most trusted ally. Equine costars such as Roy Rogers's mount Trigger, "The Smartest Horse in the Movies," and Gene Autry's four-legged friend Champion, "The World's Wonder Horse," always got billing above the female lead, whose role usually involved swooning and sighing while the cowboy had all the fun.

Many of the cowboy stars migrated to Hollywood from ranches by way of Wild West shows. A number of cowgirls ditched the rodeo or Wild West life in search of movie stardom too. Few found it. The female lead in most early Westerns qualified as little more than a supporting role.

Vivian White, c. 1935.

While cowboys became movie stars, cowgirls remained part of the scenery.

Hollywood spawned a stable of cowboy stars from John Wayne to Clint Eastwood, but the high-magnitude cowgirl star never rose. If any actress approached stardom as a cowgirl, it was Dale Evans, the fresh-faced girl-pardner of Roy Rogers. Like Annie Oakley before her, Dale Evans never ranched, never rodeoed. Her ease on horseback came mostly from Hollywood

Cowgirl rodeo suits; c. 1935;
wool, satin, rhinestones.

Charra, c. 1935.

riding lessons, and her western wardrobe courtesy of the studio costume shop. On the screen, however, Dale sang sweetly, stood by Roy through thick and thin, and her curls stayed miraculously coiffed beneath her Stetson.

Some purists began to complain that show business had transformed "cowgirl" from honest occupation to mere costume. Nowhere was that gripe more evident than in the movies, where such cowgirls as Dale Evans often "ranched" in short skirts. Dale, "The Queen of the West," had historical precedence for her wardrobe choices, however. Mexican equestriennes—some of the earliest working cowgirls—had long favored elaborate sequined *charrita* dresses. Annie Oakley opted for skirts while performing, as did Lucille Mulhall. In 1905 at a show in Madison Square Garden, Lucille's skirt got tangled in her stirrup, and she was dragged for a short distance before shaking herself free. Narrowly averting disaster, she learned the hard way that skirts and quirts aren't a natural mix.

Trousers on women remained taboo well into this century. And while many early cowgirls were willing to risk the wrath of proper society by doing so-called men's work, they stopped short of wearing men's clothes. Some cowgirls fashioned split skirts for riding. Others pulled a skirt on over their trousers whenever business took them into town. But soon, some of the gutsiest and busiest cowgirls got fed up. They discarded the oppressive dress code that interfered with their work, their fun, and their freedom.

When Prohibition-era flappers popularized bloomers and bared knees, cowgirls rejoiced. Bloomers of corduroy or satin, blouses with low necklines, and long ringlet curls peeking out from beneath wide-brimmed western hats was *the* cowgirl look of the 1920s. Trick rider Vera McGinnis did bloomers one better. Taking a pair of men's white trousers, she removed the front fly, improvised a new fastener on the

China Poblana, c. 1935.

side, and created quite a stir wearing her modified menswear at the Fort Worth Rodeo of 1927.

Jodhpurs caught on with cowgirls during the 1930s, changing the approach to equestrienne fashion altogether. Split skirts and bloomers represented attempts to make women's clothes more masculine and better suited for riding, but with the advent of jodhpurs, cowgirls began feminizing men's clothing instead—a trend that holds today.

As feminine and stylish as some individual cowgirls are, as a group they've gained a reputation as masculine, hard-looking women. But as one cowboy said of a female colleague: "If she looks tough or mean, it's because her lips are too chapped to smile."

The reason for that? For a very few, "cowgirl" isn't just a costume—it remains an occupation.

These days a woman doesn't have to be a cowgirl to dress like one. Urban cowgirls break in their designer boots on big-city pavement. All-hat-and-no-cattle types opt for designer denim and leather as shortcuts to the cowgirl mystique. But no less than real ranch women, these drugstore cowgirls count as authentic too. Today's cowgirl is where you find her. And occasionally, that's still on the range.

American National CattleWomen, Inc., an association of female ranchers, estimates that as many as 15,000 women in the United States run their own cattle operations or make their way as hired livestock hands. More than 2,000 gals carry cards certifying membership in one of the two nationally recognized women's professional rodeo associations, with a few of those earning more than $100,000 per year in

competition. Cowgirl poets gather annually in Elko, Nevada. Organizations of cowgirl artists mount group exhibitions at prestigious galleries, and big-city restaurants specialize in cowgirl cuisine. While the world still awaits the first really big cowgirl movie star, cowgirls have ridden into Nashville en masse. From Patsy Montana to Shania Twain, cowgirls sell records. And they still manage to capture America's heart.

The National Cowgirl Museum and Hall of Fame in Fort Worth, Texas, recognizes that there are many types of cowgirls—ranchers, rodeo riders, entertainers, and yes, even citified cowgirl wanna-bes. Since its founding in 1975, the Hall of Fame has inducted more than one hundred women, both living and dead, as milestone cowgirls. Alongside the names of Lucille Mulhall, Annie Oakley, and Tad Lucas, museum-goers will find nods to pioneering writer Willa Cather, artist Georgia O'Keeffe, and others who've done their part, through their lives or their work, to perpetuate and enrich the cowgirl legend.

Today, a century after Will Rogers first uttered the word *cowgirl,* the cowgirl fiction has now transcended the cowgirl fact. In Tom Robbins's novel *Even Cowgirls Get the Blues,* a character bemoaning that puzzling paradox complains: "So they let you dress up like a cowgirl, and when you say, 'I'm gonna be a cowgirl when I grow up,' they laugh and say, 'Ain't she cute.' Then one day they tell you, 'Look honey, cowgirls are only play. You can't *really* be one.' "

Oh, yeah? Just try telling that to the seven-year-old in Connecticut.

Of course, she wants to be a cowgirl! Who doesn't?!

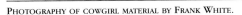

PHOTOGRAPHY OF COWGIRL MATERIAL BY FRANK WHITE.

Prairie Rose, c. 1910. **Born Ann Robbins, Prairie Rose Henderson** was a pioneer professional cowgirl also known for her flamboyant costumes like this one with its appliqué, dangles, and exotic trim.

Mexican *charrita* dress; c. 1885; black velvet, appliqué, *hilo de oro* trim, sequins, beads, rhinestones, and mother-of-pearl snaps.

Bonnie McCarroll Thrown from "Silver," 1915. After champion cowgirl Bonnie McCarroll was thrown and tragically killed in 1929, women's bronc riding events at western venues all but vanished. One popular opinion held that the furor over McCarroll's death led to the discontinuation of the event. Her contemporaries, however, attest that women's bronc riding waned because the economics no longer panned out for rodeo promoters.

Cowgirls at the Tucumcari, Round-Up, c. 1915. Identified: (from left) Dorothy Morrell, Ruth Roach, and (third from right) Prairie Rose Henderson.

The Hopkins & Allen 'Prairie Girl', 1910, chromolithograph on paper. Hopkins and Allen was a major American firearms manufacturer based in Norwich, Connecticut, from 1868 to 1915.

The Only Way, 1903, chromolithograph on paper. The Chicago & Alton Railway Company printed these images of early cowgirls in a 1904 promotional calendar.

Woman in Skirt Mounted Astride,
c. 1910

Three Mounted Women Riders,
c. 1907.

Four Mounted Riders, c. 1910.

William Henry Dethlef Koerner,
Mary Ware, c. 1934,
pastel on board.

Horseman, Ride West!

The Evolution of the Spur

Jane Pattie

Note: Torch Energy acquired the comprehensive spur collection of Joe and Hope Russell of San Angelo, Texas, in 1993. Russell's interest in collecting spurs began when he found a Spanish cavalryman's spur on his father's Cross L Ranch in southwest Texas in 1940, and fifty-three years later when the spurs became an addition to Torch's corporate collection of art and artifacts of the American West, there were more than 500 pairs and 200 singles. The nucleus of the collection is classic and contemporary cowboy spurs, but it also covers a much broader expanse—from an 800-year-old Knight Templar's prick spur and European spurs through the ages to the great-rowel spur of the Spanish conquistadors and numerous examples of Spanish colonial and Mexican spurs. It reflects the evolution of the spur that influenced those used in the American West.

Russell had acquired spurs from various notable collections. Twenty-nine spurs belonged to the late Dr. Tom Reagan of Beeville, Texas, a foremost authority on ancient, medieval, and Renaissance spurs as well as Spanish colonial and Mexican espuelas. Dr. Reagan had acquired spurs from dealers and museums and outstanding collections in Great Britain, the United States, Mexico, and South America. Seventeen Gothic spurs had belonged to the late Dr. Bashford, Dean of the Metropolitan Museum, New York.

216

California Rattlesnake Spurs by Vogt Western Silver, Ltd., with cutout and engraved silver-inlaid rattlesnake heel bands, shanks, and chap guards. Turlock, California, c. 1975, steel and silver, L 7⅝" (19.4 cm.).

Knight's Templar Prick Spur with strap loop and pyramidal point. England, c. 1125, bronze, L 5⅛" (13.0 cm.). The wearer of this spur fastened it to the foot with a leather strap that ran through the heel-band loops, over the instep, and under the sole.

The great-rowel spurs worn by the Spanish conquistadors who conquered Mexico in 1520 were the forerunners of the vaquero spurs of Mexico and California and of American cowboy spurs, but they, too, had historical antecedents. Spurs have been the universal hallmark of all manner of horsemen for 2,400 years—Greeks, Etruscans, Romans, Arabs, European knights, Spanish conquerors. Where history was made, there was the spur. Nowhere do they fit better than on the heels of a *charro* or *vaquero* or a cowboy. Just as these centaurs are brothers under the skin—or should we say sombrero or Stetson—so are their spurs similar and yet different. Each pair is a stepping stone in the history of horsemen.

When man first mounted a horse for mobility in battle, he developed goads for his heels to leave his hands free for weapons. The first spurs were probably forked sticks and short pieces of wood with bone projections at the back, tied onto a rider's feet with thongs. These early spurs had their origins in the dim past, possibly with the warlike, horseback Scythians who swept out of the Russian steppes into Persia. Horses soon spread around the Mediterranean and throughout Europe and Britain.

The earliest metal spurs date from 700 B.C. to 400 B.C., the late Bronze Age in Europe. They are known as prick spurs because of the sharp goads at the back of the simple, short heel bands. The spurs were secured by leather straps buttoned onto large studs on the ends of the heel bands. Similar spurs were used by the Greeks; however, Alexander the Great was the first military leader to use cavalry, and his soldiers rode without stirrups, bits, or spurs.

Bronze spurs from the second century B.C., with studs for fasteners, were found in Etruscan tombs near Perugia, Italy, but studs also disappeared in the second century B.C., and the ends of the heel bands curled out for the strap to pass through. Studs or buttons were not seen again until the end of the seventeenth century. The oldest spur in the Torch Collection is a bronze, pyramidal-shaped prick spur of the style worn by the English Knights Templars in the early 1200s.

Prick spurs were used until the mid-1300s, but the lengths and shapes of the prods varied. During the 1100s, heel bands were longer and the ends had plates that fastened with rivets to leather on the inside of the spurs. Spurs were worn over chain mail. The straight heel band was soon replaced by a band that curved under the wearer's ankle bones for comfort. Boots had not come into use, and leather or cloth stockings covered a horseman's feet.

Changes occurred gradually, and old

styles often overlapped the new. The most significant change in the history of the spur was the invention of the rowel. German armorers were often the innovators during the Middle Ages, and they may have been the originators of the rowel spur. However, historians give credit to the French for introducing the rowel spur to England. Rowel spurs became fairly common during the first half of the fourteenth century, but prick spurs also remained in use for a hundred years. Like the prick spurs, the bands of the first rowel spurs had depressed sides and were worn over chain mail. They were held in place by straps with hooks riveted on the ends. The hooks fastened into round openings on each end of the heel bands.

During the 1370s, the top of the heel band above the shank was often drawn up in a decoration called a crest. Centuries later, American spur makers would call a similar decoration a chap guard.

Spurs denoted rank and caste during the Middle Ages and the days of chivalry. Just as wearing spurs was restricted to a select group, so was the making of spurs. The statutes of the Guild of Spur-Makers in Paris in 1357 stated that a master craftsman could have only one apprentice who worked for six years for little or no pay. At the end of that time, the apprentice became a master.

The development of armor for both the knight and his horse greatly influenced spur styles. When heavy plate armor came into general use during the 1400s, spur shanks were long so the rider could make contact with his horse. These spurs had small rowels, and the straight shanks were often ten inches in length. They were the style worn during jousting contests, but a smaller, more utilitarian spur was popular at the same time throughout Europe.

King Charles I of Spain became Charles V, emperor of the Holy Roman Empire, in 1519, and he brought German armorers with him to Spain. During Charles's reign, Cortés landed in Mexico and during the reign of Charles and his son, Phillip II, riches from the New World made Spain a major contender for world power.

The conquistador Hernán Cortés and 508 fighting men with 16 horses sailed from Cuba in 1519 and landed on the Mexican mainland bedecked in a hodge-podge of half-armor and armed with weapons rummaged up from the armories of Spain. According to the Aztec legend, the winged serpent deity, Quetzalcóatl, would appear as a white-skinned bearded man, and the indigenous Indians who first saw Cortés astride the strange four-legged beast thought this must surely be Quetzalcóatl.

Indeed, Cortés's arrival brought about major changes, not the least of which was caused by the reintroduction of the horse to the Western Hemisphere. Following a bloody war with the Aztecs, Cortés claimed New Spain for his king and church. The Spaniards built the port of Veracruz and soon brought cattle from Cuba and the West Indies to the coastal lowlands of Mexico. They were tended mainly by black slaves from the Indies and by vaqueros of mixed blood under the watchful eye of a Castilian *caporal* (ranch foreman).

For a time after the conquest, spurs and weapons were brought from Spain and Cuba to Mexico, but blacksmiths and artisans were needed locally. Cortés established craftsmen at various locations, and

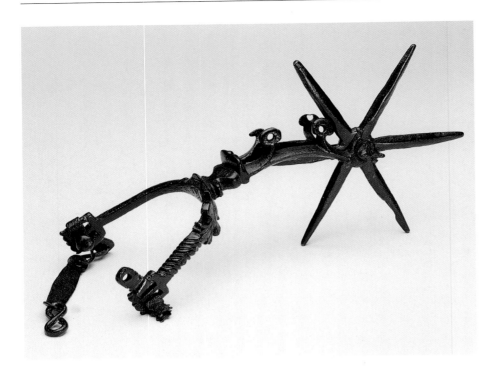

Conquistador Spur with decorative ridge along shank and 6" 6-point rowel. Spain, early 1500s, steel, L 10½" (26.2 cm.). This spur, with a small plate at the center of the heel chain, is an early conquistador spur and was brought to New Spain (Mexico).

spur and sword makers were at Amozoc, southeast of Mexico City on the road from Vera Cruz. There they made spurs and swords equal in quality to those made in Toledo. The big-rowel conquistador spur was undoubtedly the first style made in New Spain, and that spur remained popular in Spain and its colonies longer than in the rest of Europe. The early spurs of that type brought by the conquistadors have a small plate in the center of the heel chain. An example is in the Torch Collection.

The craftsmen in Amozoc also taught the Aztecs their trade. Spur making is practiced to this day by Amozoc artisans such as the Luna family whose ancestors have made spurs there for three centuries. There were 300 spur makers working in Amozoc as late as 1945, and Amozoc smiths are still noted for their fine workmanship.

Prior to 1539 all vacant land in New Spain served as common pastures, and livestock multiplied rapidly in the 1530s. Ranches developed in the 1550s along the route of conquest to Mexico City, the Camino Real, and quickly spread northward. During the 1580s and 1590s, the

Crown awarded many land grants for cattle raising. An *estancia de ganado mayor* was eventually called a *hacienda,* a ranch. The main market was for hides, and they were shipped through Veracruz to Sevilla. Sixty-four thousand cowhides were exported to Spain in 1587 alone.

Cattle ranching spread into the Mexican Highlands. The animals were gentled and kept relatively tame since they were grazed during the day and penned at night. The herdsmen worked on foot in the manner done in the Salamanca and Extremadura areas of Spain. Farther west in the Nueva Galicia area, now the state of Jalisco, work was done by mounted vaqueros. This was where the classic charro methods of handling cattle and horses developed.

During the 1600s, a short-shank spur called the Cavalier spur became popular throughout Europe. It resembled the later American cowboy spurs. It is said to have been used by the French Cavaliers, and it is thought to be the forerunner of the Mexican spurs of the eighteenth and nineteenth centuries. It had a narrow heel band and large rowels with many spokes. A small drop of steel, later called a *pajado* by vaquero spur makers, dangled from the rowel pin and jingled pleasantly against the rowel. These pajados were also called jangles, jinglers, or jingle bobs by cowboy spur makers in the West.

Noted historian and anthropologist the late Dr. Arthur Woodward, of Arizona, was of the opinion that this Cavalier spur was of Mexican origin and found its way back to Europe rather than coming from Europe to Mexico. Whatever its origin, it was one of the first styles to return to the use of studs,

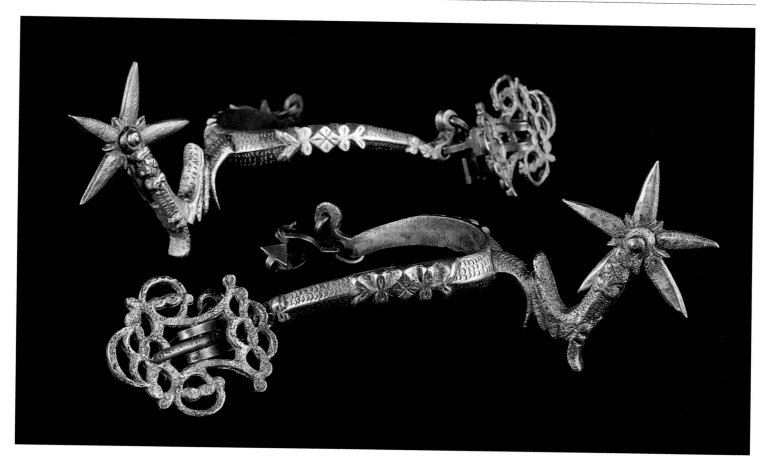

later called strap buttons, rarely seen since Roman times.

Amozoc remained the primary bit- and spur-making center in New Spain, and two other major areas developed—one around Guadalajara and Mexico City, the third in Sonora.

In 1721, the Catholic Church was granted rights to establish missions to the north in today's Texas. Cattle from the eastern lowlands spread up the Gulf Coast into Texas, and the Spanish ranching presence was established along the San Antonio River where the padres founded their missions. Each mission owned a small herd of cattle. Mission Espíritu Santo moved to its present location near Goliad in 1749, grazed 20,000 head of cattle within a decade, and was the first large ranch in Texas.

The mission system also introduced ranching to Alta California. The Franciscan friars established five missions along the Pacific coast between 1769 and 1772. Together, they owned 205 head of cattle. In 1776 Don Juan Bautista de Anza brought thirty families from Sonora and Sinaloa to settle in California. Some of the men were dusky vaqueros, and they brought their knowledge of horses and cattle with them.

Vaqueros were a colorful lot. A vaquero's typical dress consisted of a kerchief tied around his head, and on top of that sat a wide-brimmed, low-crowned hat held in place by a *barbiquejo,* a chin strap that passed just under his lower lip. His black hair hung to his shoulders. He wore a loose-fitting shirt and a red sash around his waist under a heavy belt. Knee-length pants buttoned down the side seams with a few buttons left open at the bottom. They were worn over long, white cotton drawers tucked inside of *botas,* leather leggings wrapped around his lower legs and held up with ties below the knees. His moccasin-like

Sand-Cast French Spurs with ornate buckles and star-shaped rowels. France, c. 1630, brass with some original gilding remaining, L 6¼" (15.7 cm.). Spurs like these with their inverted V-shaped shanks were popular during the early 17th century throughout England, France, Spain, and Germany.

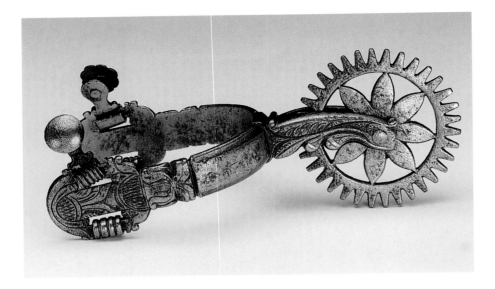

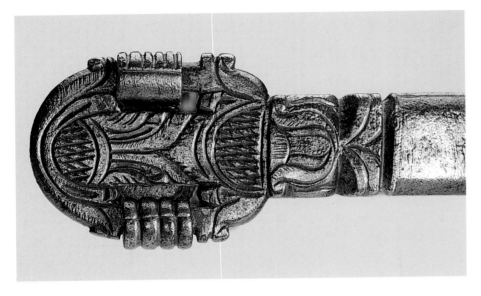

Colonial Charro Spur with incised strap plates, heel band, shank, and 2¾" disk rowel. Amozoc, Mexico, c. 1775, iron, L 6¼" (15.5 cm.).

their work. Their clothing, spurs, horse gear, and method of stock work came from Sonora and Sinaloa.

During the reign of Emperor Maximilian in Mexico from 1864 until 1867, the artisans in Amozoc began making a new style spur, now called a *charro* spur. A pair of these spurs crafted by the famous Amozoc smith Severo Balderrama was found in Maximilian's horse equipment after his assassination in 1867. They have heavy, sculptured silver bands with ornate swinging buttons. The large eight-point rowels are interlaced with silver filigree between the spokes. This style of spur has been used by Mexico's elite Charro Association since the overthrow of French rule.

The noun *charro* is a word that was commonly used in the area around Salamanca, Spain, to designate a man from the country—a rustic, a ranch cowboy. The modern Mexican charro is a gentleman cowboy. His dress, his horse, and his manner of competition—*charrería,* a sport similar to today's rodeo—are governed by a strict set of rules.

The charro spur has variations designed for their different events, much like today's cowboys have spurs for roping, cutting, or riding bulls or broncs. For instance, the charro's short-shank, small-rowel *coleadero* spur is used by a horseman when tailing a bull, throwing him by taking a wrap of his tail around the rider's right leg and stirrup leather and flipping him. This feat requires a spur that will not interfere with the procedure.

The classic Charro spur has a wide heavy heel band, swinging buttons, and often a figure-eight-shaped shank.

shoes, called *berruchis,* were made of buckskin, and he wore spurs made in Sonora.

By 1834 the California missions owned 396,000 head of cattle and 61,600 horses. For some time the good fathers had more stock than they could say grace over. When they first needed help to oversee their herds, the padres and the soldiers from the presidios, both vaqueros out of necessity, taught the art to the local Indios. It mattered not that Spanish law forbade Indians to ride horses. The mission Indians became mission vaqueros, just as their cousins had done in Mexico. Called neophytes, they were a wild, unruly bunch but adept at

Charro Spurs with silver-inlaid coiled-snake heel bands, buttons, shanks, and 8-point rowels with silver inlay. Amozoc, Mexico, c. 1885, iron and silver, L 6¼" (16.0 cm.).

According to Dr. Tom Reagan, the figure-eight shank is derived from the older kidney-shaped perforation adapted by the Spanish from the Moors. The kidney shape was popular with spur makers in colonial Chile and Argentina, but the Mexican smiths preferred the double circle or eight design.

The period from 1870 until the revolution of 1910 was the golden era of spur making in Mexico. The artisans made beautiful hand-forged spurs inlaid with silver hammered into deep-cut grooves and polished smooth. Before the popularity of inlay as decoration, the art of *pavón,* a method of bluing iron, was developed in Amozoc and used extensively. As silver inlay became popular,

the smiths inlaid their spurs and treated them with the pavón procedure to put a finish on them. The makers sometimes signed and dated their spurs. During this time, some craftsmen from Sonora and Sinaloa moved north to California, and wealthy rancheros also ordered bits and spurs from Mexico City.

The early Californians remained in contact with the Spanish and Mexican culture longer and to a greater degree than did the Texans, so today's California spurs have more nearly retained the characteristics of their Mexican antecedents. Spurs made by many artisans, such as G. S. Garcia and his sons, Abbie Hunt, and Jesús Tapia, are collectors' items.

California Spurs by Vogt Western Silver, Ltd. Stamped "VOGT" inside heel bands. Cutout bands with star and crescent moon, and overlaid engraved silver. Engraved silver on shanks and rowel disks. Turlock, California, c. 1975, steel and silver, L 6⅞" (17.6 cm.).

The classic California spur is generally of two-piece construction: the heel band and the shank. It is usually full-mounted, inlaid with silver, and often elaborately engraved and blued. It usually has stationary buttons and double heel chains. Texas-style spurs were forged of one piece of steel and have either swinging buttons or stationary buttons on turned-up heel bands. They were usually half-mounted with overlay of silver, copper, or brass, and the hand-filed steel was not blued. Cowboy spurs did not have heel chains and more often than not, they had no chap guards. They were generally plainer and more utilitarian than their California cousins.

The spurs of the northern plains were a combination of the California style and the cowboy spur. They were embellished with either inlay or overlay that was beautifully engraved and of fine workmanship. Spurs made by artists such as Phillips & Gutierrez of Cheyenne, Wyoming, and Rex Schnitger of Gillette were popular with the northern waddies, and many of the saddle shops also sold spurs made by the Texas-style makers as well as those manufactured by North & Judd and August Buermann in the East.

The early Anglo settlers who went to Texas when the land was part of Mexico often looked to the United States for their customs and lifestyle even though they were citizens of Mexico. After Texas won its independence from Mexico in 1836, more Anglo settlers came from Tennessee, Kentucky, and the southern states. The new Texans adopted the ways of the vaqueros

*Buffalo Head Spurs by North &
Judd Manufacturing Company.*
Gunmetal spurs with White Nickel
buffalo-head mountings on outside
heel bands. New Britain,
Connecticut, c. 1925, patented
March 28, 1911, gunmetal and
White Nickel, L 5⅞" (15.3 cm.).

and adapted them to suit themselves.

During the years following the Civil War
when Texans trailed hundreds of thousands
of longhorn cattle north to railheads in
Missouri and Kansas, Texas cowboys wore
leftover military spurs, Mexican spurs,
blacksmith-made spurs, whatever was available. But the Texans soon created their
own traditions in the way of horse gear,
methods of working cattle, and the style of
their spurs.

Ironically, the men who are recognized
as artists of the forge and anvil, having
earned their reputations as master craftsmen of cowboy bits and spurs, enjoyed
their popularity after the days of the big
cattle drives, near the turn of the century
and later. At first it was enough for a cowboy to just own a pair of spurs. As times

got better, custom-made spurs became the
mark of the man and fit his individuality as
well as his boot heels.

These makers of cowboy spurs were
diverse in their origins as well as their spur
designs. Before custom-makers fired up
their forges on the southern plains,
German-born August Buermann, owner of
the Buermann Manufacturing Company of
Newark, New Jersey, was selling all manner
of bits and spurs from coast to coast.
Buermann's Catalog no. 35 advertised 443
spur designs and almost as many bits.

The Connecticut firm of North & Judd
registered its Anchor Brand trademark for
saddlery hardware on April 15, 1879, but it
is said that the company began making bits
and spurs in the 1830s. North & Judd purchased the Buermann firm and its patents

Bull Head Spurs by Kelly Brothers. Full-mounted with engraved silver bull head overlays on heel bands, arrows on shanks, and silver-rimmed buttons with mother-of-pearl centers. Dalhart, Texas; c. 1919; steel, silver, and mother-of-pearl; L 6½" (16.6 cm.). Kelly did not make many spurs with mother-of-pearl buttons because they were less durable than all-silver buttons.

in 1926 and finally discontinued making bits and spurs in 1982.

The "Big Three" of the cowboy spur makers—J. R. McChesney of Oklahoma and Texas, P. M. Kelly of Texas, and Oscar Crockett of Kansas, Oklahoma, and Colorado—had their shops in cow country and kept a feel of the pulse of cowboy culture. All advertised through their own catalogs and sold through dealers and saddle shops around the country. Kelly and Crockett put their names on their spurs and McChesney stamped some of his. Many McChesneys are found unmarked, and it is my opinion that those are the spurs he made for various saddle shops. However, the McChesney styles and embellishments are easily recognizable by today's collectors.

A number of local makers developed their followings in their own areas. The Italian-born Joe Bianchi of Victoria, Texas,

made spurs for many noted ranchers along the coast and in south Texas. Cowboys in the ranch country near San Angelo had their choice of spurs and bits made by Wallie Boone or the Fort McKavett blacksmith Jess Hodge. E. F. Blanchard, maker of spurs in New Mexico and Arizona, was of Swiss and French-Canadian descent and cowboy to the bone. There was no question but that he knew what cowboys liked in spurs. There were many makers—some who became famous for their products and others only known nearer to home.

Spur making is not a dying art. There are many good cowboy spur makers today. Their workmanship is the accumulated result of every craftsman who ever fired up his forge and, with his hammer and anvil, shaped hot steel into spurs that became a horseman's pride and a collector's prize.

PHOTOGRAPHY OF SPURS BY FRANK WHITE.

Spurs by Adolph Bayers. Full-mounted with engraved silver overlay, 10-point blunt rowels, and the name "RUSTY" on the outside heel bands. Stamped "682 / BAYERS" on heel band under button swinger. Truscott, Texas, c. 1970, steel and silver, L 5¼" (13.2 cm.). Bayers made this pair of spurs for cowboy Rusty Welch, who worked for the Waggoner Ranch near Vernon, Texas.

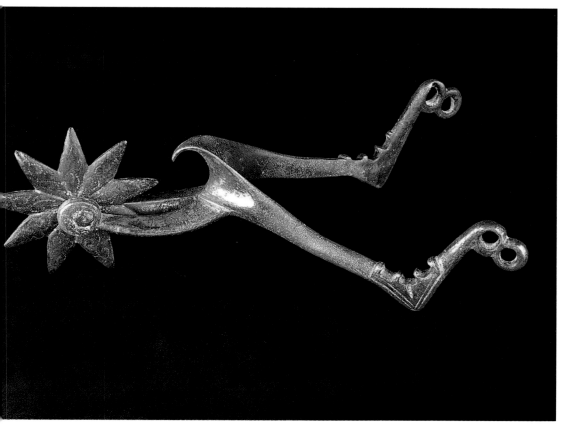

English Rowel Spur with 9-point rowel, England, c. 1376, brass, L 7¼" (18.5 cm.). The crest atop the heel band is a decorative innovation and the forerunner of the "chap guard" made by later cowboy spur makers. The Black Prince, son of Edward III of England, wore this style of spur.

*Jousting Spur with 6½" shank
and 8-point brass rowel.* Spain,
c. 1400, steel and brass, L 10½"
(26.6 cm.). This style of spur
became popular with the advent of
horse armor, making it possible for
a knight to have contact with his
mount.

*Spanish Colonial Spur with
ornate filigree strap plates,
narrow rounded heel band, and
3" 24-point rowel.* Mexico, late
1700s, iron, L 7" (17.9 cm.).

Colonial Spur with narrow rounded heel band and 24-point rowel. Pajados (jingles) and heel chain missing. Mexico, c. 1800, iron, L 7" (17.7 cm.). The workmanship and classic, elegant design of this spur indicate that it came from a master craftsman rather than a ranch blacksmith.

South American Spur with pierced heel-band terminals and large circular heel disk, kidney-shaped shank, and 4½" 8-point rowel. Spain or Argentina, c. 1800, iron, L 11¼" (28.5 cm.). The cutouts on this spur are not only decorative, but they significantly reduce the weight of the spur. The circular heel disk is typical of South American spurs and is not seen on Mexican spurs.

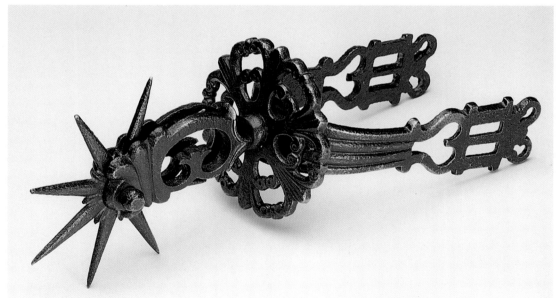

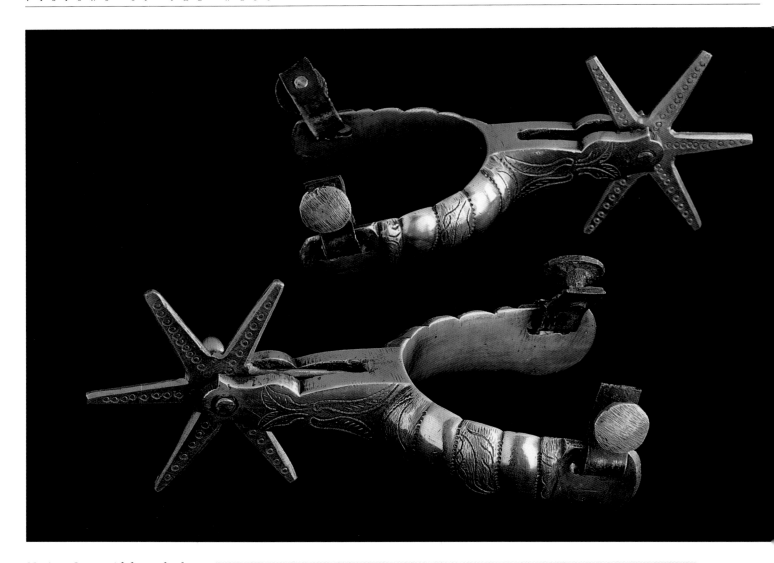

Mexican Spurs with heavy heel bands, demilune in section, with incised foliate designs and swinging buttons. Mexico, c. 1850, brass, L 6¾" (17.2 cm.). Straight shanks have 6-point rowels that are not original.

Vaquero Spurs with large swinging buttons, figure-eight shanks, and design deeply incised on heel bands. Durango or Chihuahua, Mexico, c. 1850, iron, L 7½" (19.2 cm.). Spike pins hold 3⅝" rowels with eight blunt *espigas* (spokes).

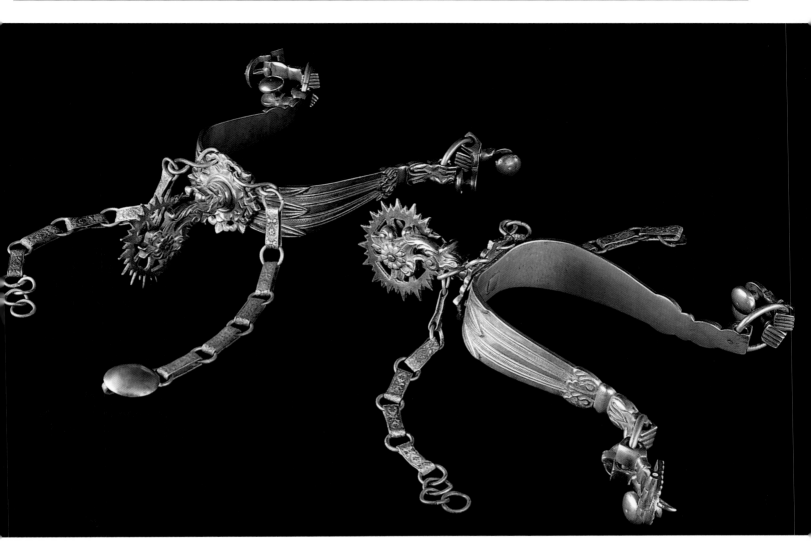

Spanish Spurs made for export to Argentina. Ornate spurs, chains, and 16-point disk rowels. Vallodolid, Spain, c. 1850, bronze, L 7½" (19.1 cm.).

Charro Coleadero Spur with rope braid heel band and gold and silver inlay; Mexico; early 1800s; iron, gold and silver; L 5⅝" (14.3 cm.). Style worn by a charro when "tailing a bull" (flipping the bull by riding up to him, catching his tail, and wrapping it around the rider's lower leg and stirrup leather. As the horse and rider pass the bull, he is pulled off his feet).

Charro Coleadero Spur. Mexico, late 1800s, iron, L 5½" (13.9 cm.).

"Dom Pedro Jr." Spurs, No. 5 in August Buermann Manufacturing Co. Catalog No. 35. Stamped with floral design and heel bands terminating in large rings that had swinging buttons. Newark, New Jersey, c. 1910, iron, L 5¼" (13.1 cm.). These spurs were named for Dom Pedro II, emperor of Brazil, 1841–89.

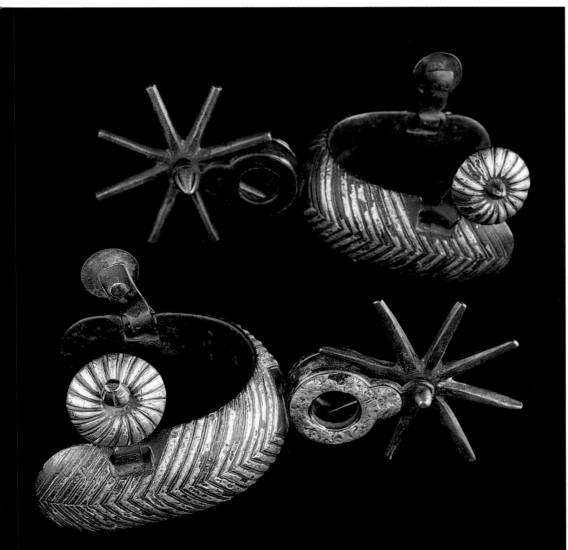

Charro Spurs with inlaid silver serpentine and geometric designs on heel bands and figure-eight shanks. Guadalajara or Zacatecas, Mexico, c. 1925, iron and silver, L 8" (20.4 cm.).

Charro Spurs with inlaid silver in repeating chevron design, figure-eight shanks, and turban-shaped swinging buttons. Puebla, Mexico, c. 1935, iron and silver, L 7" (17.9 cm.).

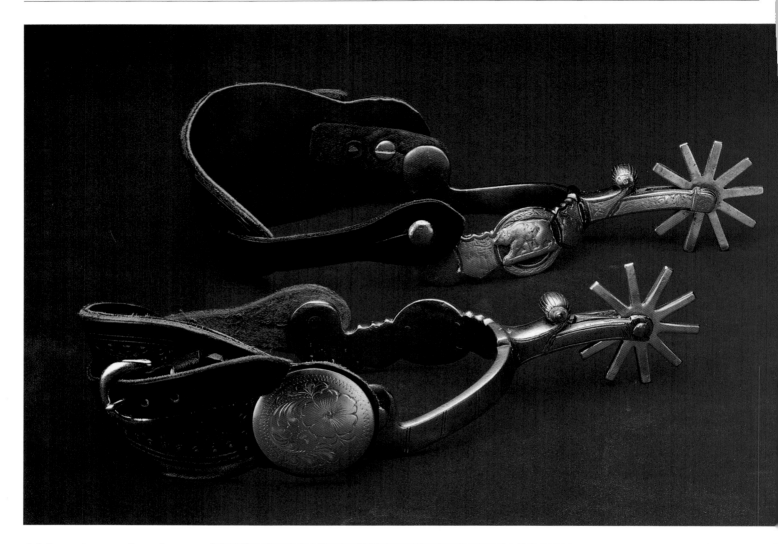

California Spurs in the early style of G. S. García. Unmarked and full-mounted with silver California bear flanked by engraved inlaid shields and chap guards. Elko, Nevada, c. 1910, steel and silver, L 7" (17.9 cm.).

O.K. Spurs by August Buermann Manufacturing Company. Four-button spurs with raised shanks and stamped "O.K." on heel bands near shanks. Newark, New Jersey, c. 1912, iron, L 5" (13.0 cm.). Buermann bought the patent for O.K. spurs from J. C. Petmecky of Austin, Texas, in 1886 and manufactured O.K. spurs, which he sold wholesale and through catalogs. Many cowboys bought these utilitarian spurs until they could afford more ornate gear.

California Spurs by August Buermann Manufacturing Company. Drooping shanks and 10-point rowels. Newark, New Jersey, c. 1900, steel, L 7⅜" (18.7 cm.). Copy of earlier style made about 1800. Buermann made spurs of this style to sell in California. The original jingles that hung from the rowel pins, known since the Middle Ages, are missing.

Gal-leg Spurs by Eduardo Grijalva. Half-mounted with engraved silver overlay and "EG" stamp on each spur. Magdalena, Sonora, Mexico, c. 1945, iron and silver, L 5⅞" (14.9 cm.). Grijalva, a Yavapai Indian, made both bits and spurs, the majority of which were sold in the United States.

Star Steel Silver Spurs by August Buermann Manufacturing Company. Engraved silver overlay and heart-shaped outside buttons. Newark, New Jersey, c. 1924, Star Steel Silver and silver, L 6⅝" (16.7 cm.). Star Steel Silver was an alloy developed for the exclusive use of the Buermann Company.

Hercules Bronze Spurs, No. 1393½ in August Buermann Manufacturing Company's No. 35 catalog. Stamped "PAT'D" and "AB" superimposed on a star at heel-band terminus, heel chains, and 20-point rowels. Newark, New Jersey, c. 1920, Hercules Bronze and nickel silver, L 6¼" (15.9 cm.). Buermann developed Hercules Bronze exclusively for his bits and spurs. This spur with its applied decoration is called "spot" style.

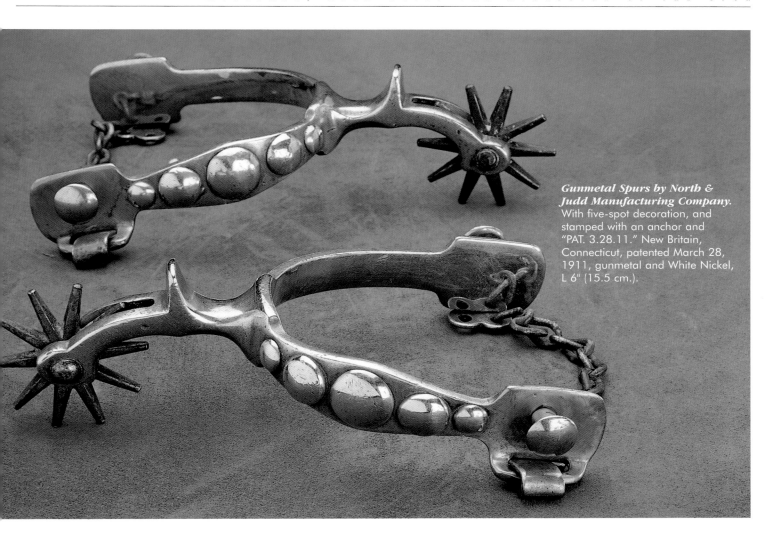

Gunmetal Spurs by North & Judd Manufacturing Company. With five-spot decoration, and stamped with an anchor and "PAT. 3.28.11." New Britain, Connecticut, patented March 28, 1911, gunmetal and White Nickel, L 6" (15.5 cm.).

Stainless Steel Spurs by Ricardo Metal Manufacturers. Engraved silver overlay, gold horse head, and faux ruby insets. Stamped in heel bands: "STERLING OVERLAY / 10K" and "Ricardo" (script). Denver, Colorado, c. 1945, stainless steel, L 5" (12.7 cm.).

Gal-leg Spurs by J. R. (John Robert) McChesney. Unmarked, shanks mounted with silver stockings and copper slippers. Paul's Valley, Oklahoma; c. 1920; steel, silver, and copper; L 5¹³⁄₁₆" (14.3 cm.). Shaped heel bands half-mounted with overlaid engraved silver scrolls on either side of a copper oval "peanut." Ends of heel bands upturned and rounded behind stationary buttons, which are typical of McChesney-made spurs. McChesney was famous for his gal-leg spurs.

Spurs by J. R. McChesney. Engraved silver shield-shaped overlay on either side of brass dot on outside heel bands, with chap guards and 14-point rowels. Pauls Valley, Oklahoma; c. 1914; steel, silver, and brass; L 5¾" (14.8 cm.).

Woman's Bottle-Opener Shank Spurs by J. R. McChesney. Full-mounted with overlaid silver arrow, copper arrowhead, bottle-opener shanks, and sawtooth rowels. Pauls Valley, Oklahoma; c. 1912; steel, copper, and silver; L 4⅜" (10.9 cm.). Spurs with bottle-opener shanks are rare because the shanks were shaped by hand and, thus, were more time-consuming to make.

Rattlesnake Spurs by Kelly Brothers. Half-mounted with engraved silver overlaid snake on heel bands and shanks, rowel pins through snake's head, and chap guard rattles. Embossed Indian-head buttons. Dalhart, Texas; c. 1920; steel, silver, and brass; L 6⅜" (16.3 cm.).

Goose Head Spurs by Kelly Brothers & Parker. Half-mounted with goose head and neck along shanks, and overlaid silver wings on heel bands. Stamped "KB&P". Dalhart, Texas, c. 1915, steel, silver, and brass, L 6¼" (15.8 cm.).

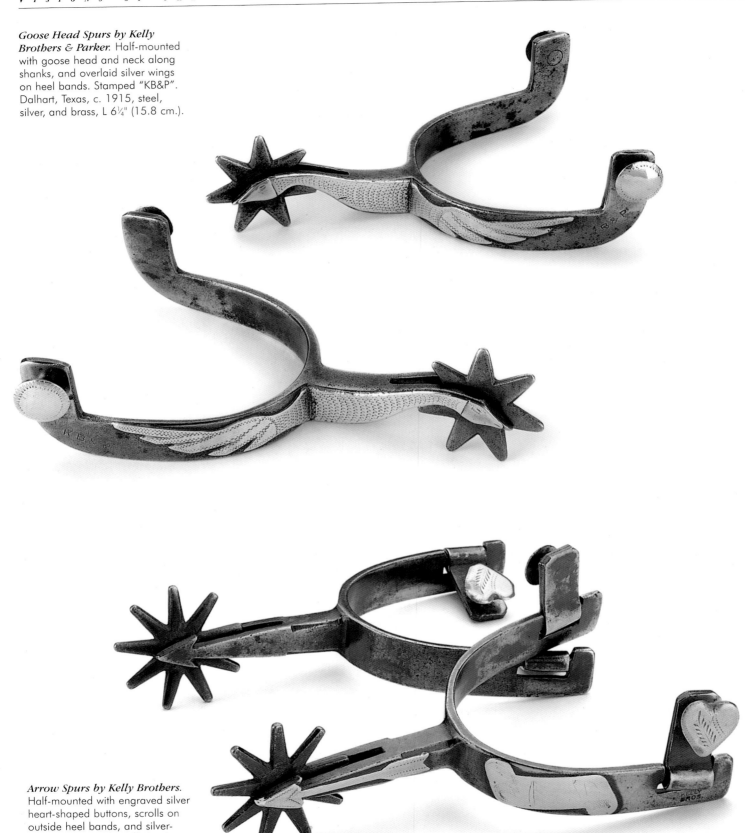

Arrow Spurs by Kelly Brothers. Half-mounted with engraved silver heart-shaped buttons, scrolls on outside heel bands, and silver-mounted arrow-shaped shanks. Stamped "KELLY / BROS." Dalhart, Texas, c. 1925, steel and silver, L 6⅝" (16.8 cm.).

Spurs by Kelly Brothers. Full-mounted with overlaid engraved silver bars on outside heel bands and shanks, chap guards, and 8-point rowels. Stamped "KELLY / BROS." El Paso, Texas, c. 1935, steel and silver, L 6½" (16.5 cm.).

"Johnnie Mullens Special" Spurs by Oscar Crockett. Half-mounted with overlaid engraved silver bars on outside heel bands and shanks. Stamped "CROCKETT" on each spur. Kansas City, Missouri, c. 1930, steel and silver, L 6½" (16.7 cm.) This was a popular style made by both Crockett and Kelly (left). Mullens was well known as a bronc rider, rodeo producer, and arena director.

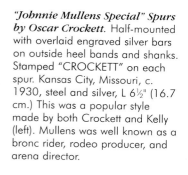

Leaf Spurs by Oscar Crockett. Half-mounted with engraved silver-leaf overlay and silver rowel-pin covers. Lenexa, Kansas, c. 1932, steel and silver, L 6⅜" (15.9 cm.). Crockett had used the leaf mounting since the 1920s when his shop was in Kansas City.

Gal-leg Spurs by Oscar Crockett. Unmarked, with engraved silver overlay and 8-point rowels. Kansas City, Missouri, c. 1931, steel and silver, L 6⅛" (15.4 cm).

Number 1614 Spurs by Crockett Bit & Spur Company. Outside heel bands and shanks completely overlaid with engraved silver. Flower-shaped rowels. Boulder, Colorado, c. 1947, stainless steel and silver, L 6¼" (16.0 cm.). Stamped "ST" for stainless steel.

Victoria Shank Spurs by Joe Bianchi. Full-mounted with plain silver overlay on heel bands and base of shanks. Mexican coins cover outside buttons and rowel pins. Stamped "JBIANCHI" on one spur and "VICTORIA" on the other. Victoria, Texas; c. 1925; steel, silver, and coins; L 6¼" (13.0 cm.). Joe Bianchi was famous for his "bottle-opener" shanks. Bianchi made these spurs for Will Cotulla, whose initials "W.C." are stamped on buttons. Cotulla, Texas, is named for his family.

Spurs by Jess S. Hodge. Unmarked and full-mounted with overlaid silver bars on heel bands, teardrop-shaped rowel-pin covers, and 16-point rowels. Overlaid silver longhorn head along top of heel band with nose down top of shank. Fort McKavett, Texas, c. 1940, steel and silver, L 4⅞" (12.3 cm.).

Number 4 Drop Shank and Chap Guard Spurs by Ed F. (Edward Fred) Blanchard, with 10-point blunt rowels. Yucca, Arizona, c. 1956, steel, L 5½" (13.9 cm.). Slanted swinging buttons are typical of Blanchard spurs, which were popular with cowboys because the slanted buttons and wide heel band kept them in place on their boots. Blanchard's early spurs were usually mounted, but his later work had a sleeker, more modern look.

Spurs by J. O. (James Oscar) Bass. Overlaid engraved silver bars on shanks and heel bands. Stamped "No. 299 MADE BY / J.O. BASS TULIA, TEX." Tulia, Texas, c. 1920, steel and silver, L 6" (15.3 cm.). The shaped button straps are typical of Bass designs.

TOOLS OF TRIUMPH AND TRAGEDY

Firearms in the American West

RICHARD C. RATTENBURY

Commencing with the first Spanish incursions in the 1490s, firearms played a fundamental role in advancing and protecting Euro-American expansion in the New World. Firearms were, in fact, among the most sophisticated and influential technologies first brought to the Americas, and their impact continued on a succession of frontiers over a period of nearly four centuries. By 1800, as adventurous and enterprising Americans began probing the approaches of the trans-Mississippi West, firearms were a long-established and very integral part of frontier material culture and the westering experience.

The first explorers and frontiersmen entering the trans-Mississippi West found an essentially untouched and expansive environment occupied by a rich diversity of new peoples and wildlife. These Americans carried single-shot, muzzle-loading flint-lock rifles and pistols, little changed in half a century. They were soon to realize that they needed weapons better adapted to new conditions—arms convenient for carriage on horseback over long distances, arms powerful enough for the large game met with on the plains, and arms of sufficient firepower for defense against an often-superior and fast-moving adversary.

As it happened, there was—for Euro-Americans—a fortuitous coincidence of parallel development between expansion in the West and advances in arms technology in the East that actually accelerated the conquest of the last continental frontier during the course of the nineteenth century. Indeed, the West provided a valuable "proving ground" for eastern gunsmiths and arms manufacturers, and, in turn, their increasingly sophisticated products helped the advancement of both

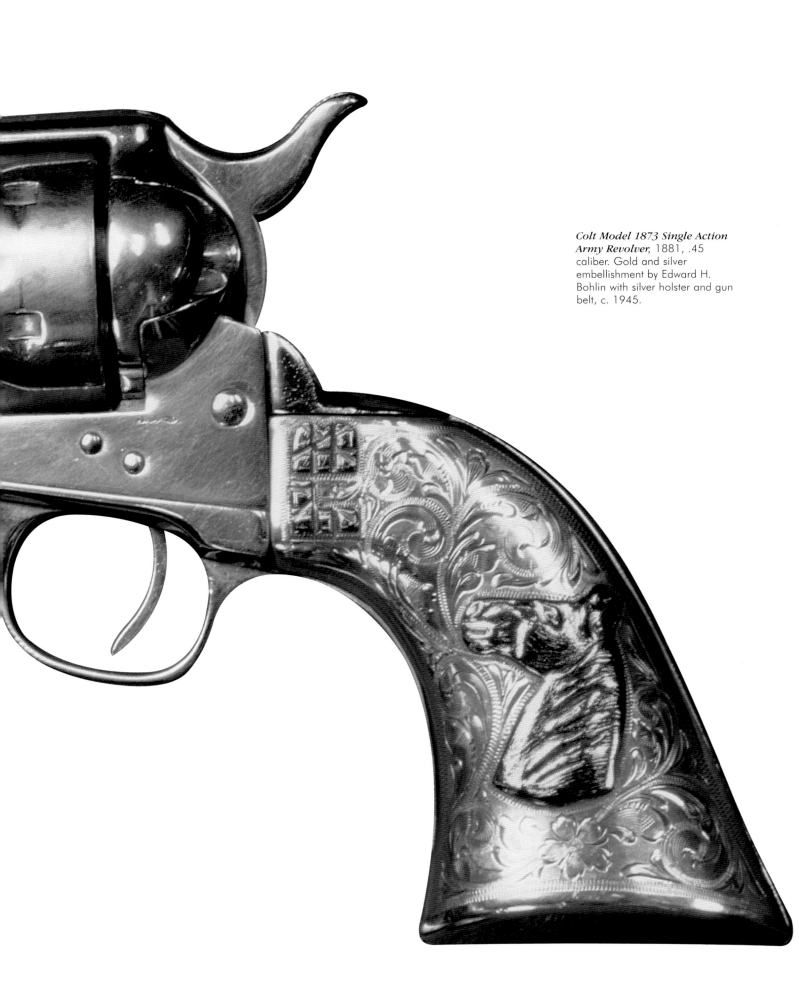

Colt Model 1873 Single Action Army Revolver, 1881, .45 caliber. Gold and silver embellishment by Edward H. Bohlin with silver holster and gun belt, c. 1945.

Colt Model 1873 Single Action Army Revolver, 1881, .45 caliber. Gold and silver embellishment by Edward H. Bohlin with silver holster and gun belt, c. 1945.

the military and civilian frontiers to a remarkable degree.

Nearly all American arms of the late colonial and early federal periods were patterned on European designs. The notable exception was the famed Pennsylvania rifle—or Kentucky rifle, as it is more commonly known today. The Pennsylvania rifle was the first truly American firearm, having evolved during the eighteenth century in response to a wilderness environment and colonial economy east of the Appalachian Mountains. Its rifled barrel (cut with interior spiral grooves that caused the projectile to spin and stabilize in flight) was adopted to provide deadly accuracy in a forested and sometimes dangerous frontier realm. Far more accurate than the common smooth-bore musket, its long barrel and compara-

tively small bore (usually from 42 to 46 inches and from .36 to .46 caliber) also were conservative of limited supplies of powder and lead. In both flint and later percussion ignition, it was the first significant firearm carried into the trans-Mississippi West by the explorers and free trappers.

As these Americans moved onto the Great Plains and into the Rocky Mountains in greater numbers, however, they found the Pennsylvania rifle inadequate for the environment. Its caliber was generally too small for the buffalo, elk, and grizzly bear so often encountered. Its relatively delicate construction proved inadequate for the rough usage required, and it was too long to be carried handily on horseback. What was needed was a sturdier rifle of shorter length and larger caliber. Necessity and environment again dictated specific design adaptations, and there evolved another distinctly American arm—the Mountain, or Plains, rifle.

Similar in form and line to the Pennsylvania rifle, the Plains rifle was, however, shorter, heavier and of larger bore (usually ranging from .53 to .58 caliber). Often called the "Mountain Man's Choice," these powerful and rather plain rifles were popular in the West from the early 1830s through the 1860s. While many Plains-style rifles were produced by gunsmiths in eastern Pennsylvania, the best examples were developed and manufactured in and around St. Louis, Missouri. Certainly the most influential among the western makers were famed brothers Jacob and Samuel Hawken, whose dedicated clientele included frontiersmen the likes of Jim Bridger and Kit Carson—men who sometimes staked their lives on the rifle's unexcelled power, accuracy, and rugged dependability. It was these qualities that inspired frontiersman William Hamilton to observe, ". . . *in those days* [1842] *the best rifles used were the Hawkins* [sic] *and they carried three hundred and fifty yards.*" The practicality and popularity of the Plains rifle as a hunting arm may be understood in the fact that not a few gunsmiths, such as J. P. Gemmer of St. Louis and J. C. Petmecky of Austin, Texas, were still producing the style as late as 1870, nearly two decades after more advanced breech-loading arms had become available.

Technical advances in firearm design and function, of course, commenced early in the nineteenth century. Among the first milestones was the innovative breech system created by John H. Hall and adopted by the U. S. Army in 1819. Hall rifles and carbines were the first semi-practical breech-loading arms in America; the U.S. Dragoons employed improved versions of the Hall carbine in the West well into the 1840s. Far more influential in the story of firearms development, however, was the advent and widespread adoption of percussion ignition during the late 1820s and 1830s. Percussion arms utilized an explosive fulminate of mercury compound fixed in small, virtually weatherproof copper caps that were placed on a short tube, or "nipple," at the rear of the weapon's chamber. When struck by the hammer, the percussion cap sent a spurt of flame through the nipple, igniting the main powder charge and discharging the arm.

Percussion ignition represented a radical improvement over the flint-and-steel locks that had served for two centuries. Its reliability in inclement or windy conditions was especially appreciated among western plainsmen and hunters. Percussion locks were phased into use on most arms between 1830 and 1835, and they were commonplace in the Far West by 1840. Coupled with the extraordinary mass-production techniques then developing in the American arms manufacturing industry, this new and simplified ignition system contributed directly to the development and relative perfection of breech-loading and repeating firearms between the mid-1830s and the early 1860s. This was especially important to westerners, as increased firepower was sometimes crucial to their very survival.

Early percussion, breech-loading guns, in which a paper- or linen-wrapped cartridge containing the powder charge and projectile was introduced at the rear of the

Plains Rifle by A. E. Dinzel of St. Louis, Missouri, with checkered stock, c. 1845, .50 caliber.

barrel and mechanically sealed (instead of being rammed down from the muzzle), represented a marked improvement in the speed with which a weapon could be loaded, discharged, and reloaded—particularly while moving on horseback. The rate of fire for the average rifleman was increased from two well-aimed shots per minute to as many as four or five. For both the soldier and the frontiersman, such an equation was most attractive, and it would prove a life saver in a number of unequal contests with Native Americans in the West.

It fell to noted gunsmith Christian Sharps, during the late 1840s and early 1850s, to perfect the first truly practical single-shot, breech-loading shoulder arm. Sharps devised a lever-actuated, falling-block design so robust that it would easily accommodate the high-powered metallic cartridge loads developed a quarter century later. Sharps arms, in a variety of rifle and carbine configurations from .36 to .56 caliber, won immediate converts on the antebellum frontier—from the abolitionists of Bleeding Kansas to the stage guards of the Butterfield Trail. They served prominently

throughout the Civil War with Federal cavalry and sharpshooter units, and were even copied by Confederate armorers.

As will be seen, later Sharps sporting rifles, taking powerful metallic cartridge loads, became the decided favorite of professional buffalo hunters in the West. While a number of innovative breech-loading arms emerged during the Civil War years, none remotely approached the Sharps in popularity or production, and it had no serious rival in the West (other than the Remington Rolling Block single-shot) prior to the failure of the venerable business in 1883.

The first example of a percussion repeating arm that enjoyed wide manufacture was the pepperbox pistol. In vogue from the 1830s to the 1860s, it incorporated a cluster of four to six barrels that rotated around a central axis and were successively fired by a single hammer. While the double-action pepperbox pistol provided greatly increased firepower compared to typical single-shot pistols, it was distinctly muzzle-heavy and difficult to shoot with any accuracy. Nevertheless, these pistols, particularly those manufactured by

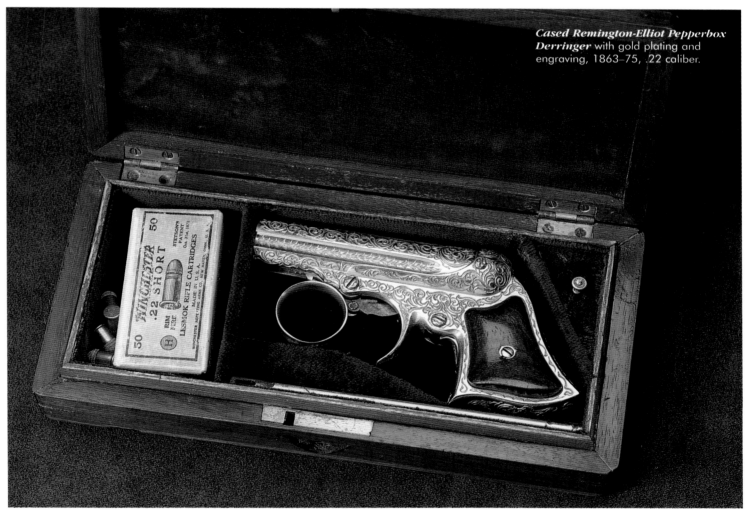

Cased Remington-Elliot Pepperbox Derringer with gold plating and engraving, 1863–75, .22 caliber.

the firm of Allen and Thurber, enjoyed wide popularity among California gold seekers and overland emigrants, successfully competing with most early revolving-cylinder arms. Less effective, and not terribly common during the 1840s and 1850s, was the application of percussion ignition to multibarreled longarms, which usually incorporated from two to four tubes (rifled, smooth, or in combination) in a cluster typically rotated by hand and discharged by a single percussion lock.

The truly practical formulation of a percussion repeater came in 1836 with Samuel Colt's patent for small arms incorporating a revolving cylinder having five or six chambers holding charged rounds ready to fire. Born near Hartford, Connecticut, in July 1814, Colt created an industrial empire based on revolving cylinder, repeating firearms that would play a prominent role in western settlement. During a sea voyage in 1830–31, he fashioned a wooden pistol with a multichambered cylinder intended to fire successive charges. Back in the United States, Colt had working models perfected while he supported the endeavor with demonstrations of nitrous oxide (laughing gas) as the "Celebrated Dr. Coulte of New York, London, and Calcutta."

Colt received a patent for his invention in February 1836, concurrent with the fast-developing revolution in Texas. The destinies of Colt's nascent Patent Arms Manufacturing Company and republican Texas were to be inextricably linked during their early years, as the two enjoyed a mutually advantageous relationship. Colt's revolutionary product provided the young republic and frontier state with the fire-power necessary to advance and defend itself, while Texas afforded the struggling arms maker a realistic testing arena and his most enthusiastic market.

Colt's Paterson revolvers (as well as rifles, carbines, and shotguns) commenced manufacture in 1837 to little public acclaim. The Republic of Texas was among the first government entities to recognize the merits of the Colt system, ordering 180 of the .36 caliber Holster Model revolvers for its fledgling navy in 1839. Issued to various Texas warships, these guns performed reasonably well in several engagements against Mexico. Colt was so pleased by the Texas purchase that he commemorated the republic's naval victory off Campeche (May 1843) with an engraved scene of the battle that was impressed on the cylinders of the future 1851 Navy, 1860 Army, and 1861 Navy Model revolvers. Some of these Paterson Colt revolvers later served with the Army of Texas and with various quasi-military adventures, such as the ill-fated expeditions to Santa Fe and Mier.

Most significant historically, however, were the revolvers reissued to the Texas Rangers, for it was with this force that the Colt revolver first won its reputation as a weapon ideally suited to mounted combat. Received in 1843, these Paterson Colts made history with the Ranger contingent commanded by Colonel John Coffee Hays in several uneven encounters with depredating Comanches. Most dramatic was the engagement in which Hays and fourteen Rangers routed some eighty Comanche warriors in a running battle in July 1844. This and other victories against considerable odds reinforced the advantage of the Colt revolver's firepower. Colt again

Colt Third Model Dragoon Revolver, 1860, .44 caliber.

demonstrated his debt to Texans for proving and popularizing his invention—all of the later Walker and Dragoon Model Colts would carry a cylinder scene commemorating the so-called "Hays Big Fight." Colt himself referred to the Paterson Holster Model revolver as the "Texas Arm," while present-day collectors know it generically as the Texas Paterson.

Although Colt's Paterson enterprise failed in 1842, his revolvers had amply demonstrated their superiority in mounted combat and won the devotion of frontiersmen across the Southwest. Not inappropriately, it was former Texas Ranger Samuel H. Walker who, in responding to the exigencies of the Mexican American War, put Colt back in business. In November 1846, Captain Walker collaborated with Colt for the production of 1,000 improved revolvers. Familiar with the frailties of the Paterson arm (sometimes referred to by less-enthusiastic patrons as "Colt's Patent Wheel of Misfortune"), Walker specified a massive new design with a nine-inch barrel and a six-shot cylinder chambered for a .44 caliber conical bullet. Observing the four-pound, nine-ounce weapon in action, Texas Ranger John S. "Rip" Ford claimed the new Walker Colt was as powerful as the U.S. Model 1841 "Mississippi" rifle. With minor modifications, this weapon inaugurated the era of perfected revolver design and manufacture.

Samuel Colt opened a new factory at Hartford, Connecticut, in 1848 and reestablished regular production under the name Colt's Patent Fire Arms Manufacturing Company. Within a few years, his handguns were preeminent among U.S. military sidearms and rapidly supplanted pepperbox pistols in the civilian market. Among the first weapons produced were the large-frame Dragoon Models that enjoyed both military and commercial sales in the West. In concert with the California gold rush and increasing western migration, the innovative arms maker also introduced a series of improved pocket and holster revolvers—most notably the .36 caliber Model 1851 Navy. Prior to the Civil War, this was by far the most popular handgun in the West, about which traveler Frederick Law Olmsted observed:

"Of the Colt's we cannot speak in too high terms. . . . There are probably in Texas about as many revolvers as male adults, and I doubt if there are one hundred in the state of any other make. . . . A border weapon so reliable in every sense would give brute courage to even a dyspeptic tailor."

Although other eastern arms manufacturers such as the Remington and Whitney firms competed for the western market, the Navy Colt dominated in the region through the 1860s.

Upon such success, Colt opened the

Colt Model 1873 Single Action Army Revolver with carved mother-of-pearl grips, 1903, .45 long caliber. This gun belonged to Sheriff Lorenzo Delgado of Las Vegas, New Mexico.

largest, most advanced private armory in the world at Hartford in 1855, a facility making full use of the machinery and mass-production principles of the "American System of Manufacturing." It would serve the nation well during the Civil War, providing the Union with more than 250,000 arms in a period of four years. Although Samuel Colt, inventor and consummate salesman, died in 1862, the future of his enterprise was assured, at least in part, by a growing and appreciative frontier clientele.

Colt revolvers remained preeminent among such arms throughout the West for the rest of the nineteenth century. Of signal importance was the justly famed Model 1873 Single Action Army revolver, the first large-caliber, solid-frame Colt handgun designed for metallic cartridges and produced in extensive quantity. The Single Action Army was well balanced, mechanically reliable, powerful, and accurate. The military adopted this revolver as its standard sidearm during the Indian Wars period, and the weapon had little real competition from rivals put forward by

Remington and Smith & Wesson.

Known generically as the Peacemaker, Plough Handle, Hog Leg, or simply "six-shooter," the Colt Single Action (in its many different calibers, barrel lengths, and design variants) was also the preferred handgun of outlaws, lawmen, and the majority of cowboys across the West between 1875 and 1900. In 1878 the Colt firm shrewdly chambered the revolver for the Winchester .44/40 cartridge, the standard chambering employed in the widely popular Model 1873 Winchester carbines and rifles. Westerners could then carry one standard cartridge for both sidearms and longarms, a decided advantage in regions where ammunition supplies often were less than dependable.

In the late 1870s Colt's introduced its first double-action revolvers, in which hammer cocking, cylinder advance, locking, and discharge all were accomplished simply by squeezing the trigger. But, while these Lightning and Frontier Model revolvers enjoyed brisk production and sales, they had little appreciable effect on the popular-

Colt Model 1877 "Lightning"
Double Action Revolver, 1882,
.41 caliber.

ity of the venerable Single Action Army among pistol-packing westerners during the remainder of the century.

During the 1850s other successful attempts were being made to increase the firepower and efficiency of American arms. Signal advances came from the partnership of Horace Smith and Daniel Wesson, who first joined forces in 1854–55 to produce a novel lever-action repeating pistol with an integral tubular magazine beneath the barrel. A direct predecessor of the famed Winchester line of repeating rifles, this relatively impractical weapon was perhaps more important for its use of self-consuming ammunition—a hollow, conical bullet holding its own powder charge and fixed with its own primer. Within two years, the partners had reestablished themselves in Springfield, Massachusetts, and developed a remarkable new revolver.

This diminutive "tip-up" design used revolutionary .22 caliber rimfire, self-contained metallic cartridges (combining the primer, powder charge, and projectile in a single unit) and incorporated a cylinder having completely bored-through chambers that loaded at the rear. Yet, however important technologically, these small-caliber handguns were not greatly favored in the West. Mark Twain, who traveled overland to California in 1861, remembered his S & W Model No. 1 tip-up revolver as a "*. . . seven-shooter, which carried a ball like a homeopathic pill, and it required the whole seven to make a dose for an adult.*"

Smith & Wesson's introduction of the large-frame Model No. 3, .44 caliber American and Russian revolvers in the early 1870s, however, was received by experienced westerners with considerable respect and enthusiasm. The "break-top" action of these revolvers allowed the simultaneous ejection of all spent cartridge cases, greatly facilitating the reloading process. The army purchased 1,000 First Model American revolvers in 1870–71 and distributed them among cavalry units across the West. The troopers found them powerful and accurate, but ordnance reviewers felt the weapons were perhaps

too complicated and prone to breakage—particularly as compared to the solid-frame Colt Single Action Army revolver that appeared late in 1872.

Although the Colt won out as the military's standard sidearm, Major George M. Schofield nevertheless managed to promote his improvements to the Smith & Wesson. Between 1875 and 1877, the army bought several thousand .45 caliber Schofield Smith & Wesson revolvers, but these never truly threatened the dominance of the Colt. Outside the military, however, the large-frame S & Ws were carried by all manner of westerners, from outlaw John Wesley Hardin to scout and showman Texas Jack Omohundro.

While Smith & Wesson prospered with their revolvers, another man picked up their initial work with the lever-actuated, tubular magazine pistol. Former shirt manufacturer Oliver Winchester was not an arms inventor but an astute businessman with an eye for opportunity. He formed the New Haven Arms Company in 1857 to produce the Volcanic repeating pistol, which, while impractical as a handgun, provided the basic design elements crucial to Winchester's future success. In 1860 shop

superintendent B. Tyler Henry adapted the Volcanic action to a rifle configuration firing self-contained .44 rimfire cartridges of his own design. The lever action Henry repeating rifle, with fifteen rounds in its tubular magazine, provided a radical advance in firepower. Produced in comparatively limited numbers and challenged by the seven-shot Spencer repeater, the Henry nevertheless won many devotees in the West and set the stage for Winchester's unequaled popularity among manufacturers of repeating longarms.

The lever-action repeating rifle that proved most successful and popular on the frontier was the .44/40 caliber Model 1873 Winchester. No less a western personage than W. F. "Buffalo Bill" Cody extolled it as "The Boss" among weapons. Available in both rifle and carbine configuration, its use was so widespread that Winchester later proclaimed it "The Gun That Won The West"— although the previous Model 1866 Winchester could lay equal or better claim to the title historically. Because both of these repeaters were underpowered in comparison to available single-shot rifles, Winchester introduced the scaled-up Model 1876 rifle, which accommodated larger and

Winchester Model 1866 Rifle with factory engraving, silver plating and silver inlay, 1868, .44 caliber.

more powerful cartridges. Known as the "Centennial Rifle," the Model 1876 was a favorite of hunter-naturalist Theodore Roosevelt. The real solution to the development of a high-powered lever-action repeater, however, was ultimately provided by western gun designer John M. Browning, whose smooth-operating, vertical-locking-bolt design put the Model 1886 Winchester rifle well beyond the competition of Marlin, Bullard, and other late-nineteenth-century competitors.

Not all westerners, of course, needed or favored a repeating rifle. For the hunter or frontiersman demanding long-range accuracy and high power, the single-shot breech-loading rifle often remained the answer. Among the best such rifles were those made by the Sharps Rifle Company of Bridgeport, Connecticut. The Model 1874 Sharps sporting rifle incorporated the familiar falling-block action of its predecessors, which was extremely strong and could withstand very high-powered cartridge loads. Another single-shot arm favored by westerners was the Remington Rolling Block sporting rifle, which also employed an exceedingly strong breech action and, like the Sharps, came in a variety of calibers, weights, and styles. These rifles were particularly popular among professional buffalo hunters during the 1870s and early 1880s.

By 1874, the "Great Buffalo Hunt" was in full swing on the plains of Nebraska,

Springfield Armory Model, 1880 Hunting Knife and Sheath.

Springfield Armory Model 1879 Rifle with bayonet and sling, 1879–85, .45-70 caliber.

Kansas, Texas, and Colorado. Using a still-hunting method known as "shooting a stand," professional buffalo hunters (who were not sportsmen but businessmen) stalked to within 100 to 300 yards of a herd and shot the leader in the lungs, causing the remaining animals to mill in confusion. The hunter then continued shooting at a measured pace until the herd scattered or all the animals were killed. This assured the maximum number of kills within the smallest possible arena, greatly aiding the skinning process that followed. Westerner Richard Irving Dodge described the result:

> *"I have myself counted 112 [buffalo] carcasses inside of a semi-circle of 200 yards radius, all of which were killed by one man from the same spot, and in less than three-quarters of an hour. . . ."*

Employing powerful Sharps and Remington breech-loading rifles, the efficacy of this deliberate hunting technique was demonstrated across the plains. While figures conflict among sources, it is likely that more than *four million* buffalo were killed by hide hunters on the central and southern plains between 1872 and 1878. On the northern plains of the Montana and Dakota Territories, the hunt concluded in 1883 with perhaps another *two million* animals destroyed. Eastern technology,

demonstrated in the refined accuracy and superior power of the Sharps rifle, may be said to have contributed in some measure to this ecological calamity in the West.

During the Indian Wars era, the U. S. Military also favored a single-shot breech-loading rifle for standard service—although their thinking was clearly outdated by the time of the Custer debacle in 1876. The first of these, which gained some renown in the famed Wagon Box Fight of 1867, were .50 caliber conversions of the Civil War rifled-musket employing the Allen "trapdoor" breech system. In 1873 regular production of this strong yet relatively simple breech design commenced with chambering for the well-regarded .45/70 Government cartridge. These improved Springfield trapdoor rifles and carbines—for infantry and cavalry, respectively—played their triumphant and tragic role in bringing the Native American peoples of the West to submission by the mid-1890s.

Beyond the significant interplay of evolving arms technology and unfolding frontier conquest, American gun makers also established an important aesthetic standard during the second half of the nineteenth century. Termed by noted arms authority R. L. Wilson as the "Golden Age

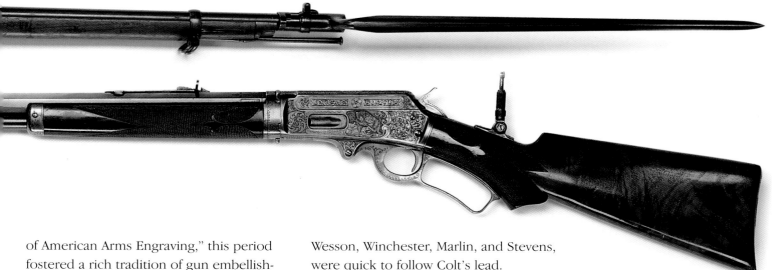

of American Arms Engraving," this period fostered a rich tradition of gun embellishment in the United States that continues to the present day. Much of the credit for this phenomenon must go to Samuel Colt. The consummate entrepreneur and promoter of his time, Colt made the presentation of lavishly cased and ornamented guns an integral part of his marketing strategy. The recipients of his largesse were invariably men of power or fame—those who could influence government contracts or publicly promote his product. Other arms manufacturers, particularly Remington, Smith &

Wesson, Winchester, Marlin, and Stevens, were quick to follow Colt's lead.

The blossoming of American gun embellishment would not have been possible, however, without the influx of skilled German emigrant craftsmen who lavished their old-world talents on the New World's machine-made firearms. Among these artisans were such talented notables as freelancer L. D. Nimschke, who engraved all manner of arms from those of Remington and Deringer, to those of Sharps and Winchester; Gustave Young, who created masterworks for both

Marlin Model 1893 Lever Action Rifle with factory engraving and checkered burl walnut, 1893–1935, .38-55 caliber.

Marlin Model 1893 Lever Action Rifle (above, detail).

Colt and Smith & Wesson; and the famed Ulrich dynasty, which for three generations enhanced the arms of Winchester and Marlin. These and other prominent artisans developed and usually practiced an engraving pattern known as the "American Style," which consisted of crisp and flowing scrollwork of foliate or "donut" motifs set off on a punched-dot background. More elaborate work incorporated paneled game scenes—invariably of western animals such as buffalo, bear, and elk—that sometimes were rendered in gold inlay. While most such work was reserved for costly presentation arms, it was available on special order to anyone willing to bear the cost.

Although the art of arms embellishment in America may have been founded on European aristocratic tradition, it was nevertheless more democratized, and it found many devotees in the frontier West. Most appreciative of finely ornamented firearms was a cadre of westerners that might be called the "frontier fraternity"—a mixed group consisting of military officers, sport hunters, ranchers, lawmen, and showmen. Notable among the owners of such fine arms were Generals Philip H. Sheridan, Nelson A. Miles, and George A. Custer; ranchmen and hunters Granville Stuart and Theodore Roosevelt; law officers William "Bat" Masterson, Bill Tilghman, and numerous Texas Rangers; and Wild West showmen "Buffalo Bill" Cody, "Pawnee Bill" Lilly, Doc Carver, and Captain Jack Crawford. The rarity and historical association of such embellished weapons adds yet another dimension of appreciation to the fascinating saga of firearms in the frontier West.

As the real "Wild West" grew quiet in the 1890s, a new technological era opened in the American firearms industry—one that would have far greater implications for the military of a burgeoning world power than for the civilian population of a former frontier. With the westering experience already passing into myth, historian Frederick Jackson Turner, writing of the colonial and federal periods in America, cited the ax, the plow, and the Pennsylvania rifle as the three tools decisive in taming the eastern frontier environment. In much the same vein, historian Walter Prescott Webb later singled out barbed wire, the windmill, and the Colt revolver as the technologies crucial in conquering the Great Plains environment. Beyond the factual and theoretical appraisals of such historians, it can be said that particularly significant nineteenth-century firearms—such as the Hawken rifle, the Colt revolver, the Sharps rifle, and the Winchester carbine—are today inextricably associated with the symbolism and myth of the frontier experience, having become virtual icons in the West of popular imagination.

SUGGESTED READING

Garavaglia, Louis A., and Charles G. Worman. *Firearms of the American West, 1803–1865.* Albuquerque, N.M.: University of New Mexico Press, 1984.

———. *Firearms of the American West, 1866–1894.* Albuquerque, N.M.: University of New Mexico Press, 1985.

Wilson, R. L. *The Peacemakers: Arms and Adventure in the American West.* New York: Random House, 1992.

PHOTOGRAPHY OF FIREARMS BY BAKÓ/BECQ WORLDWIDE AND FRANK WHITE.

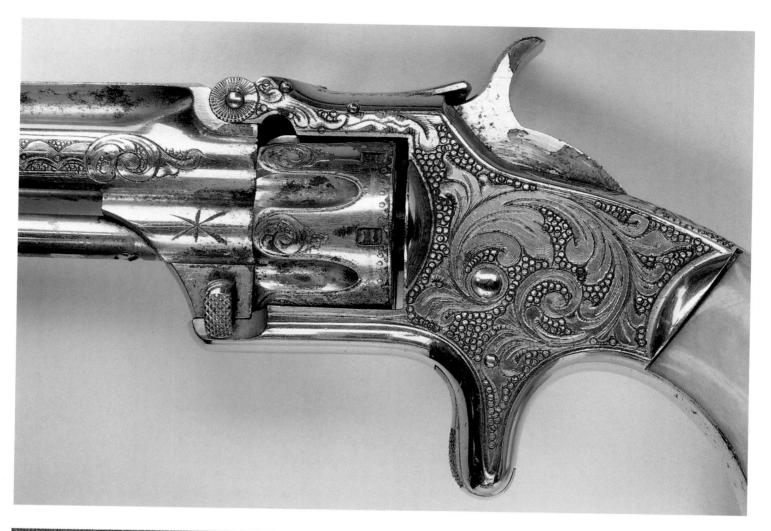

Model No. 1, Third Issue Revolver with factory engraving and ivory grips, 1868–80, .22 caliber.

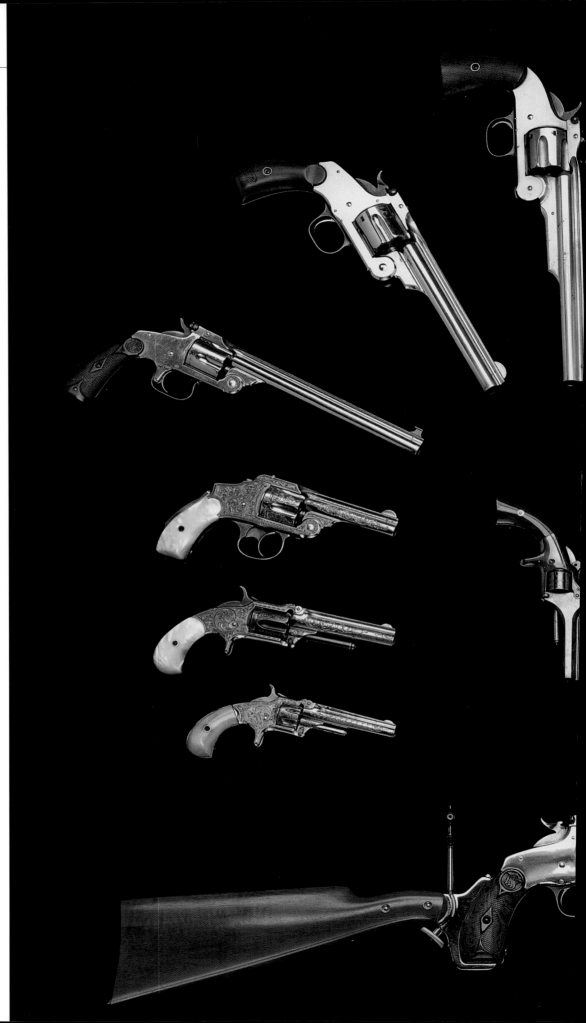

SMITH & WESSONS

Left half top to bottom:

Model No. 3 First Model Single Action Revolver, 1870–72, .44 caliber.

Model 3 Russian Third Model Single Action Revolver with martial marks, 1874–78, .44 caliber. Issued to the State of Maryland.

Single Action Mexican Model Revolver with 7-inch barrel and added trigger guard, c. 1890, .38 caliber.

Single Action Second Model 38 Safety Revolver, 1887–90, .38 caliber.

Model No. 1½ Second Issue Revolver with factory engraving and mother-of-pearl grips, 1868–75, .32 caliber.

Model No. 1, Third Issue Revolver with factory engraving and ivory grips, 1868–80, .22 caliber.

Along bottom:
Model .320 Rifle with red rubber stock and grips and tang sight, 1879–87, .320 S&W rifle caliber.

Inside left, Model No. 1, First Issue Revolver, 1857–60, .22 caliber.

Model No. 3 Second Model Single Action Revolver with carved American eagle on ivory grips and 8-inch barrel, 1872–74, .44 caliber.

First Model Schofield Single Action Revolver with martial marks, 1875, .45 caliber.

Second Model Single-Shot Pistol with 10-inch barrel, 1905–9, .22 caliber.

Single Action Second Model Revolver, 1877–91, .38 caliber.

Hand Ejector Model of 1903 Revolver, First Change, 1904–6, .32 caliber.

Double Action Fourth Model Revolver with engraving, gold wash and mother-of-pearl grips, 1895–1909, .38 caliber.

Inside right:
Model No. 1, Second Issue Revolver with mother-of-pearl grips, 1860–68, .22 caliber.

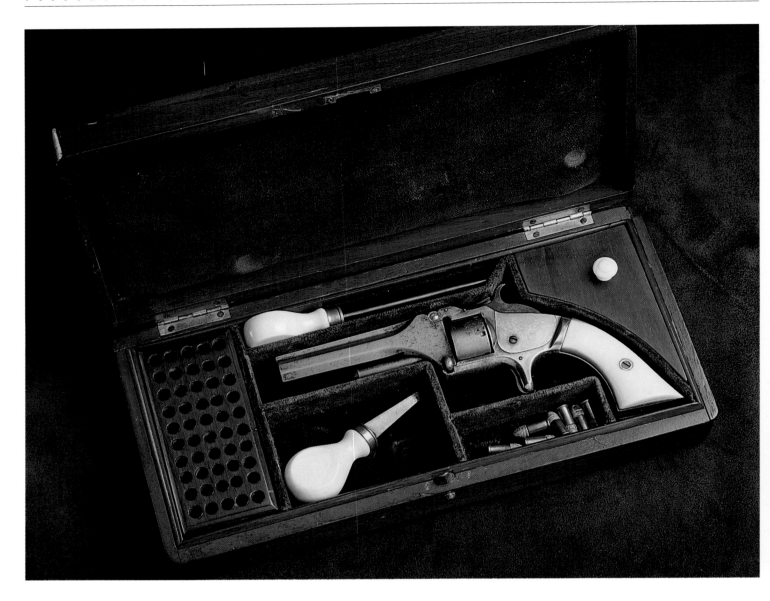

Cased Smith & Wesson Model No. 1 Second Issue Revolver with accouterments and ivory grips and handles, c. 1864, .22 caliber.

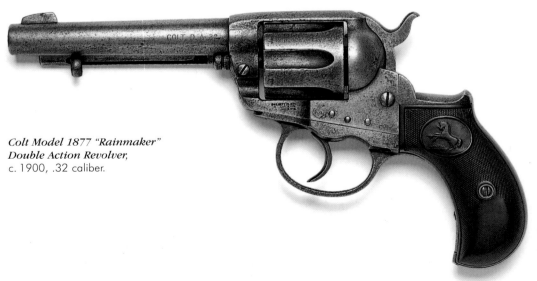

Colt Model 1877 "Rainmaker" Double Action Revolver, c. 1900, .32 caliber.

Smith & Wesson Model 3 Schofield First Model "Wells Fargo" Revolver with martial marks and painted Wells Fargo case, 1875, .45 caliber.

Single Action Second Model 38 Safety Revolver, 1887–90, .38 caliber.

Colt Model 1873 Single-Action Army revolver with eagle-carved ivory grip, 1907, .45 caliber.

Colt Model 1849 Pocket Revolver with ivory grips, 1866, .31 caliber.

Colt Model 1860 Army Revolver, 1861, .44 caliber. This revolver belonged to Pvt. Louis P. Barho of the Eighth Texas Cavalry, Terry's Texas Rangers.

***Cased Colt Seventh Model 1855
"Root" Side-hammer Pocket
Revolver*** with accouterments,
c. 1868, .31 caliber.

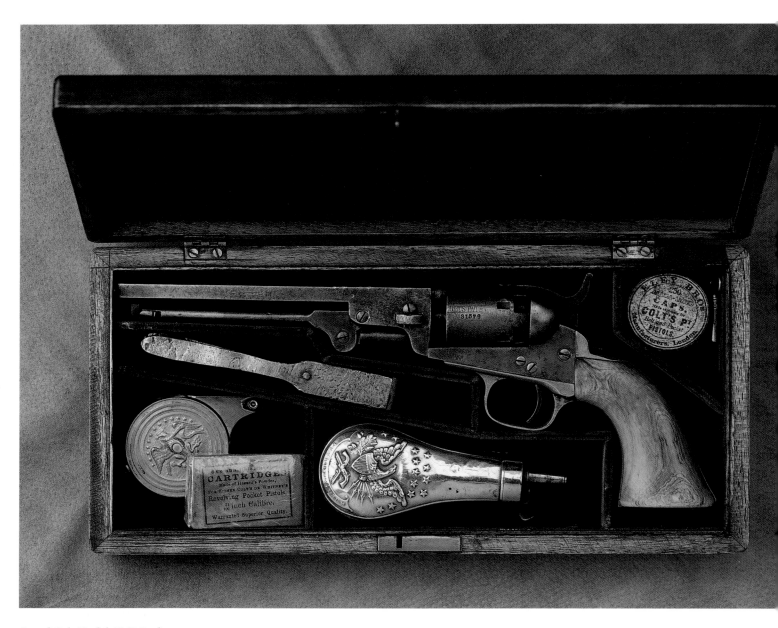

Cased Colt Model 1849 Pocket Revolver with accouterments, 1863, .31 caliber.

Cased Colt Model 1873 Single Action Army Revolver with ivory grips and accouterments, 1881, .45 caliber.

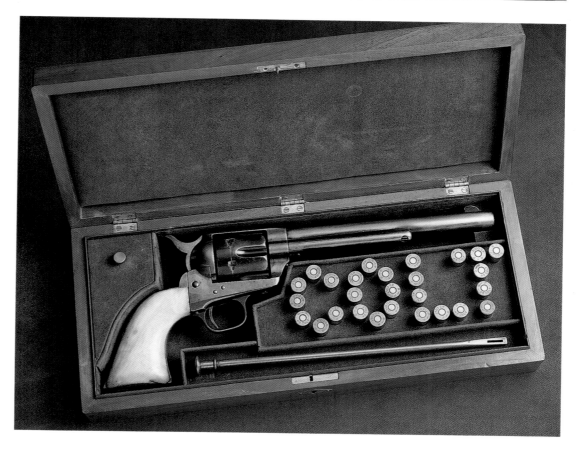

Cased Colt Model 1851 Navy Revolver with engraving and accouterments, 1863, .36 caliber.

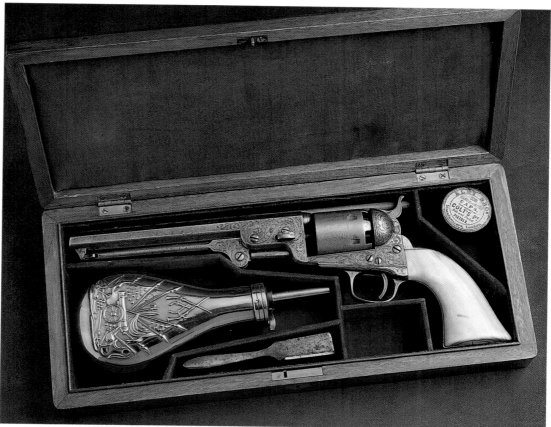

New Haven Arms Co. Volcanic Lever Action No. 1 Pocket Pistol with silver plating, ornate arabesque engraving and two-piece ivory grips, c. 1858, .31 caliber.

William W. Marston Three-Barrel Derringer with scroll-engraved frame and silver-plated barrels, c. 1869, .32 caliber.

***Stevens Vernier Hunter's
Pet Pocket Rifle No. 34-1/2***
with front globe sight and
special trigger guard, c. 1885,
.22 long caliber.

Stevens-Gould No. 37 Pistol,
c. 1900, .22 long rifle caliber.

Sharps Model 1874 "Old Reliable" Hunter's rifle, c. 1877, .40-50 Sharps necked caliber.

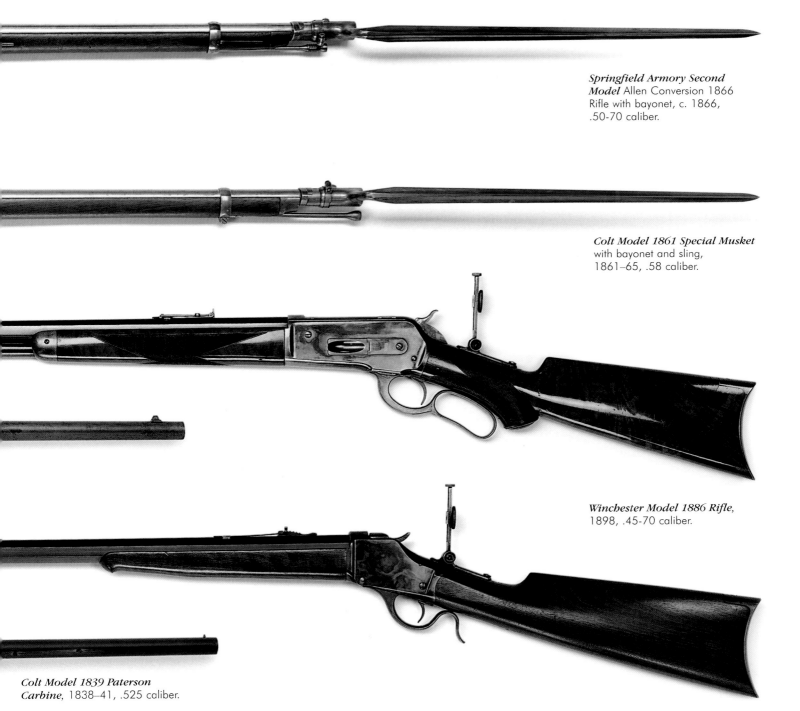

Springfield Armory Second Model Allen Conversion 1866 Rifle with bayonet, c. 1866, .50-70 caliber.

Colt Model 1861 Special Musket with bayonet and sling, 1861–65, .58 caliber.

Winchester Model 1886 Rifle, 1898, .45-70 caliber.

Colt Model 1839 Paterson Carbine, 1838–41, .525 caliber.

Winchester Model 1885 Single Shot High Wall Rifle with vernier tang sights, 1898, .38-55 caliber.

Winchester Model 1894 Takedown Rifle, 1898, .30-30 caliber.

Winchester Model 1873 Rifle, 1892, .38-40 caliber.

Henry Rifle with brass frame, 1865, .44 caliber.

Winchester Model 1886 Rifle,
1896, .45-90 caliber.

Winchester Model 1866 Carbine,
1872, .44 caliber. This carbine
once belonged to Temple
Houston, Sam Houston's son.

José Arpa y Perea, *A Laborer,
San Antonio, Texas,* c. 1903,
oil on canvas, 36" x 24"
(91.3 x 61.1 cm.).

THE SEARCH FOR TEXAS

BECKY DUVAL REESE

Herbert Read wrote of the history of art as a categorization of modes of visual perception. Art history results from the many ways in which we have seen the world—and from our desire to discover and construct a credible world. What we see *must* be made real; art so seen *becomes* reality.[1]

What then is the reality of Texas and the art of Texas? The state and its myths are so entwined that often it is difficult to separate them: Which is fact? Which fiction?

By the close of the frontier in the 1890s Texas had a well-established mystique. Dime western novels, Remington illustrations, letters home from soldiers and immigrants melded Texas and the West into one in the popular culture. A century later, while researching his novel *Texas,* James Michener remarked, "The one thing I've been most surprised by is that Texans actually believe the myths about their state." Because Texas myths are so much a part of our world, it is no wonder Texans don't wish to separate the two. Throughout the state's history, images made tangible by the many artists who immigrated to, traveled around, settled in, and chose to live in Texas helped us to know and understand our past.

Texas impressed early visitors by its size and scale, and some recorded their impressions of the land and the people they encountered. After a tour of the American West, nineteenth-century French actress Sarah Bernhardt quipped, "After Paree, I would like to be a Texan best of all."[2] On the other hand, during a posting to Texas, General Phil Sheridan wrote, "If I owned Texas and Hell, I would rent out Texas and live in Hell."[3] About Texas and the West in general, Frederic Remington said, "With me, cowboys are what gems and porcelains are to others."

EXPLORATION

Far, far; the eye strains; it is a
kind of warm pursuit to look on
farther; it is as if one hunted the
distance; one grows eager; then
sated, then tired with one's
acquisitions of spaces.
—SIDNEY LANIER, LETTERS FROM
TEXAS, 1872[4]

The art of Texas is as broad-based as
the state itself, yet Torch Energy has taken
the challenge of collecting the state's art—
and, in the process, is succeeding mightily.
But where to start searching for the art of
Texas?

Torch Energy began with the work of a
West Point classmate of Robert E. Lee. In
1848 U.S. Army Captain Seth Eastman
(1808–1875) received orders to Texas. For
seven years Eastman had taught topo-
graphical drawing at the United States
Military Academy where his book on the
subject became the academy textbook.
Eastman was an accomplished artist by the
time he reached the Texas frontier at Camp
Houston (later renamed Fort Martin Scott)
where he worked closely with the army's
Corps of Topographical Engineers.
Eastman painted Torch Energy's watercolor
View in Texas . . . Miles North of San
Antonio probably at the same time as the
watercolor *View of Texas about 65 Miles*
North of San Antonio in the collection of
the San Antonio Museum of Art.[5] The two
paintings have several similarities: they
have nearly identical titles and are the same
size, they show a consistent landscape, and
each includes small-scale figures. The
verso of Torch Energy's painting reveals

the inscription, "Mary H. Eastman from her
husband." Eastman's romantic images
depict a Texas now long vanished.

IMMIGRATION

And tell them of our going to
Texas. The news from there is
very favorable, and we are
looking forward to a pleasant
future.
—HERMANN LUNGKWITZ[6]

After revolution created the new
Republic of Texas, vast lands became available for settlement. Famines and revolu-
tions in Europe provided the human capital
who wanted—even desperately needed—to
start anew. In September 1844, Henri Castro
led the first of several hundred French and
Alsatian colonists to settle in the new town
of Castroville west of San Antonio. Among
Castro's settlers was Jean Louis Theodore
Gentilz (1819–1906), who immediately
began contributing to the pictorial history
of the new republic. Gentilz, who had studied in Paris at L'École Impériale de
Mathématique et de Dessin, was now
located near San Antonio. He recorded the
town's architecture, native costumes, and
local customs. Documenting what he saw
provided Gentilz the subject matter that
endured for his long and prolific lifetime.
Corrida de la Sandía, San Antonio is such
a painting: horsemen race across the picture as a lone rider holds aloft the game
ball, a watermelon. Genre scenes of mid-
nineteenth-century Texas became a Gentilz
specialty, one in which he trained his students, most particularly his niece Louise
Andrée Frétellière (1856–1940), one of his

most devoted students. Her painting *Marriage Procession, Mission San Juan Capistrano* owes much to Gentilz, with whom she painted regularly. Louise's paintings of everyday life show us the life, ritual, and architecture of Texas in the late-1800s.

Immigration to Texas increased dramatically in the 1840s, making Galveston the second largest point of entry for immigrants to the United States. Whereas in 1836 Germans in Texas numbered about 200, within ten years more than 7,000 additional Germans were new Texans. The Society for the Protection of German Immigrants to Texas, an organization of German noblemen seeking to relieve population and political pressures while partaking of a bit of land speculation, brought most of them to Texas even though the society bankrupted itself in the process.

Outstanding among the German artists immigrating to Texas were Karl Friedrich Hermann Lungkwitz (1813–1891) and Friedrich Richard Petri (1824–1857). They met and became close friends at the Academy of Fine Arts in Dresden, where they took part in the street fighting of 1849 while students. Government reprisals soon forced the two to immigrate to America. But before leaving Germany, Lungkwitz married Richard's sister, Elisabet, and in 1850 they left Germany together. It took Petri and the Lungwitzes more than ten months after their arrival in New York to settle on a 320-acre farm near the Pedernales River, a few miles southeast of Fredericksburg. Lungkwitz's painting *Above the Falls of the Pedernales River* is a subject he painted frequently. Lungkwitz and Petri made a living farming their land, but the two artists also found time for their art.

Elisabet Ney, *Portrait of Mrs. Dibrell*, 1900, plaster, 8½" diam. (21.6 cm.).

Lungkwitz's bucolic nineteenth-century landscapes of the Texas Hill Country married a style of romanticism with natural realism. Petri's finely crafted, classic draftsmanship in the *Portrait of Susanna Queisser,* daughter of his sister Bertha who remained in Germany, demonstrated the skill he learned at the Dresden academy.

The most accomplished sculptor to immigrate to Texas in the mid-nineteenth century was Elisabet Ney (1833–1907), whose determination gained her entrance to the Munich Academy, where in 1852 she became the first woman to enter the sculpture department. For this daughter of a German stone-carver, trampling tradition made life worthwhile. Always outside the traditional, Ney met and ultimately married a philosophy student, Edmund Montgomery, and in 1869 they left politically charged Germany and Ney's already prominent studio life for the United States.

Julius Stockfleth, *The S. S. City of Berlin*, n.d., oil on canvas, 22¼" x 36" (56.8 x 91.7 cm.).

The couple settled in Texas after 1873, but not until after 1890 did Ney return to creating art. She practiced a neoclassical style of sculpture—a style that looked to Greek and Roman precedents. With her white marble portraits of famous statesmen transformed into heroic figures, Ney found herself as successful in Texas as she had been in Germany. Her life-size figures of Sam Houston and Stephen F. Austin now

preside over the rotunda of the State Capitol while other important works are in the collection of the National Museum of American Art in Washington, D.C. Ney's medallion, *Portrait of Mrs. Dibrell*, was a fitting thanks to Ella Dibrell, the person most responsible for preserving Elisabet Ney's Austin studio as a museum.

Marine painter Julius Stockfleth

(1857–1935) left an island village in the North Sea in 1883 to make Galveston his home and the portraiture of ships his specialty. *The S.S. City of Berlin* illustrates the photographic precision characteristic of marine paintings. Stockfleth also produced views of Galveston prior to the 1900 hurricane that remains the greatest natural disaster ever to strike the United States. More than 6,000 died in that storm, and

Stockfleth's precise paintings now are the visual archives of pre-hurricane Galveston—its architecture, harbors, and ships—the primary records of a city prior to disaster.

The arrival in San Antonio in 1899 of the Spanish painter José Arpa y Perea (1858–1952) further demonstrates the continuing fascination of artists with Texas. A three-time recipient of the Prix de Rome,

Karl Hermann Friedrich Lungkwitz, *The Old Pinta Crossing on the Guadalupe,* c. 1857, oil on canvas, 22⅛" x 16" (56.0 x 40.8 cm.).

Arpa had represented Spain in the 1893 World's Columbian Exposition in Chicago. He taught at the Academy of Fine Arts in Mexico City and periodically traveled from there to San Antonio, permanently settling in the Alamo City in 1923. Arpa painted *A Laborer, San Antonio, Texas* (1903) during one of his extended visits to the city. The finely realized painting recalls the work of such seventeenth-century Spanish masters as Ribera and Murillo. Arpa's dark and light palette produced a dramatic composition, which ultimately elevated the subject, the common man, to near-sainthood. Arpa's early painting revealed his strong roots in the Spanish academic tradition just as it demonstrated his mastery of portraiture as metaphor.

SETTLEMENT

I was raised for the most part by old women. I use the words "raised" and "old" with deliberateness, for they go together. I was raised, also, by two old Texans, one a great-grandmother who had frontiered it in an Erath County dugout, had killed a panther with an ax and made her own soap almost to the day of her death. . . . I have always had a fondness for old women. I [have] collected their images, the Sixties, Seventies, and Eighties of the Nineteenth Century, those simpler times, particularly as they were lived in my own part . . . of this vast state where I feel most at home."
—CLARA MCDONALD WILLIAMSON[7]

After 1836, signs reading "Gone to Texas" frequently appeared on homes and shops in the United States, notifying all interested that the former residents and owners had chosen to start anew where they believed land and opportunity abounded. Frequently, too, the readers of the "GTT" signs thought they stood equally for "gone crazy," for the less venture-some—or less indebted—believed published descriptions of Texas as a wild, violent, inhospitable land.

One not deterred by rumors, how-ever, was Robert Jenkins Onderdonk (1852–1917) who accepted an invitation from friends living in San Antonio to visit the growing city. Too, Onderdonk had read booster advertising of Texas as "a commonwealth of unlimited resources; with an unrivaled climate, inhabited by a brave, impulsive, usually courteous people, who are anxious for others to share the state's advantages with them." So, Onderdonk moved his family from Maryland to Texas—and struggled for survival for the rest of his life. Teaching, forming art leagues, working as curator of art for state fairs in Dallas, painting china tiles in St. Louis, Robert Onderdonk worked hard at his art. His subjects ranged from quick sketches of the architecture of San Antonio and the surrounding landscape to portraits and genre scenes. He painted *Market Plaza* (1880) shortly after his arrival, showing the exotic nature of Onderdonk's adopted home. He recorded the dress and customs of the day, captur-ing a peaceful setting on San Antonio's old Military Plaza where wares and conversa-tion were exchanged—and time passed in the Spanish tradition.

Another artist migrant was Charles Franklin Reaugh (1860–1945), who made Texas his home and the recording of the Texas landscape—especially that of the Panhandle—his life's work. Reaugh's family moved to Terrell in the 1870s when he was a boy of sixteen, and he soon began to camp on the *Llano Estacado,* the Staked Plains. In 1884–85 Reaugh began the serious study of art, first at the St. Louis School of Fine Arts and later, in the winter of 1888–89, at the Académie Julian in Paris. He returned to Texas and to the Panhandle, where Palo Duro Canyon and longhorn cattle inspired him. *Lipan Flat* combines Reaugh's love of the Texas landscape with his delight in the longhorn. On his frequent plein-air sketching trips, he worked with pastels on small sheets of sketching paper, producing fresh, quick studies that pictured Texas at the turn of the century. Reaugh once wrote: "No other medium can so truthfully give the freshness and bloom of childhood complexion, or the feeling of air in landscape."8

Clara McDonald Williamson (1875–1976) was a Texas settler who late in life, untrained and unschooled in art, began putting on canvas images from her pioneer days, images she called her "memory pictures." *The Duck Pond* (1948) was one such remembrance, showing a Texas seen through the innocent eyes of a young girl.

Entering the twentieth century, Texas artists participated fully in creating a cultural life for the state. Robert Julian Onderdonk (1882–1922) followed in his father's footsteps. After his father's tutoring, Julian went to New York where he studied, as had his father before him, at the Art Students League and with William Merritt Chase. Julian worked in and traveled between New York, Dallas, and San Antonio for several years before settling permanently in the Alamo city where his art reached maturity. Embracing an impressionist style, Julian captured the Texas landscape as no other artist had before him. Frequently he painted Texas Hill Country scenes:

Charles Franklin Reaugh, *Untitled,* n.d., pastel on sandpaper, 2⅜" x 5" (6.0 x 12.6 cm.).

Charles Franklin Reaugh,
Lipan Flat, n.d., oil mixed with
sand on canvas mounted on board,
9¼ x 19¼" (23.5 x 48.9 cm.).

*In the spring, when the wild flowers
are in bloom, it is riotous: every tint,
every hue, every shade is present in
the most lavish profusion, and even in
the dead of summer, when one would
imagine that any canvas could only
convey the impression of intense heat,
the possibilities of the landscape are
still beyond comprehension. One has
only to see it properly to find that
everything glows with a wonderful
golden tint which is the delight and the
despair of all who have ever tried to
paint it.*[9]

His pastoral paintings earned Julian the
label "bluebonnet painter," a distinction he
forever disdained. *A Sunny Afternoon on
Eagle Hill, Southwest Texas* (1911) illustrated
his penchant for the Texas Hill Country and
the mastery with which he put on canvas
what he saw before him. Julian Onderdonk
died at an early age, but the "bluebonnet"
style of painting continues in Texas—a testament to one of Texas's outstanding artists.

Two of Frank Reaugh's students,
Edward G. Eisenlohr (1872–1961) and
Reveau Bassett (1897–1981) recorded in
oils and pastels the rural Texas landscape
prior to urbanization. Bassett painted
Cathedral Mountain Near Alpine, Texas
(1925) during one of the famous Reaugh
art campouts in West Texas. Certainly the
work, with its broad swath of color and
abbreviated design, has a sense of plein-air
painting. Eisenlohr's *As Seasons Change*
(1935) guides the viewer down the path
into a Texas farm scene painted with
bravura brushmarks that reveal the hand
of an artist confident in his subject matter
and in his approach to composition.

Olin Herman Travis (1888–1975) and
his wife Kathryne Hail Travis were important to the burgeoning cultural life of Dallas
in the 1920s and '30s. They met while students at the Chicago Art Institute, and
together they founded the Dallas Art
Institute in 1924. Olin Travis's forte was
landscape painting; he often sketched the
land in numerous small, quick oil studies,

Edward G. Eisenlohr, *As Seasons
Change*, c. 1935, oil on canvas,
20" x 24¼" (51.8 x 61.6 cm.).

Dawson Dawson-Watson,
Mission San Juan Capistrano,
1932, oil on canvas, 36⅛" x 30⅛"
(91.8 x 76.7 cm.).

which served as outlines for his larger paintings. *The Brook* (1926) is a fully realized work painted in colors—reds, purples, browns, blues, and greens—that showcase the proficiency of Travis's ability to convert the land he has seen into a study for quiet contemplation.

English-born artist Dawson Dawson-Watson (1864–1939) immigrated to the United States and by 1927 settled in San Antonio, where he shared with San Antonio–born Max F. Mayer (1887–1947) an affinity for painting and architecture of the area, especially the missions before their restoration. Dawson-Watson's painting *Mission San Juan Capistrano* (1932) and Mayer's watercolor *Mission Espada with*

Praying Nun (1932) offer two artists' lyrical interpretations of the Spanish missions. Both Dawson-Watson and Mayer were well trained, both had traveled and studied in Europe, and Mayer was in the first class of graduates in architecture from Texas A&M. A practicing architect, Mayer returned to record in watercolor the architecture and landscape of his native Texas at the onset of the Great Depression.

Regionalism had a firm grip on many Texas artists in the 1930s and 1940s. A grassroots, nonpolitical movement, regionalism stylistically was devoted to realistically recording American life. The Torch Energy Collection is rich in Texas regionalist expression, with paintings and prints by Alexandre Hogue (1898–1994), William Lester (1910–1991) Everett Spruce (1908–), Otis Dozier (1904–1987), Florence McClung (1894–1992), Merritt Mauzey (1898–1973), Jerry Bywaters (1906–1989), Lloyd Goff (1917–1982), Charles Bowling (1891–1985), and Coreen Mary Spellman (1905–1978). Six paintings in the collection demonstrate the unique individuality each artist brings to his or her style of regionalist expression.

Alexandre Hogue's *Texas Front Gate* (1941) captured the regionalist's ideal world: a world that was clean, precise, and uninhabited; one that created the idea of a rural paradise. He once wrote: "The American artist in general will come of age only when he has the stamina to blaze his own trails through the part of his country in which he lives."[10] Florence McClung's *Preston Road Farm* (1940) continued a regionalist's interpretation but with a twist toward precisionism. McClung's portrait of a farm is one where tools and implements rest within a static environment, one where crisp, clearly defined edges reorder experience through a precise architectural structure. Everett Spruce's *Big Bend* (1945) took his regionalist leaning and combined it with aspects of modernism. Spruce's paintings throughout his career offer a more abstracted, fragmented interpretation of a specific locale than did the earlier works of Otis Dozier. But Dozier loosened his style over the years, and by 1976 and the completion of *Open Range,* he had joined Spruce in painting the Texas landscape with a regionalist's eye albeit with a complete understanding of the lessons of abstraction. William Lester's *Three Men and a Net* (1948) displayed his unique interpretation of the prevailing style by incorporating aspects of social regionalism within a regionalist context. Coreen Mary Spellman showcased regionalist art in her gouache watercolor *Saturday Afternoon Matinee* (1941). Turning away from the empty unsettled land, Spellman here recorded Texas city life just before World War II.

But regionalist prints best captured the stark reality of depression-era and pre-World War II days. Regionalist artists responded to shared experiences of average individuals and showed concern for the common person, whom they credited with the development of Texas and the nation. Such strong images and strong ideas struck chords within the Texas psyche. Through images of the rugged, independent Texas cowboy, or the farmer bent to his plow, or the oil-field worker on a drilling rig, regionalist recordings of the real Texas promoted a mythic Texas as well. Jerry Bywaters' *Ranch Hand and Pony* (1938), Merritt

Mauzey's *The Invasion* (n.d.), Hogue's *Oil Man's Christmas Tree* (1941), Lloyd Goff's *Design for Dallas, Texas P.O.* (1938), and Charles Bowling's *March* (1941) each paralleled the ideas and images of Thomas Hart Benton (1889–1975), whose *West Texas* (1952) illustrated what the regionalists sought—realistic images of Texas at a particular place at a specific moment in time. These works came from artists who lived in sympathy with their environment. Regionalism in Texas suited the Texas sensibility. A state viewing itself as unique found in regionalism a celebration of place as well as a celebration of egalitarian ideas.

Just as many Texas artists embraced regionalism, many also looked to innovative styles of art first exhibited in the United States at the 1913 Armory Show in New York City. The exhibition displayed major nineteenth- and twentieth-century European art movements and was critical to the wide dissemination in this country of the language of modernism. Combining the structure of cubism with the color painting of Matisse, American artists quickly created American subjects. Torch Energy's Collection includes paintings and sculpture by Texas artists Lloyd Sargent (1881–1934), Lloyd Albright (1896–1950), Harry De Young (1893–1956), William Elliott (1909–), Evaline C. Sellors (1907–1994), Marie Delleney (1903–1967), Marjorie Johnson Lee (1911–1997), and De Forrest Judd (1916–1993), who exemplify the state's search for modernism.

In the first three decades of the twentieth century, numerous artists found beauty in northern New Mexico—Santa Fe, Taos— and these villages became art centers that fed the romantic souls and yearnings of

Harry Anthony De Young,
*Muzquiz Canyon, Davis
Mountains*, n.d., oil on canvas,
45⅛" x 54¼" (114.7 x 137.5 cm.).

many artists. Lloyd Albright traveled to
that remote region and recorded scenes
imbued with fauve colors and cubism's
geometric shapes. Sargent's painting *Taos,
1929* and Albright's *Untitled (Harwood
House)* (1930) rendered romantic abstract
views of the land achieved through patterns of emotive color and distillation
of form.

Harry De Young's *Muzquiz Canyon,
Davis Mountains* (1940) seems edited
from a John Ford western. Cowboys in
ten-gallon hats look down from high in
the mountains on a cattle drive creating a

bird's-eye view of possible conflict. Rather
than a scene of potential violence, however, De Young has painted his protago-
nists in postures that reflect a sense of
relaxation instead of confrontation. William
Elliott captured the personality of his subject in the 1934 portrait *Mexican Girl*. As
the direct gaze of the young woman mes-
merizes the viewer with her strength of
character, the painting simultaneously con-
veys a sense of melancholy. Whereas
William Elliott painted a unique individual,
Evaline Sellors sought to sculpt a proto-
type. In *Dreamer* (1945), she stylized the

form for expressive purposes and avoided a strict replication of nature in order to present a figure removed from the world rather than engaged with it.

Marie Delleney taught at Texas Woman's University and spent summers studying and painting in Provincetown, Massachussetts. *Cape Cod Waterfront* (1937) came from one of Delleney's summer sojourns. Employing a style of painting that is structured on cubism and precisionism, Delleney's meticulous portrait of a place demonstrated that modernism was a vigorous force between the two World Wars, a force that sought clarity and lightness in its search for the serene.

Marjorie Johnson Lee and De Forrest Judd embraced abstract expressionist painting with gusto. Lee's *Seascape with the Sun and Lighthouse, New York* and Judd's *Rattlesnake* are paintings from 1951, and they bring the Torch Collection to the middle of the twentieth century. Lee's seascape illustrated the abstract expressionist's desire to be self-revelatory while evoking emotion through color and scale. Judd's abstract—almost mythical—rattlesnake, with its angular fragmented forms brings us

Marie Delleney, *Cape Cod Waterfront*, c. 1937, oil on canvasboard, 15⅞" x 19⅞" (40.4 x 50.3 cm.).

full circle to those outsized images of Texas that, according to J. Frank Dobie, afford Texans the ability of "bragging about the worst."

What is it about Texas art that ultimately captures our imaginations? We see the land as solace—our escape from the industrialized world. We see the West and its people as symbols of courage, self-reliance, and survival. We see Texas as a place whose past is impossible to recapture balanced by the optimism of Texans raised on the notion of potential. We see Texas as the credible realization of ourselves. We see the art of Texas glimpsed through a veil of romanticism that enables us to recall and understand our history, our myths, our psyche.

Then I really felt Texas. It was all behind me, north to south, not lying there exactly but more like looking over the car, not a state or a stretch of land but some giant, some genie, some god, towering over the road. I really felt it.
—LARRY MCMURTRY
"ALL MY FRIENDS ARE GOING TO BE STRANGERS"[11]

Thomas Hart Benton, *West Texas*, 1952, lithograph on paper, 10⅞" x 13⅞" (27.7 x 35.2 cm.) Benton did the original drawing for *West Texas* near the mesas of the Texas Panhandle. *West Texas* is his only Texas lithograph.

ENDNOTES
1. Herbert Read, *History of Modern Painting* (London: Methuen & Co. Ltd., 1959), 12–13.
2. Don Graham, *Texas: A Literary Portrait* (San Antonio: Corona Publishing Company, 1985), frontispage.
3. William H. Goetzmann and Becky Duval Reese, *Texas Images and Visions* (Austin: Archer M. Huntington Art Gallery, The University of Texas at Austin, 1983), 15.
4. Graham, *Texas: A Literary Portrait*, p. 179.
5. Cecilia Steinfeldt, *Art for History's Sake: The Texas Collection of the Witte Museum* (Austin: The Texas State Historical Association for the Witte Museum of the San Antonio Museum Association, 1993), 63.
6. James Patrick McGuire, *Hermann Lungkwitz: Romantic Landscapist on the Texas Frontier* (Austin: The University of Texas Press for the University of Texas Institute of Texan Cultures at San Antonio, 1983), 10.
7. Donald and Margaret Vogel, *Aunt Clara: The Paintings of Clara McDonald Williamson* (Austin: University of Texas Press, 1966), 14.
8. Steinfeldt, *Art for History's Sake*, p. 230.
9. *Ibid*, p. 201.
10. Rick Stewart, *Lone Star Regionalism: The Dallas Nine and Their Circle, 1928–1945* (Austin: Texas Monthly Press, 1985), 147.
11. Graham, *Texas: A Literary Portrait*, p. 13.

PHOTOGRAPHY OF TEXAS ART BY FRANK WHITE.

Merritt Mauzey, *The Invasion*, n.d. lithograph on paper, 9⅝" x 16⅞" (24.5 x 42.7 cm.).

Jerry Bywaters, *Ranch Hand and Pony*, 1938, lithograph on paper, 11¼" x 14⅜" (28.7 x 36.6 cm.).

Charles Taylor Bowling, *March*, c. 1941, lithograph on paper, 9⅜" x 13¾" (23.8 x 34.9 cm.).

Jean Louis Theodore Gentilz, *Corrida de la Sandía, San Antonio* (aka *Día de San Juan*), c. 1848, oil on canvas, 7½" x 9¹⁵⁄₁₆" (19 x 25.3 cm.).

Col. Seth Eastman, *View in Texas—Miles North of San Antonio*, 1849, watercolor on paper, 4⅞" x 7¾" (12.3 x 19.7 cm.).

Friedrich Richard Petri, *Portrait of Susanna Queisser,* c. 1850, graphite pencil with chalk, 11⅞" x 10¹⁄₁₆" (30.4 x 25.5 cm.).

Robert Jenkins Onderdonk,
Market Plaza, c. 1880,
oil on canvas, 24⅛" x 42⅛"
(61.2 x 107.2 cm.).

Robert Jenkins Onderdonk,
Old Aquaduct [sic] *Near San
Antonio Tex—1880*," 1880,
watercolor with graphite on paper,
6¼" x 8½" (15.9 x 21.6 cm.).

Karl Hermann Friedrich Lungkwitz, *Above the Falls of the Pedernales River*, 1885, oil on canvas, 19" x 27" (48.2 x 68.5 cm.).

Louise Andrée Frétellière, *Marriage Procession, Mission San Juan Capistrano*, n.d., oil on board, 10½" x 13½" (26.6 x 34.4 cm.).

Robert Julian Onderdonk, *A Sunny Afternoon on Eagle Hill—South West* [sic] *Texas,* 1911, oil on canvas mounted on board, 20" x 29⅞" (50.9 x 75.8 cm.).

Elmer L. Boone, *El Capitán,* c. 1920, oil on board, 18" x 24" (45.5 x 61.0 cm.).

Lloyd L. Sargent, *Taos 1929*, 1929, oil on board, 12" x 15⅞" (30.5 x 40.4 cm.).

Olin Herman Travis, *The Brook*, 1926, oil on painted panel door, 24" x 35⅞" (61.0 x 91.3 cm.).

Lloyd Lhron Albright, *Untitled
[Harwood House]*, 1930, oil on
panel, 24" x 30" (60.9 x 76.2 cm.).

Reveau Mott Bassett,
***Cathedral Mountain near
Alpine, Tex***, n.d., pastel on
sandpaper, 3¼" x 4½"
(8.4 x 11.4 cm.).

Max F. Mayer, *Mission
Espada with Praying Nun*,
c. 1932, watercolor on paper,
11¾" x 8¾" (29.9 x 22.4 cm.).

William Elliott, *Mexican Girl*, 1934, oil on board, 16" x 12" (40.6 x 30.8 cm.).

Merritt Mauzey, *A Church in Galveston*
n.d., oil on canvas, 24¼" x 30"
(61.5 x 76.4 cm.).

Lloyd Lozes Goff, *Design for Dallas, Texas P.O.*, c. 1938, graphite and gouache on paper, 10⅛" x 25" (25.5 x 63.4 cm.).

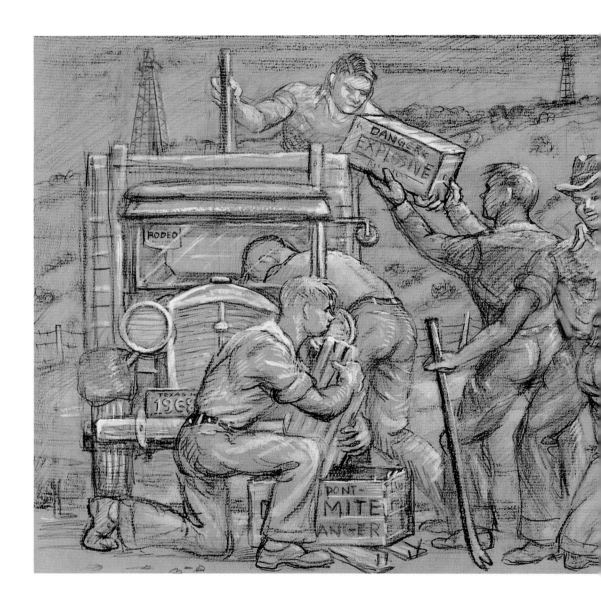

Florence McClung, *Preston Road Farm*, 1940, oil on canvas, 21" x 23⅛" (53.4 x 58.9 cm.).

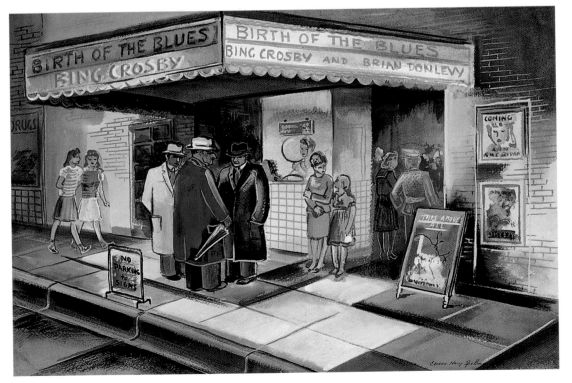

Coreen Mary Spellman, *Saturday Afternoon Matinee*, c. 1941, 13⅞" x 20¾" (35.5 x 52.7 cm.).

William Alexandre Hogue, *Texas Front Gate*, 1941, oil on canvas, 24" x 36" (60.9 x 91.4 cm.).

William Alexandre Hogue, *Oil
Man's Christmas Tree*, 1941,
lithograph on paper, 14⅜" x 9⁷⁄₁₆"
(36.7 x 24 cm.).

Everett Spruce, *Big Bend*,
1945, oil on board, 24" x 36"
(60.8 x 91.5 cm.).

Evaline C. Sellors, *Dreamer*, 1945,
limestone, 13½" ht. (35.1 cm.).

William Lewis Lester, *Three Men and a Net*, 1948, oil on board, 24" x 33⅞" (60.8 x 86.3 cm.).

Clara McDonald Williamson,
The Duck Pond, c. 1948, oil and
graphite on board, 17⅞" x 23"
(45.3 x 59.8 cm.).

Marjorie Johnson Lee, *Seascape
with the Sun and Lighthouse,
New York*, 1951, oil on canvas,
20⅛" x 24" (50.9 x 61.0 cm.).

De Forrest Hale Judd,
Rattlesnake, 1951, oil on board,
24" x 30" (61.1 x 76.3 cm.).

Janet Turner, *Once A Boat*, 1951, egg tempera on panel, 20¼" x 30⅛" (51.1 x 76.6 cm.).

Mary Doyle, *Magueys Near Fort Davis*, 1960, serigraph, 14⅞" x 22¾" (37.7 x 57.7 cm.).

Otis Dozier, *Open Range,*
1976, oil on canvas, 24⅛" x 35⅞"
(61.3 x 91.1 cm.).

BIOGRAPHIES

Andrew Bakó and **John Becq** (photo), principals of Bakó/Becq Worldwide, are an award-winning team of international advertising and corporate photographers based in Calgary, Canada. They have traveled the globe for more than twenty years providing stunning images for an impressive list of clients such as Gulf Canada Resources, Coca-Cola, Occidental Petroleum, The Bank of Montreal and Air Canada. John Becq felt honored to have worked on *Visions of the West.*

Gary Faye is an award-winning Houston-based photographer specializing in nature photography. His images have appeared in books and magazines including American Airlines' in-flight magazine, *American Way,* and an edition of Henry David Thoreau's *Walking.* He has a B.S.E.E. from the University of Colorado, Boulder, an M.S.E.E. from the University of California at Northridge, and a B.F.A. from the Art Center College of Design in Los Angeles. Faye worked as an assistant in the Ansel Adams Yosemite Workshop and has taught photography and juried shows in numerous workshops in California, Texas, and Colorado. He is represented by Photography West in Carmel, California, Afterimage Gallery in Dallas, and Harris Gallery in Houston.

Gloria Fraser Giffords received her B.F.A. and M.A. in art history from the University of Arizona. She is the author of *Mexican Folk Retablos* (Albuquerque: University of New Mexico Press, rev. ed. 1992); *Images of Popular Devotion* (Fort Worth and Dallas: InterCultura and the Meadows Museum, 1991); and numerous other essays and articles on Mexican religious art and architecture. Besides her research and writing on this subject, she is also a practicing art conservator, a fellow with the American Institute for Conservation specializing in oil paintings and polychrome statuary. She resides in Tucson, Arizona.

Gail Gilchriest's book about women of the West, *The Cowgirl Companion,* was published by Hyperion in 1993. A native of Silsbee, Texas, she is also the author of *Bubbas & Beaus,* a tribute to Southern men. Her journalism and essays have appeared in *Elle, Sports Illustrated, Texas Monthly,* and the *Houston Post.* Gilchriest graduated from the University of Texas and now lives and works in Los Angeles as a screenwriter.

Emma I. Hansen is curator of the Plains Indian Museum at the Buffalo Bill Historical Center in Cody, Wyoming. A member of the Pawnee tribe, Ms. Hansen has advanced degrees in sociology and anthropology from the University of Oklahoma and a research specialization in the arts and cultures of Plains Native people. She has taught at the University of Oklahoma and Dartmouth College and curated several exhibitions on Plains cultures, including *Powerful Images: Portrayals of Native America,* which is touring the United States and Canada from 1998–2001.

Gilberto M. Hinojosa is a professor of history and dean of the College of Arts and Sciences at the University of the Incarnate Word in San Antonio, Texas. He received his undergraduate degree from Our Lady of the Snows, his M.A. from St. Mary's University, and his Ph.D. from the University of Texas at Austin. He has written extensively on Mexican American life in the Southwest and has published several award-winning books on the subject.

George O. Jackson is an award-winning photographer whose images have appeared in numerous international publications and museum exhibitions. In addition to his decade-long *Essence of Mexico* Project, he is developing a collection of surrealistic photomontage images in his "Embrujo Mexicano" portfolio and a collection of Houston architectural images. His varied background includes art gallery management and conceptualization and design for The Gage Hotel in Marathon, Texas, and the Hofbrau Steakhouse and Cadillac Bar in Houston. Jackson also introduced the Smoke'N' Pit barbecue, at the time a new concept in outdoor cooking now adopted by the entire industry.

William Loren Katz, author of almost forty books on African Americans, began his research as a high school student during World War II. His best-known works are *The Black West* (Touchstone); *Black Women of the Old West, Black Indians: A Hidden Heritage, Proudly Red and Black* (all Atheneum); and *Black People Who Made the Old West* (Africa World Press). He has lectured widely in Europe, Africa, the United States, and on television.

Patricia Nelson Limerick was born and raised in Banning, California, and is a western American historian. She received her B.A. in American Studies in 1972 from the University of California, Santa Cruz, and her Ph.D. in American Studies in 1980 from Yale University. From 1980 to 1984, Limerick taught at Harvard University as assistant professor before becoming a history professor at the University of Colorado at Boulder. Her best-known work is *The Legacy of Conquest,* which has had a major impact on the field of western American history. Her pieces have also appeared in numerous publications including the *New York Times* and *USA Today.* In 1995, she was named a MacArthur Fellow.

Jane Pattie of Aledo, Texas, is an award-winning freelance writer and photographer. Her byline has appeared nationally and internationally on more than 2,500 magazine articles and half a dozen nonfiction books, including *Cowboy Spurs and Their Makers,* (Texas A&M University Press). Her favorite subjects are wildlife and western history, and she is a past board member of Western Writers of America, Inc. Jane and her husband, Lyle, have raised quarter horses for a number of years, and that led to interest in spurs and the men who made them.

Richard C. Rattenbury is curator of history at the National Cowboy Hall of Fame and Western Heritage Center in Oklahoma City. He holds a B.A. in history from Texas Christian University and an M.A. in museum studies from Texas Tech University. Formerly curator of the Winchester Arms Museum at the Buffalo Bill Historical Center, Rattenbury is the author of *Packing Iron: Gunleather of the Frontier West,* as well as several exhibition catalogs and more than thirty articles on historic firearms and western material culture.

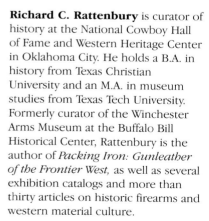

Becky Duval Reese is the director of the El Paso Museum of Art. With twenty years' experience in art museums at New Mexico State University, the University of Texas in Austin and El Paso, she has published extensively on American and regional art, and organized and juried over thirty exhibitions. Reese has also written and produced over ten video and film productions about art and art education. She received both her B.A. and M.A. in art history from New Mexico State University, graduating summa cum laude as an undergraduate.

Marta Turok is the president of the Asociación Mexicana de Arte y Cultura Popular (AMACUP), a non-profit organization in Mexico City helping local artisans market their products and preserve their cultures. An undergraduate NSF recipient, she worked on the Harvard Chiapas Project, graduating with a B.A. from Tufts. She also did master's course work at the Universidad Nacional Autónoma de México (UNAM). Turok worked in Chiapas from 1978–81 as an applied anthropologist with the National Indigenous Instituto (INI) and the Basic Foods Distribution Network (CONASUPO). She later worked at the Department of Popular Cultures (Dirección General de Culturas Populares) and was named its executive director in 1985. Turok has published numerous books on Native Mexican culture and craft.

Frank White shoots commercial projects for many of the world's largest corporations. He is the 1986 recipient of the Leica Medal of Excellence for Commercial Photography and has received numerous other awards for his work. During his spare time, White creates photographic art, teaches photography at Rice University, and collects antique and toy cameras. He graduated from the Rochester Institute of Technology in 1977. He lives and works in Houston, Texas.

Index

A

Abilene, Texas, 179
Académie Julian, 281
Academy of Fine Arts: Dresden, 277;
  Mexico City, 280
Acatlán, Guerrero, 123
Africa, 172
African American(s), xi, 170–95,
  179–80, 184, 186, 187
Afromestizo culture, 136
Aguasalas, 59
Alamo, The. *See* Mission: San Antonio
  de Valero
Alamo City. *See* San Antonio, Texas
Alaska, 187
Albia, California, 186
Albright, Lloyd Lhron, 285, 286, 296
Allen and Thurber, 250
Allen "trapdoor" breech system, 256
Alta California, 221
Alexander the Great, 218
Allensworth, California, 186
Alsatia(n), 276
Amatepeque, Mexico, 172
America(n): art history, xii; West, xii,
  1, 2, 11, 216, 274; dream, 2, 3; peo-
  ple, 2; industry/economy, 2, 67;
  resources, 53; continent of, 101;
  frontier, 170; labor system, 172;
  Revolution, 173, 176; cowgirl,
  196–215; female role of, 198, 207;
  firearms, 212, 244–73; cowboy
  spurs, 216; spur makers, 219;
  firearms in, 244, 246, 247, 253, 258;
  revolver, 253; gun makers, 256;
  gun embellishment, 257, 258;
  immigration to, 277; recording life
  in, 285; artists, 284, 285. *See also*
  United States/U.S.
American National CattleWomen,
  Inc., 206
American Style arms embellishment,
  258
Amiotte, Arthur, 12
Amozoc, Mexico, 220, 222, 223
Anchor Brand trademark. *See* North
  & Judd Manufacturing Company
Andy, Texas, 186
Anglo, vii, 2, 67, 224
Antarctica, 148
Anza, Don Juan Bautista de, 221
Apache(an): tribe, 4, 6, 8, 10, 59
Apostolic Colleges, 56
Appalachian Mountains, 196, 246
Appalachicola River, 173
Arabian horsemen, 218
Arapaho tribe, 4, 8, 10, 13. *See also*
  Native American artifacts
Argentina, 223, 229
Aridamerica, 97, 104
Arizona, 56, 172, 182, 184, 220, 226,
  243
Arkansas River, 4, 7, 10
Arkansas, 186
Armory Show (1913), New York City,
  285
Army, U.S., 173, 247, 250
Arpa y Perea, José, 275, 279–80
Art Students League, New York City,
  281
"Art Unbounded" (essay), 1–3
Ashworth brothers, 173
Asia(n), xii, 150

Assiniboine tribe, 10. *See also* Native
  American artifacts
Assumption, The, 104
Athenaeum educational center, 176
Atl (Water), 100
August Buermann Manufacturing Co.,
  224, 225, 232, 234, 235, 236
Austin, Stephen F., 173, 198, 278
Austin, Texas, 234, 247, 278
Australia, 148, 202
Autry, Gene, 203
Aztec civilization, 53, 54, 55, 97, 100,
  102, 103, 109, 144, 172, 219, 220
Aztlán, 98

B

Bacab Gods, 100
Baja California, 56
Bakó/Becq Worldwide: photos,
  142–69, 244–73; bios, 312
Balboa, Vasco, 172
Balderrama, Severo, 222
Baldridge, Melissa, ix–xii
Banks, John Willard, 174–75, 178,
  189, 190, 191
Baptist, 186
Barho, Louis P., Pvt., 264
Barnett, Abigail, 181
Bashford, Dr., 216
Bass, J. O., 243
Bassett, Reveau Mott, 282, 297
Bayers, Adolph, 227
Beckwourth, James P., 176
Beeville, Texas, 216
Benito Juárez, Huasteca Veracruzana,
  98
Benson, Ruth, 200
Benton, Thomas Hart, 285, 288
Bernhardt, Sarah, 274
Beverly Hills, California, 173
Bianchi, Joe, 226, 242
Bible, 148, 184
Billy the Kid, 179
Black Hills, 10
Black Prince, 227
"Black West, The" (essay), 170–87
"Black West, The" (artwork): *John
  Wayne,* 171; *Blacks Fought at the
  Alamo Too!* 174–75; *The Cattle
  Drive,* 178; *Bill Pickett, First Bull-
  Dogger, 1906,* 178; *Freedman's Aid
  School,* 180–81; *A Pool in the
  Desert,* 182–83; *Portrait of Black
  Cowboy,* 184; *Diamond Back
  Rat'ler,* 186–87; *Camping Time,*
  188; *The Red Bull,* 188; *Lone Oak,*
  189; *Stagecoach Robbery,* 190;
  *Overland Stagecoach at Fort
  Kearney, Nebraska,* 190; *Bustin' A
  Bronco,* 191; *The Rescue of Lt.
  Bullis,* 192; *Western Scene,* 193;
  Hog Butchering, 193; *Solemn
  Horse,* 194; *Rifleman,* 194; *Horse
  Race,* 194; *Hell Skull,* 195
Blackfoot, 3, 10, 11, 13, 14–15. *See
  also* Native American artifacts
Blanchard, Ed F., 226, 243
Bleeding Kansas, 248
Board House, Texas, 186
Bohlin, Edward H., 245, 246
Boley, Oklahoma, 181, 184
Booker, Texas, 186
Boone, Daniel, 176
Boone, Elmer L., 294

Boone, Wallie, 226
Boss, The. *See* Winchester rifles
Boulder, Colorado, 242
Bowie, Jim, 176
Bowles, California, 186
Bowling, Charles, 284, 285, 289
Bozeman, Montana, 184
Brazil, 232
Bridger, Jim, 247
Brown, Clara, 177
Brazil, 173
Bridgeport, Connecticut, 255
Bronze Age, 218
Browning, John M., 255
Buffalo Bill Cody. *See* Cody, William F.
Buffalo Hunt, Great, 255–56
Buffalo hunters, 8–10
Buffalo soldiers, 179, 182–83
Bull-dogging, 178, 179
Bullard, 255
Busy Bee Club, 184
Butterfield Trail, 248
Bryan, J. P., vii–viii, ix, x, xii, 146, 156
Bywaters, Jerry, 284, 285, 289

C

Caddo settlements, 6
Calendars, Native. *See* "Fiestas"
Calico Ball, 184
California, 2, 65, 176, 203; Baja, 56;
  missions, 173, 222; Spanish census
  of, 173; Pio Pico in, 176; gold
  rush/seekers, 176, 250, 251; and
  human rights, 177; and expansion,
  186, 223; and African Americans,
  186; -style spurs, 217, 223, 224,
  234, 235; settlement of, by de Anza,
  221
Camero, Manuel, 173
Camino Real, 220
Camp Houston, 276
Campeche, 250
Canada, x, 6, 11, 14, 177, 179
Canamas, 59
Candlemas, 104, 105
Carmelites, 152, 153
Carnaval (Carnival), 95, 98, 125
Carnaval Huasteco, 110, 111, 126
Carson, Kit, 247
Carver, Doc, 258
Cascade, Montana, 187
Casewit. *See* Kennard, Willie
Castile/Castilian, 219
Castro, Henri, 276
Castroville, Texas, 276
Cather, Willa, 207
Catholic(ism):
  Church/religion/beliefs, vii, 144,
  145, 156, 221; saints, xi, 109; cere-
  monies, 55; Spanish, 101, 144, 148;
  order, 102, 104; holy figures, 146;
  and Stations of the Cross, 156
Cavalry, U.S./Federal, 179, 248
Cayton, Horace and Susan, 187
Celts, 101
Cempoallapoualli, 103
Centennial Rifle. *See* Winchester rifles
Centéotl (God of Maize), 100
Central America, 97
Century Magazine, 182
Cerro de Coaztlahuacan, Guerrero,
  98
Chaacs (Gods of Rain and Thunder),
  102, 105
Chalchihuitlicue, 100
Champion. *See* Autry, Gene
Charles I of Spain, 219
Charles III of Spain, 173

Charles V, Holy Roman Empire, 219
Charro, 222–23, 231, 232, 233
Charro Association, 222
Chase, William Merritt, 281
Chay K'in, 103
Cherokee Bill, 179
Cherokee nation, 176
Cheyenne tribe, 4, 8, 10, 13, 14–15.
  See also Native American artifacts
Cheyenne, Wyoming, 186, 224
Chiapas Indians, 103
Chicago & Alton Railway Company,
  196, 213
Chicago Art Institute, 282
Chicago, Illinois, 176, 184, 280
Chief Joseph, 4
Chietla, Puebla, 137
Chihuahua, Mexico, 230
Chile, 223
China/Chinese, 2, 148
Chisholm Trail, 177
Chontal culture, 96, 119, 130
Christ/Christ Child. *See* Jesus Christ
"Christian Art and Imagery in
  Mexico" (essay), xi, 142–57:
  "Genesis," 142–45; "The Creators
  and Their Influences," 145–48;
  "The Collection," 148–49; "The
  Collection (Sculpture)," 149–52;
  "The Collection (Paintings),"
  152–156; "Conclusion," 156–57
"Christian Art and Imagery in
  Mexico" (paintings/sculpture):
  *Nuestra Señora, Refugio de
  Pecadores (Our Lady, Refuge of
  Sinners),* 143, 153, 156; *Nuestra
  Señora de Guadalupe (Our Lady
  of Guadalupe),* 145, 156; *Manus
  Incorruptae San Matrís
  (Incorruptible Hand of San
  Matrís),* 147, 153; *San Jerónimo,
  Defensor de la Fé y Abogado para
  la Buena Muerte (Saint Jerome,
  Defender of the Faith and
  Intercessor for a Holy or Peaceful
  Death),* 149; *Spanish 18th-century
  Silver Processional Cross,* 149;
  Corpus (body of Christ), 151;
  *Santa Rosa de Lima (Saint Rose of
  Lima, Perú),* 152; *San Miguel
  (Saint Michael, Archangel),* 153; *El
  Divino Rostro (The Divine Face of
  Christ),* 154; *La Mater Dolorosa
  con Instrumentos de la Pasión
  (Our Lady of Sorrows with
  Symbols of the Passion),* 155; *San
  Antonio de Padua (Saint Anthony
  of Padua),* 157; *Via Cruces No. 1
  (First Station of the Cross), Jesus Is
  Condemned to Death,* 158; *Via
  Cruces No. 12 (Twelfth Station of
  the Cross), Jesus Dies on the Cross,*
  158; *San Juan Nepomuceno (Saint
  John Nepomuk),* 159; *Ex-voto,* 160;
  *Santa Teresa de ávila (Saint
  Teresa of Avila),* 161; *Verónica o El
  Divino Rostro (Veil of Veronica or
  the Divine Face),* 161; *Carved
  Cross,* 162; *La Cruz de ánimas
  (The Cross of Souls),* 163; *La
  Inmaculada (The Most
  Immaculate Virgin Mary),* 164,
  166; *Corpus on Cross,* 165; *El Niño
  Jesús (The Christ Child),* 166; *San
  Cayetano (Saint Cajetan),* 167;
  *Jesús, San Joaquín y María (Jesus,
  Saint Joachim and [the Child]
  Mary),* 168; *San Anastacio (Saint
  Anastasius),* 169

Christian(s/ity), 55, 63, 101, 102, 105, 144, 145, 147
Christmas, 104, 113
Cincinnati, Ohio, 200
Civil War, ix, 177, 225, 248, 251, 252, 256
Clothing. See "Cowgirls"; Native American artifacts
Coahuiltecans, x–xi, 59, 62
Coastal Mixtec culture, 114–15, 116, 117
Cody, William F., 200, 202, 254, 258
Cofradías, 102
Colatlan del Río, Morelos, 108
Coleman, John, 188
Cologne, Texas, 186
Colonial churches, Spanish, 50
Colorado, 8, 177, 179, 184, 186, 226, 237, 242, 256
Colorado Pioneers Association, 177
Colorado River, 176
Colored Women's Republican Club, 184
Colt firearms, 3, 250–53, 254, 258, 264–67, 270–71
Colt, Samuel, 250–52, 257
Columbia River Valley, 10
Columbian, pre-, 142, 144, 147
Columbus, 172
Comanche tribe, 4, 8, 59, 176, 192, 250. See also Native American artifacts
Comanchería region, 8
Congress (U.S.), 2, 177
Congressional Medal of Honor, 179
Conley, Elvira, 179
Connecticut, 196, 207, 212, 225, 237, 250, 251, 252, 255
Conquest, Spanish, 53–55, 112
Conquistador(s), 101, 218, 220
Convento de las Capuchinas, 135
Cooper, Ronald, 195
Coronado, Francisco Vázquez de, 6
Corps of Topographical Engineers, 276
Cortés, Hernán, 53, 172, 219
Cotton, Walter Frank, 180–81
Cotulla, Texas, 242
Cotulla, Will, 242
Counter-Reformational dictates, 147
Cowboy Cowgirl. See Mulhall, Lucille
Cowboy, ix, 3, 217, 220, 226, 225, 226, 285
Cowgirl Championships, All Around, 202
Cowgirl Museum and Hall of Fame, National, 207
Cowgirl, origin of word, 199
"Cowgirls: The Wild, Wild Women of the West" (essay), 196–207
"Cowgirls: The Wild, Wild Women of the West" (photos/memorabilia): The Only Way, 196, 213; Admission Certificate of Jane Hughs, 198; Dismounted Woman Stroking Her Horse, 199; Sheridan Cowgirls, 200; Cowboy and Indian Series: Annie Oakley, 201; Vivian White's Professional Rodeo Cowboy Association gold card, 202; Vivian White, 203; Cowgirl rodeo suits, 205; Charra, 205; China Poblana, 206; Prairie Rose, 207; Mexican charrita dress, 208; Woman's riding vest and culottes, 209; Bonnie McCarroll Thrown from "Silver," 210; Cowgirls at the Tucumcari Round-Up, 211; The Hopkins & Allen 'Prairie Girl', 212; Woman in

Skirt Mounted Astride, 214; Three Mounted Women Riders, 214; Four Mounted Riders, 214; Mary Ware, 215
Cradleboards. See Native American artifacts
Crawford, Captain Jack, 258
Crazy Horse, 4
Creek Nation, 173
Cripple Creek Barroom (film), 203
Crockett Bit & Spur Company, 242
Crockett, Davy, 172, 176
Crockett, Oscar, 22, 241
Cross L Ranch, 216
Cross, Carved (sculpture), 150, 162
Crow tribe, 10, 14–15. See also Native American artifacts
Crowell, Reid Kendrick, 185
Cuba, 219
Cuicatec culture, 136
Curtis, Edward S., 107
Custer, George A, General, 256, 258
Czechs, xii

D

Dakota Territories, 10, 256
Dakota tribe. See Native American artifacts
Dalhart, Texas, 226, 239, 240
Dallas Art Institute, 282
Dallas, Texas, 280, 281, 282
Dalton gang, 179
Dance of Moors and Christians, 102
Dawson-Watson, Dawson, 284
Day of the Dead, 104
De Young, Harry Anthony, 285, 286
Dead-eye Annie. See Oakley, Annie
Deadwood Dick. See Love, Nat
Dearfield, Colorado, 186
Deep South. See South (U.S.)
Delgado, Lorenzo, Sheriff, 252
Delleney, Marie, 285, 287
Deloria, Philip, 2
Denver, Colorado, 177, 184, 186, 237
Depression, Great, 285
Deringer, 257
Derringer pistol, 249, 268
Dibrell, Ella, 277, 278
Dinzel, A. E., 248
Disciples of Jesus, 145. See also Apostles
Diseases, European-introduced, 144
Dixon, Carl, 194
Dobie, J. Frank, 288
Dodge City, Kansas, 179
Dodge, Richard Irving, 256
Dom Pedro III of Brazil, 232
Doyle, Mary, 310
Dozier, Otis, 284, 285, 311
Dragoon revolver, 251. See also Colt firearms
Dragoons, U.S., 247
Drake, Sir Francis, 172
Dresden, Germany, 277
Druid religion, 113
Durango, Mexico, 230
Du Sable, Jean Baptiste Point, 176
Dusky Demon, The. See Pickett, Bill

E

Earth, 100
East (U.S.), vii, ix, xi, 180, 184, 224, 198, 244, 256
Easter Week, 104, 105, 108, 113, 114–15, 116, 117, 118, 128, 129
Eastman, Mary H., 276
Eastman, Seth, 276, 290
Eastwood, Clint, 203
Edison Company, 203

Edward III of England, 227
Ehecatl (Wind), 100
Eighth Texas Cavalry, 264
Eisenlohr, Edward G., 282, 283
El Paso del Norte, 58
El Paso, Texas, 67, 241. See also Mission: Corpus Christi de la Ysleta; Mission: Nuestra Señora de la Limpia Concepción del Socorro
El Reino de Nuevo México, 56
Elko, Nevada, 207, 234
Elliott, William, 285, 286, 298
England/English, 2, 8, 146, 179, 202, 216, 218, 219, 221, 227
Espíritu Santo Bay, 60
Estevanico, 172
Etruscan(s), 218
Euro-American(s), xi, 2, 3, 8, 10, 11, 13, 244
Europe(an), vii, xii, 1, 53, 220; art, 1, 3, 146; origin, 2; goods, 8, 142; and Druid religion, 113; culture, 142, 172; diseases/famines/revolutions in, 144, 276; art, influence of, 148; in the West, 170; in Africa, 172; and "maroon societies," 173; emigrants, 180; and African Americans, 187; spurs, 216–21, 227–28, 231; knights, 218; Bronze Age in, 218; firearm designs, 246; arms embellishment, 258; artistic study in, 285; art movements, 285. See also Euro-American(s)
Evans, Dale, 203, 205
Extremadura, Spain, 220

F

Far West. See West(ern)
Faye, Gary, xi, 67, 312; images, 51–93
Federation of Black Women's Clubs, 184
Female Conqueror of Beef and Horn. See Mulhall, Lucille
Fernando de Béxar, town of, 64
Fields, Mary, 187
Fiesta de la Santa Cruz (Holy Cross), 112, 113, 122, 123, 124
Fiesta de la Virgen de la Asunción (Virgin of the Assumption), 136
Fiesta de la Virgen de la Candelaria (Virgin of Candlemas), 128
Fiesta de la Virgen de Guadalupe (Virgin of Guadalupe), 140
Fiesta de la Virgen del Rosario (Virgin of the Rosary), 138–39; 140
Fiesta de San Bartolo (Saint Bartholomew), 97, 141
Fiesta de San Juan Bautista (Saint John the Baptist), 107, 132, 133
Fiesta de San Francisco Asis (Saint Francis of Assisi), 137
Fiesta de San Manuelito (Saint Manuelito), 131
Fiesta de San Mateo (Saint Matthew), 106
Fiesta de San Pedro (Saint Peter), 96, 119, 130
Fiesta de Santa María Magdalena (Saint Mary Magdalene), 136
Fiesta de Santiago Apóstol (Saint James), 102, 103, 134, 135
Fiesta del Cruz del Ocho (Cross of the Eighth of May), 98
Fiesta del Inicio de la Siembra, La (Beginning of the Planting Season), 152, 155
Fiesta del Niño Cieguecito (Little Blind Child), 135
"Fiestas: Where Contemporary

Mexican Tribes and Ancient Customs Meet" (essay), xi: "On Myth and Ritual," 94–97; "Native Myths and Rituals before the Conquest," 97–99; "Creation Myths," 100; "The Discovery of Maize Myths," 100–101; "Syncretism: The Grafting of Ancient and Spanish Rituals," 101–2; "Native Calendars and Fiestas," 103–4; "Fiesta Cycles," 104; "Yaxk'in or the Sun Cult: Purification and Penance," 104–5; "Tzolk'in or the Day Count: An Agricultural Almanac," 105–6; "Festival Secularization," 106; "Photographer's Statement," 107–13
"Fiestas: Where Contemporary Mexican Tribes and Ancient Customs Meet" (photos): Huasteco (Huastec), 95; Turcos Quejandose al Presidente Municipal Acerca de Las Travesuras de Los Insoportables Negritos (Turks Presenting Their Case to the Village Mayor Regarding the Unbearably Annoying Conduct of the Negritos), 96; Maringuilla, 97; Danzando Con El Oso (Dancing with the Oso), 98; La Danza de los Tlacololeros (The Dance of the Tlacololeros), 98; Niños Pintados de Negro y Amarillo Contra Una Puerta Verde (Children Painted Yellow and Black Against a Green Door), 99; Señor Santiago, Montado en Su Caballo (Saint James, Astride His Horse), 102; Voladores (Flyers), 103; Una Ofrenda de Agradecimiento a Todos Los Ángeles en el Cielo (An Offering of Gratitude to All of the Angels in the Sky), 106; Viejita Trique (Little Old Trique Woman), 107; El Milagroso (The Miraculous One), 108; Carnaval Huasteco (Huastecan Carnival), 110; Comanches, 111; Amarrando Una Flor de Yuca (Tying a Yucca Flower), 112; Cerro de Cruzco (Place of the Crosses), 113; Apóstoles (Apostles), 114–15; Procesión de Huaves (Huave Procession), 116; El Calvario (Mount Calvary), 116; Cruces Huaves (Huave Crosses), 118; Fariseos (Pharisees), 117; Turco (Turk), 119; La Danza de Los Ormegas (The Dance of the Ormegas), 120; Negritos Bailando Los Listones (Negritos Dancing the Ribbon Pole), 120; Pasando et Pañuelo (Passing the Scarf), 120; San Juan Ahuacatlán (Festival of the Beginning of the Planting Season), 120–21; La Ofrenda (The Offering), 122; Tecoani (One Who Draws Blood), 123; Tecoani Acateco (Tecoani from Acatlán, 123; Tecoaliztli (The Act of Drawing Blood), 124; Diablos Recibiendo Una Bendición (Devils Receiving a Blessing), 125; Hombre con Penacho de Estrella Pintado de Negro y Ruedas Amarillas (Man Wearing a Headdress with a Star, Painted Black with Yellow Circles), 126;

Diablo Carnavalero (Carnival Devil), 127; *Papalotero,* 127; *Penitentes (Penitents),* 128; *Un Castillo Chispando (Castillo Shooting Sparks,* 128; *Penitente Encruzado (Crucified Penitent),* 128; *José Lachineer, Capitán de Los Negritos (José Lachineer, Captain of the Negritos),* 130; *San Manuelito (Saint Manuelito),* 131; *El Señor del Perdón (Our Lord of Forgiveness),* 131; *El Paso de un Torito Chispando (The Pass of a Torito Shooting Sparks),* 132–33; *Conchero,* 133; *La Piedad (Piety),* 134–35; *Quetzales Haciendo la Reverencia (Quetzales Practicing Reverence),* 135; *La Procesión del Niño Cieguecito (Procession of the Blind Child),* 135; *La Iglesia de Santa Maria Magdalena (The Church of Mary Magdalen),* 136; *Un Torito Desintegrando (A Torito Exploding),* 136; *Un Tecuane (A Tecuane),* 137; *La Danza de los Bixanos (The Dance of the Bixanos),* 138–39; *Danzantes en el Atrio de Una Iglesia (Dancers in a Churchyard),* 140; *La Danza de Los Malinches (Dance of the Malinches),* 140; *Danzando en el Fuego (Dancing in the Fire),* 140–41
Firearms. *See* "Tools of Triumph and Tragedy"
First Baptist Church, 184
Five Civilized Nations of the Southeast, 176
Flappers, Prohibition-era, 205
Flathead tribe. *See* Native American artifacts
Fletcher, Francis, 180
Florida, 172, 173, 176
Ford, Barney, 186
Ford, John, western, 286
Ford, John S. "Rip," 251
Fort Grant, 182
Fort Martin Scott, Texas, 276
Fort McKavett, Texas, 226, 243
Fort Worth Rodeo, 206
Fort Worth, Texas, 202, 207
France/French, vii; 8, 219, 221, 220, 222, 226, 274, 276, 281
Franciscan(s), 56, 59, 65, 221
Fredericksburg, Texas, 277
Frétellière, Louise Andrée, 276–77, 293
Frontier, 55–57, 170

G

Galveston, Texas, 277, 278
Garcia, Abbie Hunt, 223
Garcia, G. S., 223, 234
Garcia, Jesús, 223
Gemmer, J. P., 247
Gentilz, Jean Louis Theodore, 276, 290
Georgia, 176
German(y), 67, 219, 221, 225, 257, 277, 278
Ghost Dance, 11
Giant (film), 193
Gibbs, Ezekiel, 193
Gibbs, Mifflin, 186
Giffords, Gloria Fraser, xi, 312; essay, 142–57
Gilchriest, Gail, xi, 312; essay, 196–207
Gillette, Wyoming, 224

God the Father, 154
Goddesses, 98, 101, 144
Gods, 98, 100, 101, 102, 105, 106
Goff, Lloyd, 284, 285, 300–301
Gold Mountain, 2
Golden Age of American Arms Engraving, 256–57
Goliad, Texas, 67, 221. *See also* Mission: Nuestra Señora del Espíritu Santo de Zúñiga; Presidio Nuestra Señora de Loreto de La Bahía
Government cartridge, 256
Gray, Reva, 200
Great Britain. *See* England/English
Great Depression, 285
Great Dismal Swamp, 173
Great Lakes, 10
Great Plains, 4, 6–8, 246, 258
Greece/Greek, 218, 278
Griggs, Sutton, 186
Grijalva, Eduardo, 235
Gros Ventre tribe, 10
Guadalajara, Mexico, 145, 221, 233
Guadalupe, Convent of, 153
Guerrero, Vicente, 173
Guild of Spur-Makers, 219
Gulf Coast, 60, 104, 221
Gun That Won the West. *See* Winchester rifles

H

Hail Marys, 153
Hall, John H., 247
Hamilton, William, 247
Hanging Judge. *See* Parker, Isaac
Hansen, Emma I., x, 312; essay, 4–15
Hardin, John Wesley, 254
Hartford, Connecticut, 250, 251, 252
Hastings, Fox, 200
Hawken rifle, 258
Hawken, Jacob and Samuel, 247
Hays, John Coffee, Colonel, 250
Henderson, Prairie Rose. *See* Robbins, Ann
Henry rifle, 254, 272–73
Henry, B. Tyler, 254
Hercules Bronze, 236
Highland Plateau, 98
Hinojosa, Gilberto, x–xi, 313; essay, 50–67
Hispanic(s), vii; pre-, 104, 105, 109
Hispañola, 172
Hodge, Jess S., 226, 243
Hog Leg. *See* Colt firearms
Hogue, William Alexandre, 284, 285, 303, 304
Hollywood, California, 170, 203
Holy Cross, 101
Holy Cross Day, 104
Holy Family, 154
Holy Land, 156
Holy Roman Empire, 219
Holy Week. *See* Easter Week
Honduras, 172
Hopkins and Allen, 212
Horace, 113
Horse(s), Spanish, 102
"Horseman, Ride West! The Evolution of the Spur" (essay), xii, 216–26
"Horseman, Ride West! The Evolution of the Spur" (images): California Spurs, 217, 224, 234, 235; Knight's Templar Prick Spur, 218; Conquistador Spur, 220; Sand-Cast French Spurs, 221; Charro Spurs, 222, 223, 231, 233; Buffalo Head Spurs, 225; Bull Head Spurs, 226; Spurs, 227, 232, 239, 241, 243;

English Rowel Spur, 227; Jousting Spur, 228; Spanish Spur, 228, 231; Colonial Spur, 229; South American Spur, 229; Mexican Spurs, 230; Vaquero Spurs, 230; "Dom Pedro Jr." Spurs, 232; O.K. Spurs, 234; Gal-leg Spurs, 235, 238, 241; Star Steel Silver Spurs, 236; Hercules Bronze Spurs, No. 1393-1/2, 236; Gunmetal Spurs, 237; Stainless Steel Spurs, 237; Woman's Bottle-Opener Shank Spurs, 239; Rattlesnake Spurs, 239; Goose Head Spurs, 240; Arrow Spurs, 240; "Johnnie Mullens Special" Spurs, 241; Leaf Spurs, 241; Number 1614 Spurs, 242; Victoria Shank Spurs, 242; Number 4 Drop Shank and Chap Guard Spurs, 243
Houston, Texas, x, xi
Houston, Pam, 198
Houston, Sam, 273, 278
Houston, Temple, 273
Howell-Sickles, Donna, 198
Huastec, 97, 98
Huasteca Hidalguense, 95, 98, 110, 126
Huastecan Nahua culture, 98, 110, 126
Huasteco-mestizo culture, 111
Huautla (Hidalgo Shrovetide), 106
Huehuetla, Hidalgo, 128
Hughs, Jane, 198
Huitzilopochitl, 101, 102

I

Iberia, 54, 172
Igualapa, Guerrero, 131
Illinois, 176, 280
Immaculate Conception, (sculpture), 150, 164, 166
Independence Heights, Texas, 186
Indian(s), 1, 2, 3, 50–93, 103, 107, · 112, 144, 170, 192, 202, 222, 252, 256
Inter-Ocean Hotel, 186
Irish emigrants, 2
Italo-Byzantine style, 156
Italy, 218, 226
Itzam Na, 105
Ixcatepec, Huasteca Veracruzana, 111

J

Jackson, George O., Jr., xi, 96, 313; photos, 95–141; essay, 107–13
Jackson, Oliver and Minerva, 186
Japan, 148
Jaranames, 59
Jazz Age, 202
Jesuits, 56, 152, 173
Jesus Christ: as Sun God of Creation, 101; and Candlemas, 105; and Easter Week, 105; and Apostles/disciples, 105, 145; and Mary, 144, 153; retablos of, 147; *The Christ Child* (sculpture), 150, 166; *Corpus* (sculpture), 151; . . ., *San Joachim and [the Child] Mary* (painting), 153, 168; *Divine Face of* (painting), 154; in the Holy Family, 154; Passion of, in artwork, 156; and Stations of the Cross, 158; *Corpus on Cross* (sculpture), 165
Jesús, San Joaquín y la Niña María (painting), 153, 168
Joseph, 153, 154
Judd, De Forrest Hale, 285, 287, 309
Jueves de Carnaval (Carnival Thursday), 127

K

Kansas, 6, 7, 8, 177, 179, 181, 225, 226, 241, 248, 255
Kansas City, Missouri, 241
Karankawa Indians, 60
Katz, William Loren, xi, 313
Kelly Brothers/P. M. Kelly, 226, 239, 240, 241
Kelly Brothers & Parker, 240
Kendleton, Texas, 186
Kennard, Willie, 179
Kentucky, 224
Kentucky rifle. *See* Pennsylvania rifle
Kiowa tribe, 4, 8, 10, 14–15. *See also* Native American artifacts
Koerner, William Henry Dethlef, 215

L

L'école Impériale de Mathématique et de Dessin, 276
La Inmaculada (sculpture), 150, 164, 166
Lakota tribe, 6, 7, 10, 11, 12, 13, 14–15. *See also* Native American artifacts
La Mater Dolorosa con Instrumentos de la Pasión (painting), 152, 155
Lame Deer, 6
Landa, Bishop, 105
Langston City, Oklahoma, 181, 184
Lanier Sidney, 276
Laredo, Texas, 173
Las Vegas, New Mexico, 252
Lassoer in Lingerie. *See* Mulhall, Lucille
Last Sacrament, 160
Latin America, 142
Latin text, 153
Lee, Marjorie Johnson, 285, 287, 308
Lee, Robert E., 276
Leidesdorff, William, 176
Lenexa, Kansas, 241
Lengua franca, 62
Lent, 104
Leon, Ponce de, 172
Lester, William Lewis, 284, 285, 307
Lilly, "Pawnee Bill," 258
Limerick, Patricia Nelson, x, xii, 313; essay, 1–3
Little Big Horn, 4, 256
Little Rock, Arkansas, 186
Little Sure Shot. *See* Oakley, Annie
Llano Estacado, Texas, 281
Logan, Greenbury, 173
London, England, 202
Lone Star Republic. *See* Texas
Lord's Prayer, The, 153
Los Angeles, California, 173, 177, 184
Lost days, 103
Love, Nat, 177
Lucas, Barbara "Tad," 200, 202, 207
Lumholz, Carl, 107
Luna family, 220
Lungkwitz, Hermann, 276, 277, 279, 288, 293

M

Madison Square Garden, 179, 202, 205
Magdalena, Sonora, Mexico, 235
Maize Mountain, 101
Marines, U.S., 173
Marlin arms manufacturer, 255, 257, 258
Maroon societies, 173
Marston, William W., 268
Mary (Missouri slave), 177
Mary, the Mother of Jesus, 101, 105, 144, 147, 153, 154

Mary, The Most Immaculate Virgin (sculpture), 150, 164, 166
Maryland, 280
Mason, Biddy, 177
Mason-Dixon line, 196
Mason, May, 187
Massachusetts, 253, 287
Masterson, William "Bat," 258
Matisse, 285
Mauzey, Merritt, 284, 285, 289, 299
Maximilian, 222
Maya(n) civilization, 97, 100, 101, 103, 105
Mayer, Max F., 284, 297
McCabe, Edwin P., 181, 184
McCarroll, Bonnie, 210
McChesney, J. R., 226, 238, 239
McClung, Florence, 284–85, 302
McGinnis, Vera, 205–6
McMurtry, Larry, 288
Medicine Lodge Creek, 4
Mediterranean, 218
Meso-America(n), 53, 56, 97, 98, 100, 101, 102, 103, 104
Mestizo (Mexican), 2, 61, 63, 108, 135, 137, 146, 148. *See also* Mexic(o/an)
Mestizo-penitent culture, 128, 129
Mestizo-Tlaxcalteco culture, 127
Methodist Episcopal Church, 184
Metropolitan Museum, 216
Mexic(o/an), 2, 219; religious art-works, x, 3, 153, 156; religions, xi; country/people/cultures of, xi, 2, 67, 97, 108, 113, 144, 146, 223; forebears, xii; border of, 2; central, 53, 56, 61, 62, 67, 100, 142; American residents, 67; fiestas/celebrations of, 96, 105; Conquest of, 105, 112, 142, 217, 219; northern, 107; folk cultures/heritage, 107, 113; photography, 110; Indians, 110; southern, 142; Christianized, 144; clergy, 145; mining towns, 146; independence from Spain, 146; art/artists, 146, 148, 149, 157; economy, 148; and antislavery, 173; War, 176; Pio Pico of, 176; report of, by George Saunders, 177; and 101st Rodeo, 179; women in, 198; rodeo originated in, 202; caballeros, 202; equestriennes, 205; Highlands, cattle ranching in, 220; vaqueros, 221, 222; Charro Association of, 222; Texas revolution/independence from, 224, 250; American War, 251. *See also* "Christian Art and Imagery in Mexico"; "Fiestas"; "Horseman, Ride West!"
Mexico City, 53, 98, 146, 220, 221, 223, 280
Meyers, Betty, 200
Micheaux, Oscar, 187
Michener, James, 274
Middle Ages, 219, 235
Mier expedition, 250
Miles, Nelson A., General, 258
Military Plaza, 280
Milky Way, 100
Mill City, Texas, 186
Miller, Zack, 177, 179
Minnesota, 10
Mirror of the Times (newspaper), 177
Misión: Nuestra Señora de Guadalupe, 58; Espíritu Santo de Zúñiga, 60
Mission: Corpus Christi de la Ysleta, 51, 58, 68; San José y San Miguel

de Aguayo, 52, 53, 54–55, 59, 72–73, 74–75, 76–77, 78, 79, 80–81, 82–83; Nuestra Señora de la Limpia Concepción del Socorro, 58; Nuestra Señora del Perpetuo Socorro, 58; Nuestra Señora de la Purísima Concepción de Acuña, 59, 60, 69, 88, 89; San Antonio de Valero (the Alamo), 59, 64, 67, 69, 70, 71, 174; San Francisco de la Espada, 59, 66, 90; San Juan Capistrano, 59, 61, 92, 93; Nuestra Señora del Espíritu Santo de Zúñiga, 64–65, 91, 221
"Missionary-Led Indian Communities, The" (essay), x, 50–67: "The Conquest and Colonial Era Setting," 53–55; "The Frontier," 55–57; "The Missionary-led Indian Towns," 58–67
"Missionary-Led Indian Communities, The" (photos). *See* Misión; Mission
Missions, Spanish, 3, 50–93
Mississippi rifle, 251
Mississippi River, 6, 179; Valley, 176
Mississippi, 177, 244, 245
Missouri, 177, 241, 225, 248, 247, 280
Missouri River, 7, 10
Mix, Tom, 199
Mixtec civilization, 97, 105
Montana, 10, 184, 187, 256
Montana, Patsy, 207
Montejo, Francisco de, 172
Monterey, California, 173
Montgomery, Edmund, 277–78
Montgomery, John, Captain, 176
Moore, Deacon Eddie, 178
Moors, 101, 102, 172, 223
Morgan, Ike Edward, 171, 193, 194
Mormons, 177
Morning Star, 100
Morrell, Dorothy, 211
Moses, Phoebe Ann. *See* Oakley, Annie
Mountain rifle. *See* Plains rifle
Mulhall, Lucille, 198–200, 205, 207
Munich Academy, 277
Murillo, 280
Myths/mythology. *See* "Fiestas"

N

Nahua culture, 95, 106, 112, 113, 120–121, 122, 131
Nahua Guerrerense culture, 98, 106, 123, 124
Nahuatl civilization, 100, 103
Nanahuatl, 101
Nashville, Tennessee, 196, 207
National Cowgirl Museum and Hall of Fame, 207
National Museum of American Art, 278
Native American artifacts (photos): clothing/accessories, 5, 12, 16, 17, 18, 19, 22, 23, 24, 25, 29, 30–31, 32, 33, 38, 39, 40, 44, 48; weapons/accessories, 8, 20–21, 28–29, 42; saddle/accessories, 7, 45, 49; rattle, 9; storage bags, 9, 13, 21, 32, 41, 43; backrest, 11; tobacco bag, 13, 20, 24; spoon, 13; cradle-boards/cover, 26, 27, 46; moc-casins, 34–37; doll, 41; bonnet case, 47
Native American Plains: Central Plains region (Omaha, Pawnee, Ponca), 7; Missouri River region (Arikara, 7; Hidatsa, 7, 10; Mandan, 7, 10; Northern Plains region, 7, 10, 13);

Southern Plains region (Osage, 7; Tawakoni, 7; Waco, 7; Wichita, 7, 12)
Native American(s), vii, viii, x, xi, 3, 4, 172, 179, 248, 256. *See also* "Indians"; "Missionary-led Indian Communities"; "People without Borders"
Nature, forces of, 98
Navy, U.S., 173, 250, 251
Nebraska, 7, 10, 202, 255
Negro, Pietro Alonzo il, 172
Negroes, reports of, 172, 177. *See also* "Black West, The"
Nemontemi, 103
Nevada, 184, 207, 234
New Britain, Connecticut, 225, 237
New Haven Arms Company, 254, 268
New Jersey, 225, 232, 234, 235, 236
New Mexico, 2, 6, 8, 56, 58, 172, 173, 226, 250, 252, 285
New Spain, x, 50, 52, 53, 56, 148, 219, 220, 221. *See also* Mexic(o/an); Texas
New World, 170, 172, 173, 219, 244, 257. *See also* America(n); Mexic(o/an); United States (U.S.)
New York (City), 1, 179, 186, 199, 202, 216, 277, 281, 285
Newark, New Jersey, 225, 232, 234, 235, 236
Ney, Elisabet, 277–78
Nicodemus, Kansas, 179
Nimschke, L. D., 257
Niña (ship), 172
Ninth Regiment, U.S. Cavalry, 179
Nizza, Father Marco de, 172
Nordhaus, Hannah, 3
North America(n): vii, viii, ix, x, xi. *See also* West(ern)
North & Judd Manufacturing Company, 224, 225, 237
North Carolina, 173
North Sea, 279
Norwich, Connecticut, 212
Nueces River, 176
Nueva Galicia, Jalisco, Mexico, 220

O

O'Keeffe, Georgia, 207
Oakley, Annie, 200–201, 202, 203, 205, 207
Ocelotl (Jaguar/Tiger), 100
Ohio, 200
Ohio Valley, 176
Oklahoma, 7, 8, 10, 14, 176, 179, 180, 181, 184, 199, 226, 238, 239
Old Time Drivers Association, 177
Old West, 3
Oldham, Texas, 186
Ollin (Movement), 100
Olmec civilization, 97, 103
Olmsted, Frederick Law, 251
Olvera, Isabel de, 173
Omohundro, Texas Jack, 254
Oñate, Juan de, 56, 172
Onderdonk, Robert Jenkins, 280, 292
Onderdonk, Robert Julian, 281, 282, 294
101st Ranch, 179
Orient, 148
Our Lady of Guadalupe (painting), 145, 156
Our Lady of Sorrows with Symbols of the Passion (painting), 152, 155
Our Lady, Refuge of Sinners (painting), 142, 153, 156, 160
Ovanda, governor of Hispañola, 172

P

Pacific Coast, 104, 221
Pajalaches, 59
Palo Duro Canyon, Texas, 281
Pame culture, 140
Pame region, San Luis Potosí, 140
Pampopas, 59
Panama, 172
Paris, France, 219, 274, 276, 281
Parker, Isaac, 179
Parsons, Lucy Gonzales, 186
Passion of Christ, 155, 156
Patent Arms Manufacturing Company, 250, 251
Paterson firearms. *See* Colt firearms
Pattie, Jane, xii, 313; essay, 216–26
Paul's Valley, Oklahoma, 238, 239
Pawnee tribe, 10
Pecos River, 192
Pedernales River, 277
Penetaka, Comanche, 4
Pennsylvania rifle, 246, 247, 258
"People without Borders: Natives of the North American Plains" (essay), 4–14: "The Great Plains and Its Traditions," 6–7; "Buffalo Hunters on Horseback," 8–10; "End of an Era," 10–11; "Art: The Fabric of Life," 12–14
"People without Borders: Natives of the North American Plains" (photos). *See* Native American artifacts
Persia, 218
Peru, 172
Perugia, Italy, 218
Petmecky, J. C., 234, 247
Petri Lungkwitz, Elisabet, 277
Petri, Friedrich Richard, 277, 290
Philippines, 148
Phillip II of Spain, 219
Phillips & Gutierrez, 224
Pickett, Bill, 177
Pico, Pio, 176
Pinotepa de Don Luis, Oaxaca, 114–15, 116, 117
Pitalaques, 59
Pizarro brothers, 172
Plains, Great, 6–7
Plains Indians. *See* Native American artifacts; Native Americans
Plains rifle, 247, 248
Plateau tribes (Nez Perce, Yakima), 10. *See also* Native American arti-facts
Platte River, 7, 10
Plough Handle. *See* Colt firearms
Polk, U.S. President, 176
Pontiac, Chief, 172, 176
Potawatomie, 176
Prairie Madonna, 198
Presidio Church, San Elizario, 85
Presidio de Béxar, 60, 64
Presidio Nuestra Señora de Loreto de La Bahía, 57, 60, 63, 67, 84, 86, 87, 91
Prix de Rome, 279
Procession of the Blind Child (paint-ing), 104, 135
Professional Rodeo Cowboy Association (PRCA), 202
Prohibition-era flappers, 205
Provincetown, Massachusetts, 287
Puebla, Mexico, 146, 233
Pueblo culture, 6, 56, 58, 172

Q

Queen of the Range. *See* Mulhall, Lucille

Queen of the West, The. See Evans, Dale
Queisser, Bertha, 277
Querétaro, 56
Quetzalcóatl/Quatzalcóatl, 100–101, 219
Quiautl (Rain), 100
Quiviran tribe, 6

R

Rattenbury, Richard C., xi, xii, 313; essay, 244–58
Read, Herbert, 274
Reagan, Tom, Dr., 216, 223
Reaugh, Charles Franklin, 281, 282
Red River, 176
Reese, Becky Duval, xii, 314; essay, 274–88
Remington arms manufacturer, 251, 252, 257
Remington illustrations, 274
Remington rifle, 248, 255, 256
Remington, Frederic Sackrider, x, 1, 3, 170, 182–83, 274
República de Indios, 54, 65
Republic of Texas, 250
Republican River, 7
Resa, Juan Guerra de, 173
Reyes, Francisco, 173
Ribera, 280
Ricardo Metal Manufacturers, 237
Richards, Ann, 198
Rifles. See "Tools of Triumph and Tragedy"
Rio Grande, 4, 56, 58, 59, 179, 202
Rituals, Native. See "Fiestas"
Roach, Ruth, 200, 211
Robbins, Ann, 207, 211
Robbins, Tom, 207
Roberts, Texas, 186
Rocky Mountains, 6, 8, 179, 246
Rodeo, 202
Rogers, Roy, 203, 205
Rogers, Will, 186, 198–99, 207
Rome/Roman(s), 101, 218, 221, 278
Roosevelt, Theodore, 186, 199, 255, 258
Rufus Buck gang, 179
Runyon, Grace, 200
Russell, Charles, x, 1, 3, 170
Russell, Joe and Hope, 216
Russia(n), 218, 253

S

Sacrament, Last, 160
Sacramento, California, 176
Sacred Cross, 105
Sacred Lodge Dance. See Sun Dance
Saint Anastasius (painting), 152, 153, 169
Saint Anthony of Padua (painting), 156, 157
Saint Cajetan (sculpture), 149, 150, 167
Saint Francis, 104
Saint Isidore the Husbandman, 101, 104
Saint James Methodist Church, 177
Saint James the Apostle, 101, 102, 104
Saint Joachim and the Virgin as a Child (painting), 153, 168
Saint John Nepomuk (painting), 152, 159
Saint John the Baptist, 104
Saint Joseph and Yaxk'in, 105
Saint Matris, The Incorruptible Hand of (painting), 147, 153
Saint Michael the Archangel, 101, 104

Saint Michael, Archangel (painting), 152, 153
Saint Peter and Saint Paul, 104
Saint Rose of Lima, Perú (sculpture), 150, 152
Saint Teresa of Ávila (painting), 161
Saint Theresa, 153
Salamanca, Spain, 220
Salt Lake Valley/City, 177
San Angelo, Texas, 216, 226
San Antonio Museum of Art, 276
San Antonio River, 59, 65, 221; Valley, 61; mission towns, 64, 67
San Antonio, Texas, 64, 67, 173. See also Mission: Nuestra Señora de la Purísima Concepción de Acuña; Mission: San Antonio de Valero (the Alamo); Mission: San Francisco de la Espada; Mission: San José y San Miguel de Aguayo; Mission: San Juan Capistrano; "Search for Texas, The"
San Bartolo Zoogocho, Sierra Ixtlan de Juárez, Oaxaca, 97, 141
San Carlos, 182
San Elizario Presidio Church, 85
San Fernando, 65, 67, 173
San Francisco, California, 172, 173, 176
San Jose, California, 173, 177
San Juan Ahuacatlán, Sierra Norte de Puebla, 120, 121
San Juan Atzingo, Estado de Mexico, 133
San Juan Chamula, Chiapas, 132
San Juan Copala, Oaxaca, 107
San Mateo del Mar, Ismo de Tehuantepec, Oaxaca, 116, 118
San Pedro Huamelula, Oaxaca, 96, 119, 130
Sand Creek, 4, 10
Santa Ana Chiauhtempan, Tlaxcala, 127
Santa Anna, 176
Santa Barbara, California, 173
Santa Fe, New Mexico, 250, 285
Santa María Huazolotitlán, Costa Chica, Oaxaca, 136
Santiago Yancuictlalpan, Sierra Norte de Puebla, 102, 103, 135
Sargent, Lloyd L., 285, 286, 295
Satanta, 4
Saunders, George, 177
Scandinavians, xii
Schnitger, Rex, 224
Schofield, George M., Major, 254
Schreyvogel, Charles, 3
Scythian horsemen, 218
"Search for Texas, The" (essay), xii, 274–88: "Exploration," 276; "Immigration," 276–80; "Settlement," 280–88
"Search for Texas, The" (artwork): A Laborer, San Antonio, Texas, 275; Portrait of Mrs. Dibrell, 277; The S. S. City of Berlin, 278–79; The Old Pinta Crossing on the Guadalupe, 279; Untitled, 281; Lipan Flat, 282; As Seasons Change, 283; Mission San Juan Capistrano, 284; Muzquiz Canyon, Davis Mountains, 286; Cape Cod Waterfront, 287; West Texas, 288; The Invasion, 289; Ranch Hand and Pony, 289; March, 289; Corrida de la Sandia, San Antonio (aka Día de San Juan), 290; View in Texas—Miles North of San Antonio, 290; Portrait of

Susanna Queisser, 291; Market Plaza, 292; Old Aquaduct [sic] Near San Antonio Tex—1880, 292; Above the Falls of the Pedernales River, 293; Marriage Procession, Mission San Juan Capistrano, 293; A Sunny Afternoon on Eagle Hill—South West [sic] Texas, 294; El Capitán, 294; Taos 1929, 295; The Brook, 295; Untitled (Harwood House), 296; Mission Espada with Praying Nun, 297; Cathedral Mountain near Alpine, Tex, 297; Mexican Girl, 298; A Church in Galveston, 299; Design for Dallas, Texas P.O., 300–301; Preston Road Farm, 302; Saturday Afternoon Matinee, 302; Texas Front Gate, 303; Oil Man's Christmas Tree, 304; Big Bend, 305; Dreamer, 306; Three Men and a Net, 307; The Duck Pond, 308; Seascape with the Sun and Lighthouse, New York, 308; Rattlesnake, 309; Once a Boat, 310; Magueys Near Fort Davis, 310; Open Range, 311
Seattle Republican (publication), 187
Seattle, Washington, 187
Sellar-Bullard family, 179
Sellors, Evaline C., 286–87, 306
Semana Santa. See Easter Week
Seminole Indians, 173, 192
Senegambia, 173
Serra, Father Junípero, 172, 173
Sevilla, Spain, 220
Shadowcatcher. See Curtis, Edward S.
Shankleville, Texas, 186
Sharps rifle, 248, 255, 256, 257, 258, 270–71
Sharps Rifle Company, 255
Sharps, Christian, 248
Sheridan, Kansas, 179
Sheridan, Philip H., General, 258, 274
Shrovetide, 104, 105, 106
Sierra Leone, 173
Sierra Nevadas, 176
Sinaloa, Mexico, 221, 222, 223
Single Action Army Revolver. See Colt firearms
Sioux, 1, 10, 14–15; Brule, 6. See also Sitting Bull
Sitting Bull, 4, 200
Six Nations of the Northeast, 176
Slave code, 177
Slavs, xii
Smartest Horse in the Movies. See Rogers, Roy
Smith & Wesson, 252, 253, 254, 257, 258; firearms, 260–63
Smith, Horace, 253
Smith, Isaac, 186–87
Socorro, Indian community of, 67. See also Mission Nuestra Señora del Perpetuo Socorro
Sonora, Mexico, 2, 56, 65, 221, 222, 223, 235
Sorrowful Mother, The (painting), 152, 155
South (U.S.), 179, 180, 181, 224
South America(n), 216, 229
South Dakota, 6, 10, 13, 187. See also Native American Plains
Southwest, American, 8, 50, 52, 177, 198, 251
Spain/Spaniards/Spanish: exploration, vii, xi, 2, 6; governmental structure, x, 53; forebears, xii; missionaries, 1; colonists, 1; culture, 2, 223; mis-

sions/churches, 3, 50, 285; army, 6; settlements, 8; Crown, 52–53, 54, 55, 56, 57, 173, 220; economy, 53; Inquisition, 101; horse, 102; and Dance of Moors and Christians, 102; Conquest, 112; dominance of Mexico, 142, 146; Catholic(ism), 101, 144, 148; origins of art, 146; religious art of, 147, 148; text, 153; led New World, 172; census of California, 173; kings, 173, 219; conquistadors, 101, 218; ranching, 221; law and horses, 222; artists/masters, 279, 280. See also "Horseman, Ride West!"; "Missionary-led Indian Communities, The"
Spellman, Coreen Mary, 284, 285, 302
Spellmon, Fronzell L. "Doc," 192
Spencer repeating rifle, 254
Springfield rifle, 256–57, 270–71
Springfield, Massachusetts, 253
Spruce, Everett, 284, 285, 305
Spurs, xii, 3. See also "Horseman, Ride West!"
St. James Church, 184
St. Louis School of Fine Arts, 281
St. Louis World's Fair, 199
St. Louis, Missouri, 176, 247, 248, 280
Stagecoach Mary. See Fields, Mary
Star Steel Silver, 236
Stetson, 205, 218
Stevens arms manufacturer, 257
Stevens Gould. See "Tools of Triumph and Tragedy"
Stevenson, James, Colonel, 176
Stockfleth, Julius, 278–79
Stuart, Granville, 258
Sun Cult, 104–5
Sun Dance, 10, 14
Suns, 100
Swearingen, Johnnie, Rev., 188
Switzerland/Swiss, 226
Sydney, Australia, 202

T

Tamoanchan, 101
Taos, New Mexico, 285
Taxco, Guerrero, 103, 128, 129
Ten Bears, 4
Tennessee, 177, 196, 207, 224
Tenochtitlán. See Mexico City
Tenth Regiment, U.S. Cavalry. See Buffalo soldiers
Teotihuacán, 106
Teozintli, 101
Tepehua culture, 125
Tepehua region, Huasteca Veracruzana, 125
Tepehua-mestizo culture, 128
Tercer Viernes de Cuaresma (Third Friday in Lent), 131
Terrell, Texas, 281
Texas (book), 274
Texas/Texana/Texans, vii, ix, 223; furniture, ix, x; art/artists, xii, 3; state/cities of, 6, 7, 8, 10, 216, 226, 247, 256; early, 50; east, 59, 173; south, 59–60, 226; central, 65; coast, 67; west, 67, 282; population of, 173; revolution/independence from Mexico, 176, 224, 250; and slaves, 177; and expansion, 186; and women/cowgirls, 198, 202, 207; southwest Texas, 216; missions in, 221; ranching in, 221, 225; Rangers, 250, 251, 258, 264; Republic of, 250, 276; firearms in, 250, 251; Army of, 250; frontier,

276; Hill Country, 277, 281, 282; Panhandle, 281, 288; *Llano Estacado,* 281. *See also* "Horseman, Ride West!"; "Missionary-led Indian Communities, The"; "Search for Texas, The"; "Tools of Triumph and Tragedy"
Texas A&M, 285
Texas Woman's University, 287
Tezcatlipoca (Smoking Mirror), 100
Theatines Regular Clerks, 149
Tiger-Tecuan complex, 105
Tilghman, Bill, 258
Tlahuica-Ocuilteco cultures, 133
Tlalixtac, Sierra Cuicateca, Oaxaca, 136
Tlaloc (God of Rain), 100, 101, 106
Tlapanec culture, 134
Tobacco bags. *See* Native American artifacts
Toledo, Spain, 220
Toltec civilization, 97
Tonacatepetl Mountain, 101
Tonalpoualli (calendar), 103
Tonatiuh (Sun, Fifth Creation), 100
Tonantzin (Mother of the Gods), 101, 144
"Tools of Triumph and Tragedy: Firearms in the American West": (essay), 244–58
"Tools of Triumph and Tragedy: Firearms in the American West" (photos): Colt Model 1873 Single Action Army Revolver (detail), 245; Colt Model 1873 Single Action Army Revolver, 246; Plains Rifle, 248–49; Cased Remington-Elliot Pepperbox Derringer, 249; Colt Third Model Dragoon Revolver, 251; Colt Model 1873 Single Action Army Revolver, 252; Colt Model 1877 "Lightning" Double Action Revolver, 253; Winchester Model 1866 Rifle, 254–55; Springfield Armory Model (hunting knife and sheath), 255; Springfield Armory Model 1879 Rifle, 256–57; Marlin Model 1893 Lever Action Rifle, 256–57; Marlin Model 1893 Lever Action Rifle, 257; Model No. 1, Third Issue Revolver, 259; Smith & Wessons, 260–61; Model No. 3 First Model Single Action Revolver, 260; Model 3 Russian Third Model Single Action Revolver, 260, Single Action Mexican Model Revolver, 260; Single Action Second Model 38 Safety Revolver, 260; Model No. 1, Second Issue, 260; Model No. 1, Third Issue Revolver, 260; Model .320 Rifle, 260–61; Model No. 1, First Issue Revolver, 260; Model No. 3 Second Model Single Action Revolver, 261; First Model Schofield Single Action Revolver, 261; Second Model Single-Shot Pistol, 261; Single Action Second Model Revolver, 261; Hand Ejector Model of 1903 Revolver, 261; Double Action Fourth Model Revolver, 261; Model No. 1, Second Issue Revolver, 261; Cased Smith & Wesson Model No. 1 Second Issue Revolver, 262; Model No. 3 Second Model Single Action Revolver, 262; Smith & Wesson Model 3 Schofield First Model "Wells Fargo" Revolver, 263; Single Action Second Model

38 Safety Revolver, 263; Colt Model 1873 Single-Action Army Revolver, 264; Colt Model 1849 Pocket Revolver, 264; Colt Model 1860 Army Revolver, 264; Cased Colt Seventh Model 1855 "Root" Side-hammer Pocket Revolver, 265; Cased Colt Model 1849 Pocket Revolver, 266; Cased Colt Model 1873 Single Action Army Revolver, 267; Cased Colt Model 1851 Navy Revolver, 267; New Haven Arms Co. Volcanic Lever Action No. 1 Pocket Pistol, 268; William W. Marston Three-Barrel Derringer, 268; Stevens Gould No. 37 .22 Caliber Rifle, 269; Springfield Armory Second Model, 270–71; Colt Model 1861 Special Musket, 270–71; Winchester Model 1886 Rifle, 270–71; Sharps Model 1874 "Old Reliable" Hunter's Rifle, 270–71; Winchester Model 1885 Single Shot High Wall Rifle, 270–71; Colt Model 1839 Paterson Carbine, 270–71; Winchester Model 1894 Takedown Rifle, 272–73; Winchester Model 1886 Rifle, 272–73; Winchester Model 1873 Rifle, 272–73; Winchester Model 1866 Carbine, 272–73; Henry Rifle, 272–73
Torch Energy Collection, ix, 216, 218, 220, 284, 285, 287. *See also* "Christian Art and Imagery in Mexico"; "Search for Texas, The"
Torch Energy/Advisors, vii, x, 67, 216, 276
Totonac culture, 102, 103, 135
Trail of Tears, 176
Travis, Kathryne Hail, 282
Travis, Olin Herman, 282, 284, 295
Travis, William Barret, 175
Trigger. *See* Rogers, Roy
Truscott, Texas, 227
Tucumcari Round-Up, 211
Tulia, Texas, 243
Turlock, California, 217, 224
Turner, Janet, 310
Turner, Frederick Jackson, 2, 258
Turok, Marta, xi, 314; essay, 94–106
TV Guide, 193
Twain, Mark, 253
Twain, Shania, 207
24th and 25th Regiments, U.S. Infantry Regiments. *See* Buffalo soldiers
Tzimin Chaac, 102
Tzolk'in (calendar), 103
Tzotzil Maya culture, 132

U

Ulrich firearms dynasty, 258
Union Army, 184, 252
Union City, 186
United States/U.S., vii, xi; culture of, 3, 11, 187, 224; and Native Americans, 14; military/Army, 173, 176, 247, 256; Cavalry, 179, 253; Europeans emigrated to, 180, 277, 284; Mail, 187; women in western, 196–215; rodeo in, 202; spurs in, 216, 235; Dragoons, 247; Samuel Colt in, 250; military sidearms, 251; gun embellishment in, 257; Military Academy, 276; greatest natural disaster in, 279. *See also* America(n)
University of Texas, vii
Utah, 177

V

Valdez, María Rita, 173
Vallodolid, Spain, 231
Vaquero(s), 221, 222, 224–25, 230
Veil of Veronica or the Divine Face, The (painting), 153, 161
Venus, 100
Veracruz, 220
Vernon, Texas, 227
Victoria, Texas, 67, 226, 242
Victorville, California, 186
Villa Hidalgo Yalalag, Oaxaca, 138–39, 140
Virgin Mary. *See* Mary, the Mother of Jesus
Virgin of Charity, 109
Virgin of Guadalupe, 101, 144
Virginia City, Nevada, 184
Visigoths, 101
Vogt Western Silver, Ltd., 217, 224
Volcanic lever action, 254, 268

W

Wade, Robert, 200
Waggoner Ranch, 227
Wagon Box Fight (1867), 256
Walker Model Colt. *See* Colt firearms
Walker, Samuel H., Captain, 251
Wallace, D. W., 177
Warhol, Andy, 201
Washington, 187
Washington, Booker T., 184
Washington, D.C., 278
Washita, battle of, 4
Wayne, John, 203
Weapons. *See* Native American artifacts; "Tools of Triumph and Tragedy"
Webb, Walter Prescott, 258
Welch, Rusty, 227
Wells Fargo, 263
Wesson, Daniel, 253
West(ern), vii, x, xii, 2, 3, 11, 179, 184, 198–99, 203, 205, 216, 220, 256, 258, 274. *See also* Cody, William F.; Wild West shows/showmen; "Tools of Triumph and Tragedy"; "Search for Texas, The"
West Indies, 219
Western Folklore (periodical), 157
Western Hemisphere, 219
Whitney arms manufacturer, 251
White Buffalo Woman, 6
White, Frank: photos, 142–69, 196–215, 216–43,244–73; bio, 314
White, Vivian, 202, 203
Wichita tribe, 7
Wild West shows/showmen, 196, 200, 202, 203, 258. *See also* Cody, William F.; Mulhall, Lucille
Wilhelm, German Crown Prince, 200
Williams, Cathy ("William Cathy"), 186
Williams. *See* Roosevelt, Theodore
Williamson, Clara McDonald, 280, 281, 308
Winchester arms manufacturers, 257
Winchester rifle/carbine, 252, 253, 254–55, 258, 270–73
Winchester, Oliver, 254
Winter solstice, 113
Women's Movement, 198
Woodward, Arthur, Dr., 220
World War I, 184, 186; post–, 287
World War II, pre–, 285, 287
World's Columbian Exposition, 280
World's Wonder Horse, The. *See* Autry, Gene

Wounded Knee, 4, 11
Wyoming, 186, 224

X

Xipe-Totec (Flayed God of Young Corn), 105
Xiuhpoualli (calendar), 103
Xochipilli (Aztec Flower Prince), 109

Y

Yankee, 196
Yankee Hill, Colorado, 179
Yavapai Indian, 235
Yaxk'in (calendar), 103
Yellowstone Valley, 10
Young, Gustave, 257–58
Ysleta, Indian community of, 67. *See also* Mission Corpus Christi de la Ysleta
Yukon, Alaska, 187
Yucatán, 105
Yucca, Arizona, 243

Z

Zacatecas, Convent of, 153
Zacatecas, Mexico, 56, 233
Zacualpan, Guerrero, 106
Zapotec, 97
Zapotec-mestizo culture, 141
Zapotec-Yalaltec culture, 138–39, 140
Zapotitlan Tablas, Sierra Tlapaneca, Guerrero, 134
Zihuatetla, Sierra Norte de Puebla, 131
Zitlala, Guerrero, 112, 113, 122, 123, 124
Zoque civilization, 105